AF608315

Q is for Garden

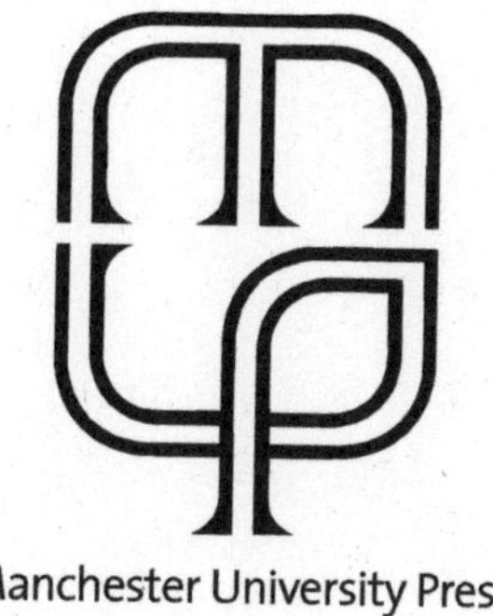

Manchester University Press

Q is for Garden

Tending the histories of queer cultivation

Jenny Chamarette

Manchester University Press

Published by Manchester University Press
Oxford Road, Manchester, M13 9PL
www.manchesteruniversitypress.co.uk

British Library Cataloguing-in-Publication Data
A catalogue record for this book is available from the British Library

ISBN 978 1 5261 9733 7 hardback

First published 2026

EU authorised representative for GPSR:
Easy Access System Europe, Mustamäe tee 50, 10621 Tallinn, Estonia
gpsr.requests@easproject.com

Typeset
by Cheshire Typesetting Ltd, Cuddington, Cheshire
Printed in Great Britain
by CPI Group (UK) Ltd, Croydon CR0 4YY

contents

prologue: broken earth

Q is for questioning.

Q is for querying.

Q is for queer.

There is a well-used phrase in queer communities. *Not gay as in happy, but queer as in fuck you.*

I am made of that joyful, defiant Q. Queer cleaves to me like soil, its earthy evidence beneath my fingernails. We are all made of earth's matter: humans in the humus. Both words share the same Latin root.

In my earliest memories, mud clung to my skin. I buried grey pebbles, waiting for prehistoric plants that never came. Inanimate objects and dormant life look the same from the outside. Once I learned the difference, I germinated seeds.

Something else grew from that connection to land and followed me into young adulthood. Having both hands in the earth – soil microbiota generating serotonin in my body – cultivated other feelings. Obsessively, I washed my hands to feel it again. Cold grit. A streak of loam. The shining crevice of rain-slicked mud. It enlivened me. Then something I couldn't name.

Sexuality begins without words. Its strange electricity caught me in snatches of queer-coded television, animation, film, art, literature. I sought it in plants, furtively scrutinising root follicles and leaf stomata, not to own but to observe. I looked for something in earth I could not find in flesh. At least, not the kind I was told to desire. In the homophobic climate of 1990s Britain's late-Conservative and early-Labour governments, I wrote diaries in ciphers; round, stone-shaped symbols, buried deep.

Black feminist thinker bell hooks describes queer life as 'the self that is at odds with everything around it and has to invent and create and find a place to speak and to thrive and to live.'[1] I felt it first, hands in the earth: both who you sleep with and how you live a life at odds. The *both, and* of it makes a place to speak from all the more urgent. And I was not at odds with plants. As my sexuality strayed from the man-made world, the soil-scents of petrichor and geosmin showed me the way.

The creative dynamics of sexuality are *old*.

Sink into it for a moment. What if you could let go of the sexualities you've been told, to listen to the ones you can *feel*? The rising sap, the mycelial network, the beetle in the magnolia flower, the dirt on your fingertips, the energetic transition from one species to another that feeds, clothes, shelters, lives, thrives, transmutes.

In the narrowest human definition of this private, consensual, regulated act, sexuality is about procreation, not co-creation. In an era of global attacks on reproductive health, gender-affirming care and basic human rights, governing doctrines of procreative sexuality at the expense of co-creative self-tending are ever more apparent. Sexuality as energy, vibrancy, agency, community, interchange, growth, is something different. Something hidden and underground, unregulated by laws or nations, cultures or religions.

Take cosexuality for example. Some magnolia species – tall, prehistoric, flowering trees – have evolved thermogenic flowers to attract the beetles who pollinate them. They hold their heat while tiny insects drowse in their warm cup. The story of the magnolia and the beetle pre-dates not just humans but *bees*. Our entire ecosystem is dependent upon acts of interspecies sex plurality. And while Charles Darwin referred disparagingly to polymorphous sexualities in his theories of evolution, more than heterosexual, more than binary-gendered behaviours and biologies have been recognised across a vast swathe of planetary life.[2]

What, then, if the querying, questioning, unbounded Q was not new but *old* – within us, between us, and beyond our horizons?

What if there were a Q, both in nature and in garden, too? Where would you find it?

I found my first answer in the broken earth.

In the winter of 2019, language came apart. The enduring tedium of this no-state is obvious to anyone who has experienced a health crisis.

When this end-point hit, it left behind a no-place. The implosion uprooted everything, unmoored my sense of self, and produced a lostness with no roadmap. I sat down in the rotting matter. In the chaos, things were unleashed. My investment in my profession, which never fulfilled its bright promise, cut loose. My quiet sexuality became loud. My gender, which had always fitted poorly, broke away from the binaries that encased it.

A wasteland is never nothing. In the routine fog of depression, where I lost speech, diurnal rhythm, sleep, there was my allotment: a scrap of tangled earth and a growing compost heap. There was the slow repetition of tasks passing time from day to night. Hands in the earth, I dug up what was buried. Flint, pottery, plastic. Mud and roots. While I weeded and kneeled, the trees witnessed my long walk back from the dead. I came back, not because of my garden but alongside it.

Towards the end of this wordless interval, I began to weave my broken plot into this book. In the warm earth, life unfurled. I nurtured it: the questioning, the querying, the queer. The Q's tenacious life force brought me back to surface. In its queer tendrils I saw the Q that had been ignored, suppressed, destroyed in the histories of cultivation. In the face of nothingness, I saw what had been hidden in me. I felt the hope and the fury too.

Because what if the Q – the nonconforming, the nonbinary, the multiple – had *always* been there, neither aberrance nor deviation, but simply part of life's entangled complexity?

What lies do we tell ourselves to keep this truth buried?

I went looking for a place wide enough to hold a life outside binaries. A *there* to point to.

In his late diaries published as *Modern Nature*, the queer filmmaker and artist Derek Jarman wrote: 'my garden's boundaries are the horizon.'[3] Prospect Cottage is demarcated by the shingle stretch of Britain's only desert peninsula. 'Desert' is often a metaphor for discarded land, but in the case of Dungeness, the ecology of its tiny microclimate is a descriptor, not a moral value. In front of the peat-black fisherman's hut a little tarmac road loops from the crags of the infamous power station to the village of Lydd-on-Sea.

Daffodils and rock roses rise improbably from the gravel. Before them, the Strait of Dover stretches towards France's coastline. What Jarman most fervently desired, while he weathered the storms of AIDS-related illness and brutal treatment regimes, was to tend his fragile life as a gardener, artist, activist. In his garden without borders sea gusts lift the shingle, salt the tongue.

There.
Right there.

The pebble ridges of Dungeness National Nature Reserve give way inland to dunes and lagoons, mudflats, salt marshes and low-lying grassy plains.[4] All of these feature in Jarman's anti-state, anti-policing film *The Garden* (1990). In the British imaginary, gardens are tied to little England, whose fences and hedges neatly mark out property ownership and white bourgeois heterosexuality. This fiction misses the point, since rural England is replete with queer storytelling, as Jarman knew well. Sacred and profane by turns, his films created utopian alternatives to rigid parables. In the ecological desert of Dungeness, Jarman recreated the abundant paradise of Eden as scrappy and riotous, a lavish stage in a wasteland, a queer recasting of Christian myth, and a wholesale rejection of the forces of government that policed and discarded queer lives in the midst of the HIV/AIDS epidemic. *The Garden* reveals riches beyond governmental controls of liveable, grievable life.[5]

When he took on Prospect Cottage and the gravelly stretches that became its gardens, Jarman was already dying. He was aware of the peninsula's environmental inhospitality and its volatile history. For millennia the Kent coast has been a battleground of invasion, occupation, and an unforgiving source of livelihood from the sea. The county known as the garden of England is also guardian, guard and border. That same horizon is now, once again, a frontline of border enforcement.

A short walk along the tarmac from Prospect Cottage, the grey warehouse of the Royal National Lifeboat Institution station rises from the peninsula's undulating creases. In recent years its lightweight vessel has assisted thousands of people, overloaded on small dinghies in the English Channel, suffering from shock and exhaustion and blocked from any safe and legal routes to asylum.

Living at odds – with state-sanctioned border enforcement, or the state-sanctioned policing of sexuality and gender – requires radical, creative and sometimes desperate acts of survival.

It is both utopian fantasy and a political act of resistance to imagine a garden beyond borders. Queer life persists by refusing enclosure, and yet it uses those walls as a trellis on which to refashion itself. Like a fast-growing vine that winds up the most inhospitable of barriers, the Q lives beyond the exclusions of binaries: cultivation/wilderness, citizen/migrant. When it must, it resists and persists within those borders, finding a place to feel the earth and take root. To live, flourish, speak. The mud caking in my palms tells me this.

Jarman's horizon too. The curve of the Earth; the spectrum of visibility we know is not an end but a reminder of our smallness. A place to resist and persist. The space between sky and sea, where the wind cradles your ear.

Do you hear it?

Q is for Garden.

If a garden is an enclosure, we can reshape its walls, replace them, pull them down entirely, in conversation with the land and its inhabitants. There are other ways of living that let us tend our tender landscapes. Other gardens that gaze out towards the blue.

introduction

This book began in the ground. Its pulse is a love of land, and an ongoing departure from the excluding norms that divide nature from culture, human from non-human, self from world. *Q is for Garden* is both a field guide and an act of recovery. An archive of what the land holds, remembers and continues to teach.

I wrote it while learning how to live a life that cannot be reduced to identity and where my worth is not determined by what I produce. While many of the binaries I undo in this book and beyond it relate to gender and sexuality, they are always about life – about who and what gets to flourish between and beyond the borders we have built. Embracing queerness and nonconforming gender, and the queer communities who live with land, was an undoing as much as an unfolding. In the company of queer lives I have found an unfastening of the binds, a balm and, eventually, a common ground.

That undoing began in a period of personal and planetary crisis. My own rupture coincided almost exactly with the COVID pandemic. Transformations, human or planetary, begin with a breaking point. The causes of mine are unclear and perhaps beside the point. What matters is what comes after: the will to begin again, and to resist the amnesia, cultural or psychological, that pretends collapse never happened.

This book is in many ways a study of life's tenacious persistence. Its 12 chapters follow the shifting cycles of a temperate garden in the northern hemisphere – think trellis, not wall – tracing how queer and non-binary lives take root and flourish across seasons, histories and soils. Though lunar cycles and equinoxes mark its rhythms, *Q* is not a queer gardening almanac. It is a meditation on growth in uncertain and sometimes hostile political and ecological climates, where frosts linger until May, heatwaves arrive in February and droughts fall in October. These errant seasons, like queer lives, trace the shapes of fluid time.

The four sections of *Q* draw inspiration from each wayward season: watery introspection in autumn, going to ground in winter, seeds of change in spring, burning fury in summer. I draw from both the stalwarts of queer garden history, like Vita Sackville-West's Sissinghurst, and the unseen connections between radical politics and ecology: the queer history of the tomato, Indigenous foraging in Palestine or Eve Balfour, the lesbian founder of the Soil Association.

These stories and histories also underpin my own story of recovery without cure. Nature did not heal me, but it was my witness. The soil told me there were older wounds. My garden taught me to trace them beyond my own plot, toward the place where sea meets stone, and growth strains against its borders. I had been there before, on another shore, watching a garden reach for its horizon.

Derek Jarman's garden of the horizon is radical because it resists. It lives in tension with walls and borders, pulling against their confines. The oldest words for garden involve walls: *jardin* (Old French), *gardo* (Proto-Germanic), *hortus* (Latin). *Pardez* in Persian, the Avestic *pairidaēza*, a compound of *pairi* (around) and *daeza* (wall). Etymologically and culturally, the garden is an enclosed space, whose origins show how power shapes what grows, and who is allowed to thrive. The garden was never innocent. Its twin pulls between abundance and exclusion are ancient and generative, and one of the earliest binaries that bind culture to cultivation. Inside, outside. My own garden, a small patch overshadowed by Victorian terraces, is no exception.

The garden's barriers are familiar terrain, in Olivia Laing's recent search for a common garden paradise in *The Garden Against Time* for instance, and before Laing in Toni Morrison's novel *Paradise* and Jamaica Kincaid's *My Garden (Book)*.[1] But enclosure is never airtight. The invertebrate renewal of waste, mycelial networks and bacterial microbiome, water tables, minerals and elements are part of the natural ecosystems upon which cultivation depends. The hermaphroditic garden snail – who I talk to, or perhaps with, in Chapter 1 – is an example of nature's many-gendered complexity in ordinary garden settings. Often regarded as a gardener's bane – I have my own ambivalent feelings too – snails are essential to soil health and aeration, moisture retention and nutrient recycling. They show what is missing, and they fill the gap. Snails are a queer signal, revealing cultivation's own hard stops.

The natural world, in all its polymorphous diversity, was never not queer. This is both about what grows in the garden and who tends it. The complex eco-social–sexual contract between plants and humans includes queer and gender non-conforming gardeners, botanists, agriculturalists, artists, writers, practitioners of plant medicines who draw on old forms of knowledge within, beside and beyond enclosure.

The long lineage of walls begins early, in mortar and in myth. For millennia, cultivation and colonisation have gone hand in hand. When the ancient Roman philosopher Cicero said 'If you have a garden and a library, everything will be complete',[2] he named the garden as part of the good life and – subtly – as the location of statecraft in the Republic, where power takes root. From the fourth century onward, the garden paradise of Christian creation myth controlled and defined women – their sexuality, their bodies, their roles.[3] Colonial Christianity made gardens in the form of plantations,[4] whose Edenic fable it used to justify the subjugation of reproductive rights for Indigenous people and slaves: extraction, incarceration, appropriation.[5] It professed civilisation while executing violence.

There are always stories of resistance, though. Places where the walls of the garden don't hold. In seventeenth-century Surinam, enslaved African and Indigenous women used their knowledge of abortifacient herbal medicines to undermine the plantation economy, preventing the birth of children conceived by rape and/or who would be condemned to lives of slavery or exploitation.[6] While new knowledge of butterflies, pollination, plants, amphibians and metamorphosis returned to Europe, this knowledge of medicinal abortifacients did not travel widely into European empires. And yet, as Londa Schiebinger shows, these suppressed stories appear in the writings of Maria Sibylla Merian, one of the few early Enlightenment women making botanical knowledge. The same partitions that contained plantations could not withhold knowledge passed from hand to hand.

Knowledge finds a way, giving hands to hold in the dark. Indigenous and global majority writers, artists, activists and ecologists continue to resist the binaries of Euro-Western thinking. Robin Wall Kimmerer's ecological intimacy, adrienne maree brown's *Emergent Strategy*, Alexis Pauline Gumbs' Black ecofeminism, Octavia E. Butler's speculative fiction: each cultivates abundant hope in times of climate emergency and a crisis of social justice. In *Q is for Garden* their open speculative imaginaries cultivate a more generous understanding of our intimacy with land. Their hands hold mine.

Life proliferates. Biology too refuses the colonial rules imposed upon it. Much of the world deviates from the binaries of sex and gender constructed by white Europeans over the last five hundred years. As Joan Roughgarden identifies, many beings – plant, animal, human – repeatedly disprove sweeping claims about sex-based binaries and biological essentialism.[7] The only incontrovertible components of biological sex are gametes: tiny haploid cells with a single chromosomal set. Big and female, like an egg or ovum, or small and male, like sperm or microspores. How gametes are produced or expressed – in the same body, in different bodies, outside or among many bodies – creates sexual diversity.

Sex is simple, but not what you think.

Gender is expansive beyond all imagining.

In 1726 the Swedish botanist Carolus Linnaeus adopted three planetary symbols to mark what he saw as the genders of flowers. Two of these signs (Mars ♂, Venus ♀) are now ubiquitous: they exist everywhere in Euro-Western culture as a shorthand for human gender. But he initially used a third: ☿ – Mercury – a hybrid messenger, conduit of the in-between. Linnaeus acknowledged a riot of floral sexuality: the polyandrous, polygynous, polygamous plant world was a new kind of sexual imaginary.[8] Even within early Enlightenment science's rigid confines, the plant world flourished, queerly.

Plant buds and severed root balls travelled in the cargo holds of European vessels scouring the world for the next new source of wealth. The captured soil gave off strange odours: potato, tomato, lemon verbena. Japanese knotweed, swamp cypress. Breadfruit, tea, tobacco, indigo, sugar, cotton, coffee, cacao. As Banu Subramaniam writes in *Botany of Empire*, colonial botany was one of the most extensive tools of imperialism. Particularly so for Britain, which extracted the world's biocapital, claimed mastery over knowledge and ultimately controlled land – as it still does – through settler-colonial and postcolonial elites. Empire policed sexuality in the same breath, ordering bodies into hierarchies, trimming diversity to fit the frame of white Christian power. And yet, what exists persists.

The Q flourishes in the cracks of empire, in the stories of the oppressed and the oppressor alike. It moves from hand to hand. Queerness is not absent from white European histories; it is simply disguised.

Take Jean/ne Baret, for example, widely described as the first European woman to circumnavigate the globe on the 1766–69 French Bougainville expedition, but who cultivated a gender far from binary. Jean/ne's story is both tragedy and strength – a reminder that even within the imperial machine, some bodies refused to fit the script. Or the late nineteenth-century lady gardeners of Kew Royal Botanical Gardens: in well-cut wool jackets, waistcoats and breeches, their gender-nonconforming attire flew under the radar of Victorian prurience. Their tweeds held cold shears and pocketbooks while cultivating specimens in service of empire, extracting knowledge and profit from Britain's overseas colonies.

Queer white histories are entangled with dominion, and the complicity of white Europeans in imperial oppression is an uncomfortable truth. Queer white Europeans belong in this story too, not because they are right, but because they exist both in tension with the walls of power and in alliance with them. Queer is not a moral value, though it frames an ethics made of attention, reciprocity, tension and refusal.

Colonial, patriarchal power rises because it pushes others down. Its walls climb higher, brick by stolen brick. Today's faux-debates about who counts as a man or woman, who belongs inside a border or is cast outside it, draw from those same foundations. Exclusion is the architecture of power. The sciences of plants and bodies serve those walls, declaring who is 'natural', who deserves rights, who is allowed to live. For half a millennium this purism of gender, sexuality, race, ethnicity, nationhood has rendered outsiders unworthy of life. And yet the ground beneath is restless.

Colonialism leaves its traces in the earth – the same earth into which I plunge my queer hands. I ask myself why – *why* – is it necessary to continue to live beneath these broken values?

The process of uncovering the Q is also about what has masked it. It is about choosing differently. And revealing how those choices have always existed.

If empire tried to police human bodies, nature kept refusing to comply. As in history, so in science: the Q resists and persists. Plant sexuality, for example, is predicated upon the ability to flourish, as well as to reproduce. This requires adaptiveness to change. Plants cosexualise with humans: they have done for millennia. As Stefano Mancuso points out in *The Revolutionary Genius of Plants*, the chilli fruit, rice blade, wheat stalk, maize shaft, sunflower and tomato are 'anthropochores',[9] plants who 'dance with humanity'.[10] Humans are the ultimate vector for plant survival.

Plants adapted to human cultivation; we, in turn, built worlds of food and faith around them.

The complex genders and sexualities of plants might have little to do with humans, if we weren't so entangled with their survival, and they with ours. As the anthropologist Anna L. Tsing says in her tracing of the matsutake mushroom's travels around the world as food, medicine and capital commodity, paying attention to mushrooms won't save us, 'but it might open our imaginations.'[11] Imagination – especially the visionary capacity to think within and beyond borders, binaries and definitions – is crucial to our capacity to live otherwise than we have been told. The standardised norms of sexuality and the biological essentialism that entrap us in exclusionary doom spirals are not just failures of science. They are failures of imagination.

I want to – am compelled to – imagine broader and more enriching parameters for science, culture and nature. I often sense the Q where metaphor and reality meet. After all, my meandering gardening life was always entangled with the queer cultivation that came before. Like these entangled life-sustaining systems, this book forks and meanders – from memoir to poetry, history to botany, animation to art.

I don't make absolute distinctions in this book between gardens and allotments, parks and landscapes, urban nature and wild cultivation, but I do try to account for ownership, profit, legal status and access – the bedrocks of aristocratic land-holding in the UK. Definitions come from the same binaries that police the borders of gender and sexuality. At the same time, they sit at the intersections of other kinds of structural disadvantage: race, ethnicity, socio-economic status, disability.

I write deliberately on queer cultivation in city and country, for example. The common association between sexuality and urban environments is so powerful that it risks eclipsing rural queer cultures; likewise there is a common but false equation between rural life and conservative strongholds of heteronormative sexuality. Neither holds true. As Jill H. Casid said in *Sowing Empire*, 'we need to queer this binary in our writing about the past as well as the present, bringing to the fore that side of the slash we may most desire to suppress or forget.'[12] I do not want to live either side of the divide. I no longer wish to suppress what does not fit into neat little boxes. I am *both, and*.

Even the word *queer* is a pliable word, liable to fall in and out of favour. The term first appears in Scottish or Low German as *quer* or *queir* from around 1500, meaning oblique, strange, off-centre. Its earlier Proto-Indo-European root is **terkw*: torsion, twisting, turning, perverse, angry. And, as Eve Kosofsky Sedgwick, the late and brilliant co-founder of queer theory, recognised, *torque*.[13] Queer twists, resists, persists. It needs something to push and pull against.

In the early nineteenth century *queer* gains traction as a term of suspicion, a word for cheats and spoilers. By the turn of the twentieth century it refers offensively to deviant sexuality, illicit sex and dubious gender.[14] Within LGBTQIA+ communities where the Q holds its place in the wider alphabetic spectrum, queer still incites difficult feelings. For certain gay men born before the decriminalisation of homosexuality in England and Wales in 1967, who survived the HIV/AIDS epidemic in the 1980s and 1990s, and who knew the word only as a code for violence, it is hard to hear. Queer has traversed and contorted the poles of pejorative and honorific. It is old, powerful and in perpetual, seasonal flux.

When my fingers seek out soil's root matter, I feel it. When my queer tendrils reach and recoil, I feel that too.

Seeking the Q in garden is about choosing *both, and*. The endgame of in/out, yes/no, either/or needn't be the only shape life takes. The Q is about those who have lived differently, who walked away from these prisons of belief disguised as fact. I do not want to choose between two equally unliveable options: forced inside the confines of the gender binary, or abandoned alone with no community and no land to love. I am looking for other ways to live. Inspired by the Black lesbian and feminist women of the Combahee River Collective, 'to be recognized as human, levelly human, is enough.'[15] Maybe what I am also looking for is to be recognised as a being – simply, levelly being – in the garden I tend and that tends me.

I keep digging. The land answers with its own scars. When there are microplastics in every part of Antarctica,[16] ocean acidification as deep as 1,500m below sea level,[17] there is no environment on Earth unmarked by human activity. By intention or effect, humans have touched every part. Nature is political because, despite the failed stewardship of white Europeans, humans were always beings in nature, not apart from it. Life is tenacious, regardless of the restrictions we impose. No wall will save us from that truth. No binary holds us separate. The life of Q – human, plant, animal, fungal – has always persisted. Sometimes it has flourished.

water::question?::autumn

1

Q is for garden (on heritage, passing and bothness)

Between the scarlet branches of the dogwood and the lilac-flowering hibiscus in my South London garden, there is an undersized lemon verbena plant. It is in the wrong place, overshadowed by the large arcs of the cherry tree that shed pink snowfall in May. Still, it shoots up tall stalks, fighting for light. I should move this little twiggy bush, which in its original location on Earth would become a tree of two metres or more. But there isn't much room in the borders of my urban garden, and I love the smell of its leaves as I brush past: a fresh, sweet, not-of-this-place scent, nothing like the earthy mildness of the other vegetation around it.

A swatch of its pruned stems has lain drying on my kitchen countertop for days. As I pull papery leaves from twiggy cuttings, a small snail shell falls onto the pages of the book in front of me. Ten minutes later, a head and two stalked eyes emerge from a thin, grey-blue body, sliding silently across the page.

This tiny hermaphrodite entered my kitchen, hidden in the leaves of a medicinal plant once thieved from South America by eighteenth-century European Spanish botanists. I love to say it this way, *thieved*, just as Jamaica Kincaid does in her book *My Garden*. As Kincaid expresses it, gardening is often a result of botanical theft.[1] In Spain, the lemon verbena became *hierba luisa*. It travelled to Paris, Oxford, London, then throughout Britain, where it became a plant of many names: *Aloysia citrodora. Aloysia triphylla. Lippia citrodora.*[2] Finally it was shipped to North America, completing the cycle of larceny by landing in the epicentre of capitalism.

Those curling leaflets shelter an intersex being. Plants, by the way, are also mostly hermaphroditic, intermingling more-than-male and more-than-female parts. An intersex snail-being and a polysexual plant-being sit on my counter-top, while I stand next to them, a human being caught up in the binaries of human sex and gender wars.

It feels obvious to say that the land is many-gendered. Sexuality is part of the contract between humans and the earth, which we either choose to cultivate or ignore. But to say that it feels obvious does not mean that it is. To say there is a Q in garden does not mean you can see it.

You could say that this is a story about snail sex. It's about other things too: what you see and what you want to see, straight lines and queer spirals, passing and tenderness. Cultivation and civilisation, nature and ornament. Both, and. But it begins with a plant, and a snail.

* * *

On a mild late October morning in 2020, dry and a brief reprieve from the month's torrents, a prominent journalist complains about queerness. I say prominent but I had not heard of him before his column erupted onto my social media timelines, reposted by outraged queers. This individual lambasted the attempts of British heritage charity the National Trust to put queerness back into the history of Knole House in Kent. Irked by an encounter with a Trust volunteer who – so he believes – has mistaken his friend's and his own matching Barbour jackets for signs of queer partnership, he describes the organisation's attention to the sexual histories of stately homes and their owners as an 'act of modern narcissism' that 'pull[s] the rug out from under our own feet'.[3] Apparently, it would be narcissistic to imagine there were queer people in the past: that vast unknown ocean of others 'who did not think like us'. To be queer is to be contemporary, without history, locked myopically in the present. To include these vagabonds of time is to uproot the nation: that bastion of identity to which the journalist clings like the last rock at sea.

Strong words, uttered with conviction.

As soon as you begin to deconstruct it, the thinness of the argument feels like punching wet toilet paper.[4] Some personal discomfort about the visibility of queer identity in historical contexts becomes a rallying cry. He pronounces: 'A nation without a history, or at least without a history that gives it a sense of roots, is not a nation at all.' Those lovely, white, straight-down-the-middle roots, which the columnist calls the origins of Britishness. Why he believes queer history – or gay sexuality – to be rootless is never made explicit. But it's all in the name – and the naming.

Back in my kitchen, I pull leaves from a plant pilfered by 250 years of colonial botany. The snail, eye stalks protruding, looks up at me. I look down at them, and I say,

'What the fuck is he talking about?'

* * *

Knole is a place familiar to my childhood in the suburban hinterland between Greater London and Kent. I studied the place for my History GCSE. But that was in the time of Section 28, the legal framework set up by Margaret Thatcher's government that criminalised the 'promotion' of homosexuality by local authorities, ergo prohibiting any mention at all. Queerness in my history lessons was outlawed. Knole is the birthplace of Vita Sackville-West, and the former home of Edward Sackville-West, Vita's cousin. Both were queer, and part of the loose association known as the Bloomsbury Group.

Eddy Sackville-West, novelist and music critic, bequeathed a substantial art collection to his former lover Eardley Knollys, who in turn bestowed it to Mattei Radev, the former lover of E. M. Forster. The Radev Collection was exhibited in the early and mid-2010s in museums and galleries throughout the UK, and contains works by Picasso, Braque and Modigliani, as well as work from Bloomsbury artist Duncan Grant. And, just for luck, a black-and-white cat with an enormous bowl of cream in poster paint by six-year-old Pat Berrisford, displayed in 1953 at the national exhibition of children's art during the Festival of Britain.[5]

Vita Sackville-West, the writer and gardener, whose open marriage to Harold Nicolson enabled her to build Sissinghurst gardens, was famously a lover and friend of Virginia Woolf, who, inspired by Vita, so it is said, wrote her 1928 novel, *Orlando: A Biography*. Vita, an openly bisexual woman, discussed her gender ambivalence in letters to her friend. She may have identified as non-binary, had the terminology been available at that time. The language might not have existed, but the concept did: the notion of a third intermediate gender was prevalent in the Europe of Woolf and Sackville-West, particularly in Weimar Germany.

Virginia certainly thought Vita lived between genders. Vita was disinherited from Knole not by virtue of her sexuality but because of her assigned gender, since the British aristocracy does not permit women to inherit wealth. She discussed her disinheritance extensively – and disinheritance is a key feature of *Orlando*, when a centuries-long legal battle ultimately dispossesses the genderqueer protagonist.

The journalist, he of tissue-thin argument, doesn't mention Vita, only Eddy – and certainly not the art collection, Vita's garden nor Virginia's great work of literature. If narcissism is self-regard, then all three figures look beyond themselves, creating kin and art in outward spirals. If there is more to know about the sexual relationships that brought these art forms into existence, wreathed by friendship, creativity and inspiration, then it is not narcissism, but life.

The Bloomsbury circles of lovers, artists, writers, gardeners, landowners and bequeathers unravel all the conventional mappings of heterosexual heritage. Their geometries break down the lines of father-to-son ownership, where each male proprietor produces male offspring-owners through assorted wives and lover-vessels. In Vita and Eddy, the vertical columns of patrilineal heritage are displaced by squares, circles, triangles.[6] Whorls and spirals.

This is what the journalist wants to straighten out, the queer Bloomsbury kinks and twirls. He wants to strafe the historical landscape, so that everything is pleasantly, heterosexually aligned. And mask queerness in the mystifying forces of inference, which is where the 'fun' is, apparently – and where ignorance must be equally enjoyable.

All the queers must be closeted again so they don't disturb the jolly straight lines.

If 'queer' is just a name or an anachronism, not an act, or a life, then it can't have existed in the past. What name could adequately describe lesbian and gay and bisexual relationships, the polyamorous dynamics of the gay salon, the mutual love and admiration between Vita and Virginia, and the gender ambivalence which inspired Virginia to write one of the most well-known works of modernist literature? Maybe they should have no name at all, conveniently swept like dust into the back of that cosy, inferential closet.

Naming is powerful. Refusing to name is also an act of power. When the lemon verbena was extracted from its cultural and geographical home alongside the historic civilisations and Indigenous societies of South America, it already had many names. Naming is an accretion of layers over time, only some of which you can see. Naming can erase a past. Not naming can do this too. Names will not save us. Not even queer ones. Naming is not the same as being.

Codicils of queer love and aristocratic wealth propagated the Bloomsbury circles of art and land, gardens and literature. These wellsprings of desire not only manifested themselves in which lover to take, but how to embody love in writing; how to pass works of art from one lover to another; how to build the rhythmic love that cultivates gardens from land.

The journalist who doesn't want to know about Eddy Sackville-West's lovers calls himself a historian. I do not know the name for a historian who wishes to eradicate whatever he finds dull or inconvenient. I did not know it was the work of a historian to erase history. Or love, for that matter.

There is something else, though. A needling. I can feel it.

The journalist's unreasoned reasoning for the strafing of history is a casual dismissal. Who one's lover is isn't interesting or important. Not real history. Who one's lover isn't is, of course, very important indeed (Barbour jackets and all). Lovers are ephemeral; not the stuff of history. Love is ephemeral too; nothing to do with heritage. And sexuality, of course, is merely who you sleep with.

Ah. There it is.

I have heard this one before.

* * *

The hot-water infusion made from lemon verbena is antipyretic, antispasmodic and has oestrogenic properties that may assist with reproductive health. For this reason, verbena is associated with the feminine. There's no reason why soothing tinctures should be the sole reserve of beings who menstruate, though.

The snail creeps along the thin edge of the kitchen paper I have set down to gather the dried verbena leaves. Their shell is glass-like, reddish brown. Even though they are less than half a centimetre in diameter, the shell's whorl is clear and distinct.

Land snails have complex reproductive sexualities. They may mate with another snail using their penis, or they may allow themselves to be penetrated by the penis of said other snail, sometimes both at the same time. Some self-inseminate instead. It doesn't really make sense to decide upon the binary gender of a snail, since they contain at least, if not more than, two.

Snail sexualities are slow, led by touch, taste and smell. After a snail picks up on the chemical traces of a potential lover, it takes some time to reach them, before they *might* begin many hours of embracing, foot to foot. This is an object of small fascination depicted in Claude Nuridsany and Marie Pérennou's 1996 insect documentary, *Microcosmos*. On YouTube there are many homages to this short sequence of snail romance; retakes and adaptations with new soundtracks added to extend the human-snail sexual metaphor.

Snail love is epic and curious. After long hours of embrace, the snail shoots a love dart into their snail-lover to test out their partner's sexual probity. A sharp structure made of chitin and calcium, the love dart's puncture is the human equivalent of being stabbed by a 15-inch knife.[7] Snail sex is a risky transaction. They don't make snap decisions about sexual partners.

If I were to talk to the snail about sex, they would no doubt be cautious. Sex and sexuality are a sensuous, dangerous, whole body-mind exercise. Besides, a snail is more likely to identify the traces of my pheromones, or feel the air vibrations of my voice, than speak. Sound in human frequency is not a virtue in the world of gastropods.

'Sexuality is who you sleep with?'

The snail waggles their eye stalks.

* * *

I have heard this claim before.

Some years ago, on the last fine, warm weekend of the year before the long descent into autumn and moonlit afternoons, a friend and I took a long walk. This old friend and I, we talked as we passed through the same Essex farmland and riversides that John Constable once painted.

I find myself re-walking this path, reliving the part of the conversation that caught me in a tender place.

We pass a flint-walled church, gothic arches echoed in the curves of sandstone plaques rising from the grassy churchyard. For reasons that are beyond me, I start to tell my friend about the choking recoil I have felt in the past during the weddings of straight friends. Not because of the weddings, or the friends who wed, but because of the tightening of a bind that leaves no room for my own queerness. A bind that feels like a metal hasp pulled tight across thick, unyielding tarpaulin, stifling weeds and wildlife against those walls.

Many times I have stood uncomfortably in other churchyards where wildflowers meet lichen-blown headstones, in that fixed position of what it is to be a particular kind of human. To be a wedding guest, commanded to fit seamlessly into a matrix of straight, often white, able-bodied life, in photographs of perfect youth, with the elderly fondly looking on. No space to be a messy, non-compliant body – to be young and in pain, or sick, or an assigned female, non-feminine body, or a sense of self that isn't framed by man–woman married partnership. This is not a criticism of my married heterosexual friends: their happiness brings me joy. As I have eased into my own queer non-compliance, the choking feeling has ebbed a little. But still sometimes, rising up from awkward angles, at inopportune moments, the tarpaulin engulfs me. The hasp seals me in the airless dark, trapped against the flint.

In that churchyard, on that fine autumn day, I don't say all this. I don't know it then, but I am trying, and failing, to talk about a particular kind of culture. Not the weddings, nor the friends, but what lies beneath. The obligatory culture of a binary-gendered, predominantly straight, white world, sedimented by ritual.

And of course I don't explain myself very well, because the friend doesn't see the bind or the tarpaulin, or the stone walls. Instead, he says: 'but why should it matter who you sleep with?'

As if to force the bind tighter, my friend turns abruptly to my concern with plants and earth, my love of gardens and allotments. He declares these things as exclusively heterosexual and bourgeois: *The Good Life* on steroids. A conclusive proof of my non-queerness. And, incidentally, my class betrayal.

As I press lemon verbena leaves into a jar, the snail curves their smelling lobes towards me. They wrap around the corner of the kitchen paper and retract swiftly, returning to the fragile safety of their glassy shell.

'Why the fuck did you tell him that?'

The snail is motionless, muffled by the home on their back.

* * *

Sissinghurst Castle, Vita Sackville-West's former home, is now a pleasure garden for most of the year. A place for lovers of plants, lovers of lovers, and lovers themselves, to seek pleasure in being with what grows there. Although I have visited many times in summer, with queer and straight friends, in autumn it is easier to see the garden's bones. Ligaments and nerve bundles too: small black signs pushed into the earth with white capitals that list the Latin binomial titles for what grows above or is hidden beneath the soil. In late November, it is easier to see the fresh planting among the perennials, some cut back, others with straggling limbs that will protect them from the frosts to come. Even on the cusp of winter, the rose garden gives off rose scent.

When Vita Sackville-West first started writing about her gardens, she was not an expert gardener. Her first garden experience was love, not mastery. The end stanza of her 1915 poem 'The Garden' is about failure: 'We waited then for them to grow/We planted wallflowers in a row/And lavender and borage blue/But love was all that ever grew.'[8] Where lavender and borage struggle by implication ('But love'), love is what grows in Sackville-West's first garden in Long Barn, two miles away from her childhood home of Knole, and 15 years before she and Harold move to Sissinghurst.

Vita's career as a garden designer did not begin with Sissinghurst; nor did her life as a writer end with it. On Sissinghurst's 20-year development in *House and Garden* in 1950, she complains about the absence of straight lines in the old Tudor walls. They are 'coffin-shaped', 'oblique', 'inexplicable'.[9] It takes queer Vita and her queer husband, Harold, in their very lavender marriage, to bring the lines into parallel, beginning the formal structure of the garden rooms, which she observes from her study in its all-seeing turret.

I find myself looking for straight lines in this bare-boned autumnal garden, but what I see are geometries, bends and returns. I see the coffin-shaped courtyard, but also the imperfect squares of the White Garden, which at this time of year is green. Delicate frothing grey-greens of artemisia and angelica, stout bottle-and-lime greens of box hedging, wavering yellow-greens of wisteria peeling away from its branches, filled with the steep sweaty scent of fallen apples. The Tudor walls are stacked with lichens and mosses; sturdy supports for the roses, clematis and old magnolias that lean between them and the tower that houses Vita's writing room and her collections of blue Tehran glass. All the garden's geometries point towards spirals, circles, helical forms. Queerness in the straight.

* * *

For a long time, queer people have clothed their queerness in straight paraphernalia. Many queer people – though of course not all – have learned to pass for straight, cisgendered, to fit in wherever they can. And that way of passing is a bind. Do it too convincingly, and the reasons for passing become obliterated. Become too obedient to straight cultures that claim to have no visible sexuality at all, and sexuality becomes only skin-deep. A cut of the cloth, not a foundation of being. Hence the barbs of my old acquaintance and the claims of the journalist-historian: to them, passing is indistinguishable from straightness. Sexuality becomes who you sleep with, and not how you show up in the world. Passing eliminates your difference, and you pay the price.

The snail's long slim body slides along the underside of the discarded branches on my kitchen countertop. They have never tried to pass for anything but themselves.

Although passing is a privilege that grants safety, sometimes it is involuntary. This is particularly difficult for people who travel across genders and sexualities. To be seen as one thing when in fact you are another, many others, carries its own form of pain. This is true for femmes and trans couples too; those who appear close to, who resemble heterosexual tropes, but are not the same. Lesbians are mistaken for sisters; trans families are mistaken for straight, nuclear ones. This may be a tool of safety in a world where the violence of gender correction hangs like dark clouds. But misrecognition, the partner of passing, drifts in the air.

Passing is, can be, a tactic of safety performed by marginalised people who are able to appear, for a while, to be straight, or white, or of a fixed gender, or able-bodied, or Anglo-European, or middle class, or permanently settled. If performed for too long or too hard, passing overloads a body, becoming self-estranging. Passing is always unstable, at risk of provoking at best suspicious and at worst hostile reactions from either of the identity groups between which the passer passes (straight/gay, white/black, working class/upper class, able-bodied/disabled).

In Nella Larsen's 1929 novel *Passing* – adapted into film by director Rebecca Hall in 2021 – middle-class Irene simultaneously adores and defends herself against narcissistic, worldly Clare. Two Black women who pass as white, permanently or temporarily, battle with their mutual attraction, amid the painful complexity of class, race and sexuality in 1920s Harlem.

Passing is about class, race, sexuality, gender, disability, global mobility. It is also part of a much longer discourse from the histories of slavery. It is a matter of repressive violence and social control. Passing reaches into any domain where social dominance is regulated by who is included and who is excluded, by virtue of their appearance. It is – can be – a source of pleasure and danger, pride and shame.

The experiences that flow beneath passing are historically powerful, life-altering. Yet it is also delicate: passing provokes pain and incites tenderness. Its instability is just as likely to wound as it is to resolve.

* * *

There is always a personal saga: a wound hidden behind wounding words. It is not my place to speculate on the origins of the ones that spiked me that autumn day. I am more interested in the wider cultural compost that feeds the story of the straight.

When the eighteenth-century Swedish botanist Carolus Linnaeus created classifications for flowering plants in the Latin binomial system, he used binary models of sexual difference to catalogue and classify plant life. Or rather: he began with the in-between – the hybrid, the hermaphrodite – but somehow, for the sake of economy, or simplicity, or familiarity, or what served the Christian European colonial models of patriarchal power in which he was steeped, the in-between fell away. In the Linnaean binomial system, gender and sexuality are almost always one or the other. Male or female. Heterosexually reproductive. According to these sorting systems, the space for the things in between closes up without trace.

No room to acknowledge that plants contain sexualities and genders infinitely more complex than a binary sexual system could ever accommodate – monoecious, dioecious, 'perfect/bisexual' (my favourite category). No room, in the formative Linnaean either/or world, to love the mingling of the organic and the ornamental: to recognise that heterosexual gender binaries are a product of the speaker, not the subject.

And according to my friend's binary system, unwitting inheritor of the Linnaean tradition, knowing about plants is bourgeois and heterosexual and therefore nothing else. The messiness of queer love in nature and cultivation is as unviable as a queer desire to speak about how plants came to be in an Essex riverside, churchyard, cottage garden, because it does not fit into the either/or world of binary thinking. Nothing queer, for my friend – and nothing therefore that was made *for* him – about deciphering the ecologies of plants, the long-fingered outcomes of European empires that imported innumerable plant species for decorative or utilitarian or even accidental reasons, regardless of their position in the ecosystem, or their capacity to accommodate, dominate, even eradicate other more fragile beings.

Botany and ecology and gardening are often associated – and for good reason – with wealthy white heterosexuality, land ownership, patrilineal heritage and colonial models of scientific classification. And so in the Linnaean binomial system they cannot also be queer. There is no Q in garden or gardening or landscape or horticulture or cultivation because this is an either/or situation. No room for both, and.

* * *

Often I cannot say the thing I want to. Words betray me. Are a hasp and a tarpaulin and a flint wall ever enough to describe the darkness through which feelings seep into the thing called erasure? My metaphor is wrong. And yet, this is the feeling that feeds on me. The hasp. The tarpaulin. The wall.

I don't know how to explain that the feeling, the darkness, the choking is not a doing or an act; that nobody ever *told* me I was the wrong body for a wedding guest. Not many, anyway: there are always a few random acts of homophobia and misogyny, even for a modestly straight-passing, vaguely womanish white person.

How can I reveal the shadows cast by walls that regiment sexuality and gender to someone who lives comfortably within its enclosures? If I point out the wall, does it start to crumble?

Is it always either/or? Or could it be both, and?

The snail's newly-emerged antennae undulate in cosine curves.

'What the fuck are you talking about, now?'

Let me try to explain.

***

Queerness does not run straight, even as it seeks to even out centuries of obliquity.

Queerness is not an either/or equation.

I doubt the journalist who dislikes the queerness of Knole would like Sissinghurst very much – it has been cared for by the National Trust since 1967. There is little inference in the Sissinghurst that Vita writes about from 1950, only clarity about struggle, time and waiting, and the energy to persist. She is clear about the physical-architectural lines drawn by her husband. How his imaginal world on paper devised the rooms and vistas of the garden, before they were created by labouring hands in earth and brick, stone and yew hedging. Vita's deference and love for her companion of decades shine out from the page.

And I see straight lines of a sort in the garden rooms of Sissinghurst. I also see mazes, turnings, oblique angles, the curve of the yew hedge, the tenderness of decay and senescence, and quiet new growth. I see circular time: the failing of plants from disease or the wrong positioning, or simply the end of their life-cycle. Before-time, in the re-shaping of the old rose garden into the White Garden, which took place during Vita's lifetime. And after-time in Delos, the Greek island-inspired corner that Vita and Harold never managed to establish successfully. It is difficult to make Mediterranean planting thrive in rich, wet Kentish Weald. But by transforming the soil structure beneath, contemporary garden designer Dan Pearson and Sissinghurst's gardeners have created a future-time for Delos, with gravel and flagstone paths that snake between sandstone follies, structural euphorbia and grasses, scented thyme and achillea.

Why should straight lines always be perfectly and only straight? Couldn't they be lines of sight, pulled off-centre by the green flesh of plants, a tangle of branches, a winding path?

Vita writes consistently about her love of Sissinghurst. Love is a prerequisite for gardening: 'One needs years of patience to make a garden; one needs deeply to love it, in order to endure that patience. One needs optimism and foresight. One has to wait.'[10] Years of getting it wrong and starting again. Years of hope, despite living through two global wars. Years of waiting. Becoming used to failure as well as success. Years of labour (not all Vita's, as she admits herself).

Time undoes straight lines. Or maybe they were never straight to begin with.

Is Vita Sackville-West un-queered by her love of plants? Or is her garden rightfully a part of the queer heritage of gardening that runs back through the nineteenth century via the likes of Gertrude Jekyll and the Kewriosities – women trained as gardeners at Kew Royal Botanical Gardens, who became sensational not because of their plant skills but because of their bloomers? And before that in queer figures like Anne Lister, Mary Delany and Jean/ne Baret? And before and after and during all that, queer Indigenous knowledge that gives much fuller room for the complexity of sexualities for all beings?

What if the queerness in gardening was a both, and situation?

The Kewriosities are another story. Q is for curious, for women's rights activist, for plantswoman, for coloniser.

* * *

Both, and.

Sexuality is both who you sleep with and how you see the world. How you love it. Straight lines, obliques, coffin-shapes. Spirals, circles, helixes. Roses and sandstone. A plant and a snail.

And passing is painful. Misrecognition hurts. The difficulty of passing (or failing to pass) and the pain of misrecognition are common experiences for many queer people. And it's funny how, the more fragile and precarious your sense of being recognised is, the more you recognise yourself. What forms an identity most powerfully is what tries to extinguish it.

And patrilineal straightness unwittingly leaves its monocultural abrasions on land and bodies, past and present. Nonetheless, things regrow from whatever is broken, or needled, or wounded. Bodies and land learn very quickly how to self-tend, uproot the damage and reseed, regrow. The fungal fingers that notice the uprooting self-tend too, mending the broken links that stretch tenderly beneath the soil for leagues in a vast mycorrhizal network.

And what comes up as queer might well have bloomed as something else at another time. *Hierba luisa. Aloysia citrodora. Lemon verbena*. These plants are connected even if the words are not.

There is a history decided by those who do not like what they see, because to see things otherwise would disturb the foundations of a straight, white, male world made in the image of sixteenth-century Europe. There is also a probing form of queer storytelling that looks for the gaps, reveals the erasures, plants wildflower meadows in churned-up terrain. Querying, spiral stories are destabilising for those who walk on the land as if land were a birthright, and not a gift.

A plant and a snail could teach a different story. About a world, and a natural history that is neither comfortable nor singular. Neither male nor female. Straight nor gay. Is more both, and. And until a new word comes along: queer.

Queerness is not so much about the naming as the feeling. Feelings. Both the feelings – my feelings – of being needled constantly, in an endless bind to an inhospitable prevailing culture, and the love, the tenderness, finding a space to grow between. A fragile helix the thickness of a snail shell, from which to emerge and retreat. To come out and go in again.

There is no need for a Q in garden, if you do not see the Q. And there is no stronger need for that Q than when it can't be seen.

'I see you.'

The snail slowly meanders across the countertop, seeking shelter.

I see the snail, too. Their many-gendered, polymorphous fragility. Shell and flesh. Eye stalks and lovedarts.

***

Both, and.

Vita Sackville-West's gardens run through her. As do her disinheritance and extraction from Knole, her childhood home; as do her wealth and status that made manual labour a thing that others do, except in times of global crisis. World War II left her with no more than blistered hands from trimming yew hedges: the same hedges which now observe perfect right-angles and geometric curves. These things coexist with her queerness. They are uneasy. They are part of the oblique, enfolded outlooks that make a life a life, and not a straightened historical certitude.

Like many people with a pot of soil or two, a handful of seeds, gardening is part of my being. It is generative and gutsy: plunging my hands into the earth is one of the most intimate acts I can imagine. That intimacy is no more governed by who I sleep with than the golden, sun-ripened sweetness of an allotment-grown tomato.

And yet.

Sexuality is not a thin cultural veneer, but grows from creativity and life force. It runs below history: it is the earth from which history grows. The land is many-gendered. They say that 'civilisation' is four days deep, but cultivation goes deeper. All these things are in unique partnership at any given time. They are not and never have been determined by the cultural misconceptions of a so-called historian. No matter how powerful the system of naming.

The seeds of my being have learned to flourish and transform under tricky environments. When I pull a weed, or plant a seed, I am not always, maybe even rarely successful in cultivating my spirit, entwined as it is with plant and animal life, lemon verbena and land snail. If my tender shoots are unwittingly crushed by the misperceptions of a friend, who himself involuntarily emulates the binary language systems of eighteenth-century botanists, or the words of a twenty-first-century journalist, that story is as personal as it is political, cultural and historical.

* * *

By the time I have screwed the lid tight on the jar of verbena leaves, labelled it and put it away on the shelf, the snail has crawled off the kitchen worktop, looking for a safe place to hibernate. I hope they find it.

I write in the spirit of defiance and gentleness. Gentleness and defiance to tend my tender plants, in my tender landscape. The tender queer garden of my life.

And I also know this from a space of deep knowing-ness, where words and names are secondary to the evolution of being. I know this in the nape of my neck and the curve of my big toe as it presses into the earth beneath me. There is, always has been ample room for queerness in the matrix of tiny microorganisms and minerals, water acidities and leaf-mould, compost and humus.

In civilisation and cultivation; nature and ornament. Both, and.

2

kewrious (on queer bodies and transgressive gardening fashion)

Once I see one snail, I see another. And another. My garden fills with slow, oozing, brittle-shelled bodies. Each year I watch as my hostas, whose delicious verdant heads rise so optimistically in early spring, are transformed into lacy strings. By the autumn, spiky stumps have replaced once luscious limes and blue-greens. Year on year, snails feast, and plants fail, and I fail at adequately protecting them. But the snails remain, cemented beneath windowsills and behind plant pots.

The young boy Jody in Derek Jarman's film *The Garden* plays with a snail companion, touching the gastropod's muscular foot to his bare cheek. A snail overhears human conversations from the safety of a flowerbed in Virginia Woolf's short story 'Kew Gardens', first printed and decorated by her sister Vanessa Bell for Hogarth Press, their publishing house. Elizabeth Tova Bailey's memoir and short film *The Sound of a Wild Snail, Eating* spend extended, illness-infused time with a snail. And Patricia Highsmith's snail companions – whom she once took to a cocktail party in a handbag full of lettuce leaves – feature prominently in her stories. Especially 'The Snail Watcher', in which protagonist Peter Knoppert is consumed, quite literally, by his voyeuristic snail fetish.[1]

I'm glad to be in the company of snails and queer snail-loving encounters, disconcertingly erotic and frustrating as they are.

Maybe the Q in Garden is not a plant, nor tendrils of a vine, but a snail trail. A silvered path that winds through the thicket of things.

* * *

I don't think much about what I wear when I garden. It's like most things: when you begin an activity, a pastime, you take what you have and you adapt, and adapting becomes a pattern of behaviour, or clothing, or ritual: like the first sip of coffee before I sit down to write as morning breaks behind the blinds.

For gardening I wear a blue cotton twill fisherman's smock that used to belong to my father, but which he never wore. The sleeves of the smock are long, so that I can roll them up in summer and down in winter. The wide collar fits a scarf underneath, or is airy when I overheat, and protects my neck from burning. The wide square pockets in the front are useful for storing tools or bits of wire or whatever I accumulate. I always wear it for gardening. It is my gardening smock.

For my lower half, I've yet to land upon my official gardening gear. Sometimes I wear walking trousers. Too short from crotch seam to waist, they slip down uncomfortably and dig into my lower abdomen when crouching and kneeling (the majority of my gardening work). The legs are long enough (just), but they are wide at the bottom, leaving unneeded fabric that catches and muddies when I dig the soil. I don't know what it's best to garden in.

Some well-cut, wide-legged twill culottes tied close at the calf would do.

* * *

The silvered snail path leads me back to the garden's word-roots and root words.

Garden: from the Vulgar Latin *hortus gardinus*, the 'enclosed garden', via the Frankish *Gardo*. The Old North French *gardin* referred to a garden, an orchard or a palace grounds. The garden is the space between the castle and the forest. There's an association, implied rather than stated, with wealth – and affluence still percolates through garden ownership. Owning a garden is also owning land, after all. The first syllable of garden is speculated to come from the Proto-Indo-European root *gher*, meaning to grasp or to enclose – found in *horticulture*, *garden* and *yard*, as well as *choir*, *Asgard* and *hangar*. The Old English *geard* also referred to a fenced garden. And *gher* means to like or to want, found in *charisma*, *greedy* and *yearn*. The old English *geard* means to strive or desire. *Gern* is the German word for enjoyment, preference. *Ich mache es gerne* means, I'll do it willingly. I'm happy to do it. The double meaning of *gher* brings pleasure and desire and garden enclosure into the same orbit, which makes sense, since *pairidaēza* in Avestan (from Zoroastrian scripture) means a walled enclosure, exceptional garden or park; a pleasure ground. Greek and Latin *paradisus* and *paradeisos* both refer to parks, orchards or the garden of Paradise. Modern Persian and Arabic use the word *firdaus*.

Pleasure and Paradise. Guarding and garden. Gardens always hold within them the promise of enclosure:

protection from the desert winds, but exclusion too. Who enters the garden, and how they enter it, is a matter the garden is already well prepared for, historically speaking. As the artist Zheng Bo says, 'a garden is more than a space to cultivate others; it is ultimately a place to cultivate ourselves.'[2] The cultivation and shaping of other human bodies is always a pursuit that takes place in the garden.

There is an image of three such bodies, guarding their gardening in breeches and boots.

These are the names of the first women gardeners at Kew Botanical Gardens. Eleanor Morland. Gertrude Cope. Alice Hutchings. Annie Gulvin. Jessie Newsham. Florence Potter. Madeline Agar.

I love their dapper look: flat caps, tweed waistcoats, knickerbockers and gaiters, with a handkerchief and a pocket-watch chain. Two of them carry a pocketbook in one hand. These three women look young – very young. They are all graduates of Swanley Horticultural College in Hextable, Kent, newly recruited to Kew from 1896 to 1897.

Do they know their own queerness in this Victorian photograph? What do they think as they stare back at the camera, bodies stilled so that their images don't blur the frame?

* * *

Eleanor Morland, Gertrude Cope, Alice Hutchings. Writing their names is important. Remembering their names is important. Saying the name, remembering the person, is like an antidote against amnesia. Not a death in the personal sense, but death as oblivion, death as the wiping out of the past which is always more complicated, more like and unlike the present than any of us can imagine. Death as the erasure of gendered complexity in the garden.

Figure 1 Three women gardeners, c.1896. Photograph, courtesy of Royal Botanic Gardens, Kew and Bridgeman Images.

Seeing these young women who might have been 18 or 19 or 20 when the photograph was taken, remembering that they had names, and lives, before and after this photograph as working women, gardeners, botanists and, later, compliant servants of empire too: all this matters. Remembering their work and their lives is an inoculation against a present moment that will always seek to erase the subtler, more intricate story.

Take the poem, for instance. 'Kewriosity' is associated with these women, reprinted in full in headlines and by-lines about them. The poem wasn't written by Alice, Gertrude and Eleanor. It likely wasn't even written about them. It was published in 1900, some years after they had already left Kew. Magazines entitled *Fun* are rarely the epitome of cutting-edge news stories. *Fun* was a direct competitor to the more well-known *Punch*. Satire's masculine violence is still there though, regardless of the entreaty to entertain.

'Kewriosity' appears in an elaborate, pantomime-like set-up of an article, which perhaps I would appreciate if I were more familiar with Victorian humour. The article is called 'The "Fun" Club: Fourteenth Meeting' and reads like a satirical character sketch of various society bodies at the time. Some figures appear over the haze of 120 years; Thomas Hardy, for example, Rudyard Kipling and William Thackeray, Leonard Henry Courtney, the politician and advocate for proportional representation, and the Scottish poet Robert Williams Buchanan, to whom the poem is apocryphally attributed. Entitled 'London's Kewriosity', it has a 5-stanza, 4-line, AABB rhyming structure, 11–12 syllables, 4 stresses. Regular as clockwork.

It's not a great poem:

> A rumour went forth and the town was aglow
> From Greenwich to Richmond, from Peckham to Bow—
> And the man-in-the-street made a fine how-de-do,
> When he heard of the ladies who gardened at Kew.

[Greenwich, Richmond, Peckham, Bow. Mostly south of the river in its pursuits then – the poor cousin of wealthy

North London. *Fun* has been described in some quarters as the poor man's *Punch*. Maybe this is why it's concerned with the man in the street. And so the poem continues:]

They gardened in bloomers the newspapers said
So to Kew without waiting all Londoners sped;
From the roofs of the 'buses they had a fine view
Of the ladies in bloomers who gardened at Kew.

The orchids were slighted, the lilies were scorned,
The dahlias were flouted, till botanists mourned.
But the Londoners shouted: 'What ho, there! Go to!
Who wants to see blooms now you've bloomers at Kew!'

So the botanists held a big meeting and said:—
'This won't do, for all London has gone off its head;
This costume we find is too painfully "new"—
It is making a "sideshow" of beautiful Kew.'

These ladies in bloomers are treated as 'freaks'
In future they'd all better garden in 'breeks'—
Now they look so like men no-one rushes to view—
And a pastoral quiet has settled on Kew.

Not a great poem. It condenses some themes, as satirical jokes usually do. It acknowledges the newspapers reporting on the agreement established in 1895 between Swanley Horticultural College and the Director of the Royal Botanical Gardens, William Turner Thistleton-Dyer (the same Thistleton-Dyer who refused to consider seriously the artist and children's writer Beatrix Potter's mycological drawings and research because she was a woman, and therefore an amateur scholar), that a small number of the college's best female students could join the staff at Kew. The media were some half a decade late on this. And of course, it follows that, when contemporary amusements like the circus, minstrelsy, vaudeville and the freak show all insisted on looking, staring and gawping as legitimate pursuits of popular life, this poem emphasises the women's appearance over any actual gardening activity. But it didn't even get that right.

The uniform worn by Morland, Cope and Hutchings isn't an adaptation of feminine dress. It is a fully masculine design: from the white cravats and collar points of their undershirts, to the waistcoat and jacket. The waistcoats act as a kind of binder; the well-cut but relaxed jackets hide the hip-to-waist ratio. The garments, hand-sewn and tailored by the women or their families, make movement easy, removing the unceasing de-mobilisation of female-presenting bodies that was a commonplace of Victorian fashion – whalebones, stays, corsetry, floor-length skirts. *Fun* magazine's man on the street loses interest in a woman who dresses like a man, moves like a man, stands like a man (hands in breech pockets, easy stare). Particularly when she – they – become indistinguishable from the masculine figures of gardeners.

Women who dress like men disappear into the background. Their gender becomes invisible. This was indeed the principle: the women appointed to work at Kew in that brief window between 1895 and 1902 would work with men, like men, indistinguishable from men, in the same uniform as men. They were first appointed as 'Garden Boys' – apprentices to the full gardener role, on wages commensurate with that status. Their boyness was intentional.

In 2021, when this photograph spread across social media, their visibility provoked queer exclamations of joy. Masculine-presenting women, shifting across the borderlands of sex and gender. A call to the non-binary, to the genderqueer.

This is a queer photograph. And this is how I see them queerly. This is who they are, at the very least because their masculine-presenting uniforms transmit the message, across 125 years, that the limiting binaries of gender presentation have always left loopholes through which nonconforming beings can pass.

Another piece in the jigsaw puzzle.

Another time and place for anachronism to do its work. A queerness that does its work above and below language, queerness that is felt in a body, expressed in a stance, communicated in stitches and breeches and cloth.

* * *

I eye the Kewriosities' breeches with envy. I would like to feel well-dressed but practical when I garden. As it is, I lose a sense of my own style, surrendered to kneeling and weeding, or sowing, or cutting back brambles, or tying fast-growing tomato plants to canes, or covering the purple-sprouting broccoli with netting to protect against marauding pigeons. What would it be like to feel good in my gardening clothes, and not like an overweight, middle-aged, unkempt creature of indifferent gender? I haven't yet clothed myself to address both my sexuality and my practicality, combining the me that gardens with the me that sees myself gardening with the me that is seen to garden.

This is in one sense no kind of problem at all: does it matter how I look, when I'm absorbed in my gardening? Does the earth care what I am dressed in, or the plants I tend? The simplest answer to these issues is no. A plant is distinctly unbothered as to whether I am dressed in petroleum derivatives or hyperfarmed and chemically over-treated cotton. But what sort of hypocrite would I be if the clothes I wear didn't have some relationship to and with the land?

I look at these three women, comfortably staring down the camera, and I feel the urge to talk about my body. This body, battered, bruised, broken, remade, reformed, deformed, unkindly loved, kindly hated, object of intense self-scrutiny, thing to be at war with, source of comfort, my only home.

I want to talk about my body because, in all the years that I've moved closer to embodied theories of thinking, living, writing, feeling, looking, hearing, seeing, failing, beginning again – I've held my own body at one remove.

In my career as a historian and philosopher of visual culture, I've wanted to put bodies back into film, back into histories of art (which, truth be told, they never actually left). And I'm left with the awareness that the discipline to which I have subjected this body that carries me is the sum of a hundred different social structures. Structures that first taught me how to be white, British, compliantly able-bodied, girl-woman, then how to be a student, scholar, academic, chronically ill person. Structures that taught me how to tolerate sitting still for far longer periods of time than my natural inclinations would normally withstand. Structures that never encouraged me to garden.

My body likes to move. And even though I love to *be* still, to relax, sometimes it seems my body no longer knows how to do this. It could, as my friend S says, fall off the ground itself. My body is not comfortably, practically clothed in a uniform that makes me capable, trustworthy, genderless, stilled before the camera lens. Though I wish it were.

My body, whose shape I definitively do not like or appreciate in its current state, was once fat, is now fat, and wasn't in between. My body that I starved of food from the age of 14, and which reacted with the traces of what calorific deprivation does to young bodies: restricted growth in the bones in my feet, enduring irritable bowel syndrome, muscle wastage from a frame that is, should be, genetically, muscular. I am the great grandchild of blacksmiths on my mother's side. I have swimmers' shoulders: rounded, muscular, with a bull-like knot of muscle leading outward from the nape of my neck that is the result of miles of front crawl, up and down the lanes of the swimming pools of London, lakes in France, the Atlantic coast in Wales and Cornwall, the North Sea at Berwick. My frame is wide, tall, sturdy, strong. Was strong. Is and was. A slipped disc, hypermobile joints in my fingers and toes, a body that feels too tall, too wide to be female, means that however I look, however I see my body, I notice what it is *not* – not slim enough, not small enough, not narrow-hipped enough, not tapered enough of waist or shoulder. Not femme. Not even butch. There is nothing new in this: it could be the story of millions.

And yet: what if I did not have to drag around the label of 'woman', or the narrow assignations of what that is supposed to mean culturally, dimensionally? What if I did not have to follow the pattern-cutting templates of the global apparel industry, who largely use only one human-sized model and then 'extrapolate' the dimensions of a proportionally larger or smaller person with equally proportional fat distribution around their hips and buttocks and breasts? When we know that genetics, hormones, health, built environment, environmental pollutants, wealth, food sources, trauma, movement patterns and occupations shape all bodies in unique combinations, the dress size of a person seems a ludicrous measurement. Throw gender into the mix – that for a woman to be a woman she must be small and compact and fit easily within UK dress sizes 6–14 – and it seems less surprising that despair creeps in from all the ways I fail at being a woman, and simultaneously refuse to be crammed into these inch-wide categories.

Can you measure a life in inches? Many people who sew their own clothes know that mass fashion is a ruse, and that compliance is optional. And it's not difficult, not even frowned upon, for someone called a woman to wear clothing gendered for men. But I'm not sure switching the poles of the binary will help me when I remain unconvinced about the purpose of gendering cloth.

And what if, rather than being scrutinised as a statistical set of measurements – Body Mass Index, waist circumference, waist-to-hip ratio, weight, height, inside leg measurement, arm length, chest circumference, breast shape, foot length, eye shape, hair texture, skin tone, nostril size, and before you think I am going too far, all of these things were indeed measured in the horrifying colonial experiments that formed the basis of racialised anthropometrics – I was instead just a body, to whose frame garments could be fitted? Because in every frame of knowledge adopted by the natural sciences, measurement has been the defining feature of its taxonomies of the natural and human world. Measurements by eye, by tool, by system have always become implements for control. Control of the size and colour of a supermarket tomato. Control of plant and insect populations and unwanted biodiversity. Control of what is deemed normal, or natural, safe or dangerous, worthy of life or condemned to extinction.

And maybe, just maybe, there is something else, too. A connection between measurement and optics. Measurement is almost always tied to looking. Observation is, after all, a cornerstone of empirical data-gathering. Looking is also a way of knowing and, by extension, owning knowledge extracted from the object being looked at. Sometimes looking claims ownership, and ownership claims determination. To look is to determine what is.

Perhaps I might not have struggled for so many years with what gender formation my body is *supposed* to be if there were no-one there to look. No human being at least. When I cut late-flowering dahlias from the allotment, their upturned faces are entirely indifferent to the label in my trousers. If my clothing were not always in service of the wider cultural frameworks that society calls gender, a woman-shaped, woman-designated person who fails (and refuses) to look or feel like a woman, maybe I would feel a little less too-wide of hip, too-broad of shoulder. If I didn't feel that vast cultural gaze turned toward me every time I put on my gardening smock and my gardening trousers, maybe I wouldn't feel quite so miserable in my own skin. Maybe I wouldn't feel the sting of being told I 'must' be transgender (with the violent threat of gender 'correction' implicit in that assertion) because of the size of my biceps – when I would rather have no binary gender at all. Maybe my body could simply be in its doing, in my garden.

If gender is in the eye of the beholder, what if we just stopped looking?

* * *

The Kewriosities are fragments of a life, and that is what is mainly present in the record. Catherine Horwood's book *Women and Their Gardens* does a good job of uncovering what happened to Annie Gulvin, Alice Hutchings, Eleanor Morland and Gertrude Cope. Fiona Davidson's recent book *An Almost Impossible Thing* traces them still further, through the archival records held at the Royal Horticultural Society Lindley Library. Horwood writes: 'After the hard work and fun at Swanley, Alice and Annie's lives were to be intertwined for many years.'[3] Alice and Annie, the daughters of middle-class families, both trained at Swanley, enrolling in February 1894. Both moved to work at Kew in 1895, after excelling in their examinations, which included both theoretical and practical portions.

Annie and Alice became highly trained professionals at a very early age: they were both in their teens when appointed to Kew. Annie left aged 20, to become head gardener, first at Iscoed, an eighteenth-century manor house in Carmarthenshire with a dilapidated and underfunded garden, then in Burstall near Ipswich in Suffolk, before ending her career in marriage in summer 1900. Alice stayed on, becoming a 'sub-forewoman in the alpine pits', before taking up Annie's post in Suffolk. Alice married William Patterson in 1902, who first directed the Agricultural School in St Vincent and then later became a government entomologist on the Gold Coast, where they were both absorbed seamlessly into the colonial matrix for the next 20 years. Annie later returned to work at Kew during World War I.

Davidson also tracks the lives of Gertrude and Annie after they departed from Kew. Gertrude worked first for cultish theosophists in a newly established college for physical education at Anstey, then as head gardener for the Cadbury family (they of chocolate fame) in Northfield, where she remained for 20 years. Annie corresponded extensively about her gardening ventures at Iscoed, and her success was noted in the *Journal of the Kew Guild* in 1898: 'many will be surprised that one of her sex so young should have conquered all the difficulties of a first situation which was evidently not of the apple-pie order.'[4] Never underestimate a young woman.

I thirst for more about Annie and Alice, Eleanor and Gertrude. These sketches of their lives, from letters and photographs and other historians, feel unfulfilled. I want to know them, because by knowing them, maybe I can also know me. Maybe I can follow the queer tendrils that unhook gender from labour, clothing, and find more ease. If Alice, Gertrude and Eleanor can stand between well-kept lawn and ivy-covered brick, comfortable, collected, ungendered for a time, then I can too. Historical images give permission to be otherwise in the now. The Kewriosities permit me to be at ease in my gardening skin. They are queer resonance, waiting to be heard. Because imagination is also a historical force. If failures of imagination have been used to suppress queer histories, reigniting that power reopens them.

But this is also the problem of working with the queer archive: how do you find what is hidden, invisible, censored?

Even with that imaginal force behind you, how do you know the queer in what you see?

By instinct?
Comparison?
Self-recognition?

* * *

The breeches worn by the lady gardeners of Kew were practical, enabling them to get on with their business in a world principally governed by white imperial men. In 1896, in that photograph, they mostly look at ease. Alice on the right has one hand plunged in the pocket of her jacket, gazing into the distance. As Catherine Horwood identifies,

'There was no question of the women wearing trousers, but knickerbockers were seen as a sensible alternative since "skirts might damage valuable plants in the crowded houses." The provision of a dressing room for the girls "lest they should be seen unsuitably attired when going to and from their work" was also the subject of some mirth in the gardening press.'[5]

Their subversion was therefore quiet: it took the gutter press four years to cotton on to their presence at Kew, by which time most had already left. They were noticed in the past tense; transformed into puff with little attention paid to fact. The puff still continues: when the photograph surfaces on social media in February 2021, it throws up all kinds of associations, questions and assumptions from the assembled crowd. Notions that the women were working class because they were working women or otherwise helpless orphans (thanks, *Oliver!*) rather than the educated middle-class women that they were. That these women were oppressed because of the practical, gender-defying clothing they wore to do their gardening work.

Oh, to be so oppressed that I wear a well-cut tweed suit with a pocket-watch chain, handkerchief and gaiters.

But here's the thing. In that terrible poem from an equally terrible journal, the Kewriosities are not castigated for their 'masculine' clothing, or for their failure to present their femininity. The poem claims them as objects of the freak show. In the end, masculine clothing shields their femininity, and neutralises them in the eyes of the public, who lose interest as quickly as it came. There's a category error of course, or maybe simply a disguise: their disappearance from the public eye isn't because of their clothing but because of their employment elsewhere, and their disappearance into colonial complicity, and the social prohibitions that made labour and marriage incompatible for women of the upper and middle classes.

By the early 1900s there were numerous agricultural and horticultural colleges across England which admitted women – some of them, like Swanley College, exclusively. Lady gardeners transformed the nature of gendered labour. Annie and Alice, Eleanor and Gertrude were some of the middle-class women who achieved it. For a short time, they were paid the same as the men. The objective of their clothing was not to highlight gender difference but to erase it. In the performance of cloth, gender neutrality lingers, deliciously, if only for a moment.

* * *

Gender takes curious twists and turns, always governed by culture.

Gendered clothing is a means of gendering gardening. And my body is not comfortable in its assigned gender when I garden. Gardening is when I feel the most gender-expansive, and the least assured of my femininity.

I want to write about my body that does not fit the categories of what is feminine, and which makes me feel like a fraud every time I wear a dress. I want to write about the body shame that still runs so fucking deep, not because this is an original discovery, but because my body – this thing, this set of parts which I have spent so many years trying to control, deny, deprive, confine, culture, restrain – is also the thing that allows me to smell, touch and taste the earth-scents of humus, compost and mud. Grass, leaves and fruit. Bitter sap and sweet sweat. My body is my own garden of delights and it is also my prison. How can that be?

My body is my greatest source of shame, and my highest source of wisdom.

How can that be?

I love seeing photographs of women and queer people at ease – whatever that ease might mean. Whether it is the wide easy stare of hands in breeches, or the sprezzatura of a queer body, such as in *Puberty*, the self-documenting photographs of queer contemporary artist Laurence Philomene tracking their transition journey using hormonal replacement therapy in gorgeous vivid colour,[6] or the expansive gestural repertoire of drag kings and queens.

And yet.

I could count on the fingers of one hand the number of photographs ever taken of me in which the me who was submitting to being photographed, and the me observing the photographic result, were at ease.

Is this what body dysmorphia means? It's certainly not a condition for which I've ever sought medical assistance. It's a body-situation I live with, that I am learning about, and perhaps eventually I will learn to accept.

It is far less difficult to admit these admittedly painful things than it used to be. It's a matter of recent years that have translated the pain from hidden shame to the practice of writing that shame, giving shape and form to shame in words. Words that become transmissible, shareable tendrils of life. Because I am not alone in this shame. Not alone in finding a place for it in my tender garden.

* * *

How many times do I have to say that queerness is not about the word? That queerness, sex and gender slide and meander across the 125 years between me and Annie Gulvin, Alice Hutchings, Eleanor Morland and Gertrude Cope. They don't have to be lesbians, but who they are, how they present, already shifts the gender binary queerly. Challenges it, and, amazingly, passes *under* the radar of social speculation until it's too late – they are already gone. Dressed in practical, dapper tweed, they can undertake their pruning and digging, cultivating and nurturing, while continuing their studies in biochemistry, botany, meteorology. Now you see me. Now you don't.

Third sexes, non-binary genders, are also part of European history. Max Hirschfeld's *Institut für Sexualwissenschaft*, burned to the ground by the Nazis in 1933, was formative in building knowledge about homosexuality, bisexuality, transsexuality, intersex lives. He is thought to have been the author of the instructional pamphlet *What People Should Know About the Third Sex*, published in Wilhelmine Germany in 1901.[7] Hirschfeld's work was formative for the work of the American sexologist Alfred Kinsey. And as So Mayer narrates in their book *A Nazi Word for a Nazi Thing*, Hirschfeld helped to build a culture of queer acceptance and then watched helplessly from abroad as the Nazis burned his institute, and its research papers, and its irrecoverable archival documents and testimonies. And yet: rising from the ashes is what queers are especially good at. Hiding in the shadows too. But it's a long time to wait.

* * *

Of course I am curious about Annie and Alice's friendship that travelled with them across the country, that led Alice to take up Annie's head gardener post in Suffolk when Annie married. Of course I want to know if, how and when their friendship might have slid between romance and sexual attraction. Of course I want to know about these things, because my secret-not-so-secret conviction is that no-one, no-one is in fact heterosexual, that heterosexuality itself is a poorly fitting construct, about as useful as a whalebone corset to a pair of pruning secateurs. There are queer pairs of nurserywomen and women farmers dotted across the twentieth century: Ada Brown and Decima Allen, Beatrice Havergal and Avice Sanders, Eve Balfour and Kathleen Carnley.[8] But Annie and Alice's queerness doesn't necessarily have anything to do with who they slept with. It's to do with what they love. And this is where the stories get complicated. Implicated.

Gardening. Dressing for the job. Education. Developing a highly skilled and physically demanding career. Challenging the socially gendered positions in which a middle-class woman would have found herself. Emigrating, with her agricultural professional education, to the colonies, to shape agricultural practices and educational practices. To shape the bodies and minds of people for whom there was no other choice. To become effective, obedient, complicit tools of empire, in order to be at greater physical liberty to travel and pursue an educated life.

What is given is also taken away.

In the 1880s, Britain was experiencing an agricultural depression. It was also busy entrenching and upholding its colonial empire, while the increasingly pressing issue of middle- and upper-class women's underemployment was gaining prominence among women's rights campaigners.

It was in the midst of these issues that Swanley Horticultural College, from which Annie, Alice, Eleanor, Gertrude and others graduated and made the transition to Kew, was founded in 1889. The agreement established between Swanley and Kew emerged in 1895, just four years after the first women entrants into the college.

It's a mistake to think that the rights of middle- and upper-class, white British women aren't also connected to the demand for skilled and educated white labour in Britain's colonies, to uphold the violent governance of that vast geographic spread. The educated woman gardener was a valuable asset to Britain's empire. When Alice married William Patterson in 1902, they travelled first to St Vincent in the West Indies, then to the Gold Coast, pursuing agricultural terraforming as 'entomologists'. Jessie Newsham, who tragically died a few days after the birth of her first child in 1908, had travelled with her husband to British Guiana.[9]

Women's rights. Imperial rule. The professionalisation of horticulture. All part of the queer strands woven into the waistcoats and turn-down shirt collars of Alice and Annie, Gertrude and Eleanor. Literally woven, since the cotton, wool and tussar silk from which their garments were likely made are, directly or indirectly, products of empire, from the origins of the yarns to the dyes with which they were coloured. Textiles which, for the most part, are extremely demanding of water resources. Tussar silk is produced mainly in Bhagalpur, West Bengal, with an industry that dates from around the time that the Kewriosities would have been sewing and fitting their uniforms. Thirsty cotton was one of the primary crops produced by transatlantic chattel slavery. And although slavery technically ended in the USA in 1865, a track record of forced labour continues in the cotton industry, particularly in the light of recent reports on the exploitation of Uyghur minority ethnic groups in the Xinjiang Autonomous Region of western China.[10]

All things come full circle in the end.

***

What kind of a queer gardener do I want to look like? Gertrude Cope or Jamaica Kincaid? Derek Jarman or Dan Pearson? Alys Fowler or Gertrude Jekyll? The rituals of clothing and appearance are both important and unimportant, about pride and about humility. Many things, mixed up together.

Why do I attend to my upper body in a very different way compared to my lower? What have my legs, hips and buttocks done to cause me such offence?

I do not know what to do with these questions. I began with Kewriosity. And I am still curious. Still curious about tweed and twill, silk and cotton. Still curious about empire and education, suffrage and domination. And about the building of colonial botanical gardens like Kew, and arboretums: those living tree-museums of the nineteenth century.

***

What does this have to do with queer gardens?

It has to do with the bodies that inhabit gardens queerly. The easy stare, the hands in jacket pockets.

I want my body to queerly inhabit my garden. With all of itself. And that means bringing my body, without breeches, without waistcoat, into the field of vision too.

I also write at a point where I have trained my body to run again, where I've committed to a regular yoga practice that has made infinitesimally small progress towards an internal body strength I didn't know I could own. Also at a point where the swimming pools have been shut for the vast majority of lockdowns since March 2020, and when I haven't been able to re-establish a swimming routine which was no small contributor to regaining my health in 2014, and 2015, and 2017, and 2019, and each of the times when I thought I had lost myself to illness. The embrace of the water on every part of my skin is something I still ache for, and which I cannot allow myself to fully grieve because it is the tiniest grievance in a vast ocean of grief over which viral, broken times have washed.

A body in water is a body of water: water meets water and is held. Some say that full body immersion brings us back to the womb. And even though my skin is already formed, in water there is an invitation, if only for a moment, to return to that protean state where everything is potential. I dream of developing gills so I never have to lift my head above the waterline again. For the webbing between my toes to grow so that my feet become wide fins. In water, I am held. I am released from the demands of being seen. Because despite water's transparency, it also refracts and distorts light, exchanging the air's clarity for shimmer. In water, I am a floating, moving body in constant change, slipping in and out of sight. Water mythologies often contain shapeshifters of this kind. In water, I become water: fluid, mutable, holding and held. Water carries me, and it carries with me the grief of this body, and the bodies that formed it. Out of water, I am forced to reckon with how to live in constant visibility.

So I am brokering, again, a different sort of relationship to my body that has become broken and healed and broken and healed and broken and healed again. A relationship that shifts along a spectrum of feminine and masculine, that is neither non-binary nor trans in as far as I can understand myself at this time. Much of the time my body benefits from cis-gendered presentation, but that doesn't begin to cover the full range of gender that it is possible for this body to inhabit.

Asking my body what queer is, my body says …

My body says … what allows me to be fluid. What allows the ocean-dwelling spirit of the selkie in me to slip away from the surface of creation and dive into the wine-dark sea of bodily experience. No wonder mermaids are trans icons: held by the water, living in a body of grace, fluid and free, and filled with the grief of living between land and sea. Their capacity to shift between species and spaces, between air and earth and water: this matters. The freedom of trans, non-binary and gender-diverse young people to make decisions about their own lives at their own pace: this matters too. Mermaids is the name of the UK charity supporting young people on their journeys through gender diversity. Holding them gently as they dive. Water is a metaphor, but sometimes, only just.

Queer is … fluidity. Oceanic feeling, like Alexis Pauline Gumbs, 'a marine mammal apprentice'. As she points out, 'if interlocking underground communication of trees, dandelion resilience, and responsive mycelium networks can inspire us to relate within and across species differently so can marine mammals.'[11] Gliding, without obtrusion, between land and water. Not being contained, nor confined, nor condemned. Many-genderedness. Many-bodiedness. Including the shame, but neither imprisoned nor silenced by it. Curiosity, exploration, expansive and spacious and trepidatious self-discovery. The building of communal seas of experience, making room for each wavelet, each current, that is different and unique and also part of the whole.

What am I saying?

I don't know.

Only my body knows.

My body does not speak a language that you will understand.

My body is Kewrious.

3

arboretum, or the feeling of trees (on genderqueer forests and herb women)

> Queerness is not a new phenomenon; that narrative is a product of colonization and is erasure in action. Queerness is as old and complex as lichen; it informs our soul's work. It is an aspect of the soul likened to the anima and animus; it is the *animx*.
>
> Pınar Ateş Sinopoulos-Lloyd, 'Queer Futurism: Denizens of Liminality'[1]

I am looking for a feeling. A feeling of trees.

What they have witnessed over the sandfly of time during which humans have existed.

The London village in which I live falls squarely within a seven-mile stretch of forest, from Deptford through Peckham and Brixton, down to Streatham, Selhurst, Beckenham and Thornton Heath. Ancient forests, filled with oak, beech and alder; the Great North Wood, as it was once called, formed part of the wildwoods of pre-Saxon Britain. Sessile oak and hornbeams grew, not far from the windless groundmist of this autumn morning. What remains of that forest murmurs beneath tarmac and railway lines; its ghosts surface in the names of streets and placenames. One Tree Hill. Honor Oak.

In the time of Henry VIII, this was prime hunting ground, and men on overburdened horses regularly chased down terrified creatures fleeing horns and hounds. In a flailing attempt to prevent food shortages and disease, the Tudor Preservation of Grain Act 1532 actively required Britain's people to destroy as much wildlife as possible. Millions of animals, including hedgehogs, pine martens and wild cats, were massacred until its repeal in the eighteenth century. The Act carries a long tail: British attitudes to what it calls vermin have formed through centuries of mass slaughter.

South of London's clay soils, the last remnants of an ancient forest survive: the High Weald, once part of the vast Andreaswald that stretched between the Downs from Hampshire to Kent. Its chalky, free-draining ground – unfriendly to farming, hospitable to trees – still holds memories of oak, lime and larch. Centuries of felling fed England's furnaces – cannonballs, ships, houses, firebacks – until the wildwood was reduced to heath and rabbit-populated plains. Later, when the forges cooled, the man-made lakes filled again with beech and chestnut, as if the forest remembered itself. By the nineteenth century, George Beauclark built his estate on the ruins of that memory; later, Edmund Loder filled it with trophies from his colonial hunting and botanical expeditions, importing azaleas and camellias from East Asia to ornament the wounds of the Weald. *Rhododendron ponticum* is now considered an invasive species in many parts of the Weald – and yet there is also a variety of rhododendron named after Leonardslee: *R. arboreum* 'Leonardslee'. There are other trees in the arboretum of course: cypresses, conifers and pines purloined from swamps and mountains across the world. The arboretum outlives the colonialists who planted it, hiding its ghosts in plain sight.

Beside the old forge lakes, between the knees of a swamp cypress uprooted from a Mississippi shoreline, sits a ghost of a being, neither man nor woman, who watches.

* * *

Humans have pinned their souls to trees: origins of the world, portals to cosmic planes, spirits of mischief and mercy, shelter and death. The *hamadryads* of Ancient Greece lived and died with their trees, more collective than individual, their queerness taken for granted. The *lilitu* and *lilu* in the ancient Mesopotamian *Epic of Gilgamesh* guarded groves in feminine and masculine forms alike. In Bantu cosmology, the *kinyamkela* is a child-spirit defending their hollow tree-home from harm. And in the Norse world, the *Yggdrasil* entwines both male and female spirits within its ash trunk – a living axis between the living, the dead and the divine. Trees and humans are intertwined: their lives and deaths become axes of the world; roots, trunk and canopy the structures of the connection between the living, the dead and the gods. To know a tree is arcane and mundane magic: layered, porous, shifting.

And they are both male and female. Both, and.

* * *

There once was a woman who identified trees and plants: a traditional herbalist, a voyager and a shapeshifter. Or rather, there was a person, who was not a cis-gendered man, born in 1740 to a family of illiterate subsistence labourers in the Loire valley in France. The average life expectancy at that time was 26, driven ever downward by brutal working conditions, poor nutrition and the feudal brutality of

Burgundian lords. Somehow this daughter of serfs escaped that miserable existence, becoming first a 'herbwoman', who drew botanical knowledge from the fields in which their parents laboured, and then, in their early twenties, became the lover, teacher, assistant, housekeeper, valet and carer of the botanist Philibert de Commerson.[2]

Commerson was an admirer of natural philosophers like Carolus Linnaeus and François Brossier de Sauvages, Commerson's professor at the University of Montpellier and a close friend of eminent Enlightenment writer and thinker Voltaire. Commerson had worked for several years under Linnaeus during compilation of the tenth edition of his *Systema Naturae*, widely understood as the first comprehensive attempt to systematically categorise all plant and animal species known to Euro-Western science.

The herbwoman's apprenticeship unfolded within this classification fever, in a world hungry to name and own. Commerson had also acquired an appalling leg injury in his early thirties on a plant-collecting expedition in the Alps of south-eastern France. A stinking, gangrenous wound like the one Henry VIII carried as he collected and discarded wife after wife, and which this gender-queering herbwoman tended from when the two met, sometime between 1760 and 1764, to Commerson's death in Mauritius in 1773.

Then, the herbwoman swapped their gender (or, at the very least, suppressed one of them) to accompany their lover Commerson as part of the crew of the ship *L'Étoile*, captained by Louis Antoine de Bougainville with its sister vessel, *La Boudeuse*. *L'Étoile* and *La Boudeuse* travelled from Nantes across the Atlantic, further and further south through the Straits of Magellan and onward to the Pacific Ocean, circumnavigating the globe from 1767 to 1769. On this voyage they collected thousands of plant species new to the Enlightenment Europeans and of eminent value to France, on its and other European nations' ever-enlarging quest for sufficient biocapital to secure food, clothing and commodities to meet the needs of their expanding empires (and a voracious desire for wealth back home).

The name of the tree-loving, gender-queering herbwoman was Jean/Jeanne Baret, though they signed their name Barret and went by Bonnefoy for a time just before joining the Bougainville expedition.[3] Jean/ne Baret is understood to be the first woman, or, as I prefer to acknowledge them, non-binary person, to have circumnavigated the globe, from 1767 when they left with Bougainville's expedition to 1775 when they returned home to France, two years after Commerson's death in 1773 on the Isle de France (now Mauritius).

Time is fluid. The eighteenth century is many human lifetimes ago. But a tree remembers.

* * *

Not all trees live forever, though. Some only for the lifetime of a human being, maybe less. The ornamental cherry whose blossom rains down pink joy on my garden every May, the weeping willow (*Salix babylonica*), birches (*Betula*) with their beautiful, beloved paper-barks, alders and poplars might live 50, 70 years. A crab apple, rowan or wild cherry could live to be a hundred. Ash, hawthorn, Norway spruce, red oak and walnut can reach 150 years; beech and maple 200. The Big Trees are the ones I see in parkland filled with fallow deer and the intention of longevity; or in the square pockets of London parks, or along roadsides in southern France or winding Scottish switchbacks: hornbeam, English oak, holly, lime, Scots pine, sessile oak, sweet chestnut, sycamore. Trees around whose span I can't fully reach, with gullies and divots in their roots, the ground around them rich in leaf litter but rarely grassy. Their lives, of 300 years or more, are more like the lifetime of Orlando, Virginia Woolf's (and filmmaker Sally Potter's) fictional polygendered aristocrat.

Beyond that, there are the Old Trees. The trees that carry an aura of spirituality simply because they exist. The yews and Austrian pine, Noble and Douglas fir, and Sitka spruce. The bald cypress: one individual in the Black River wetlands in North Carolina in the USA is currently estimated to be at least 2,624 years old.[4]

There is a reason why yews are considered the tree of life in Europe. The Fortingall Yew, which sits in the corner of a churchyard in Perthshire, is estimated to be somewhere between 3,000 and 9,000 years old; the oldest living organism in Europe. Older than Stonehenge. As old as the cultivation of squash and maize in Meso-America. In 2015, scientists from the Royal Botanic Garden in Edinburgh observed that its branches were changing sex, from male to female.[5] It is not the only dioecious tree (plant species with separate male and female individuals) to do this: Douglas firs, ginkgoes and striped maples have been known to switch, even when the tree individual has up until that point only produced haploids of one sex. This cohabitation of sexes in the same dioecious tree, known as cosexuality (which is also about the communitarian shaping of sex and sexuality across species) is thought to develop in times of stress. A branch will transition from male to female if it is at risk of dying, ensuring its survival in ripe fruit-and-seed form for future generations. One of the theories as to why the Fortingall Yew is changing sex is because of the horror of climate change.

Cosexuality is a strategy of survival. And if tree time is a foreign country, that does not mean we cannot recognise each other across the tree–human divide. Across the gulf of time. Sex. Death.

***

Baret's intimate knowledge of the oral and land-based histories of plant medicine was a vital counterpart to Commerson's university-led botanical education. Their knowledge of plant-based remedies no doubt extended Commerson's life on more than one occasion; particularly as the gangrene in his leg wound worsened. Their physical labour, pushing harder and further than Commerson himself to acquire plant specimens during the Bougainville expedition, made both Commerson and Bougainville famous. Baret's physical strength, determination, perseverance, care, literacy and skills as a botanist-cum-herbwoman made it possible, in every way, for Commerson to continue his research. Their story is one of the many thousands of underpaid, under-recognised research assistants who enabled so-called great men to take the credit for their discoveries.

Baret and Commerson joined the *Étoile*, one of the two ships of Louis Antoine de Bougainville's expeditionary voyage in 1766, but not before Commerson had outlined provision for Baret in his will, including his household possessions, 600 livres in cash and time to remain in his house to put his papers in order.[6] Aboard the *Étoile* Jean/ne more or less successfully concealed their feminine gender for 18 months, binding their breasts and dressing as a man, and acting as Commerson's eunuch-valet. The papers and journals associated with Bougainville's voyage, published in 1977 by then director of conservation at the French National

Archives Étienne Taillemite, reveal that there were early suspicions about Baret's gender, which could, if confirmed, have resulted in their being left ashore and Commerson being suspended for a month.[7] But Baret managed to remain clothed even during the disgusting hazing rituals that the ship's sailors enacted when the *Étoile* crossed the equator, which required sailors to strip naked and stand in a foetid pool of water filled with ship's waste and excrement, while the other sailors beat them with oars, offering them a welcome from 'Father Neptune'.[8]

Bougainville's journal, published on his return to France in 1771, describes the moment of Baret's eventual 'outing' as a more complex gender than they might at first have presented, not from the hazing rituals of the Europeans aboard the *Étoile* as it moved from northern hemisphere to southern, but from the Tahitians who surrounded Baret on their arrival to the island in 1767. Bougainville devises a picture of Baret stepping ashore only to be identified immediately by the Tahitian community as a woman, 'ayenene'. In guarded terms, he describes Baret's outing as a moment of risk to 'her' honour, where 'she' required protection by the first lieutenant of the *Boudeuse* from the marauding Tahitians.[9] But Bougainville was not on board the *Étoile* when Baret's gender was outed and, as historian Glynis Ridley identifies, the veracity of Bougainville's journal is compromised (Ridley suggests that the passage about revelations of Baret's gender were written later and then added to the manuscript). There are numerous other accounts, including that of the Tahitian islander Aotourou, who befriended Baret, joined the expedition and travelled to France with Bougainville's ships, which describe a very different story. The threat to Baret's safety certainly did not come from the Tahitians, who, as Aotourou describes, had identified her as *māhū* – the name for the revered third gender in Polynesian and Hawaiian Indigenous cultures.[10]

The ship's surgeon, François Vivès, writes two sneering accounts of Baret's assault in New Ireland, where, stripped of the pistols Jean/ne had been carrying for self-protection, they were set upon by the sailors and their genitalia forcibly examined. Beneath Vivès' smooth euphemisms of gunlock plates and seeking Baret's 'concha veneris', he implies serial rape, which Ridley confirms: 'historians of the expedition who argue these passages imply only an inspection and not a rape are projecting onto Baret's story what they wish had happened, as opposed to what so clearly did happen. The reality [...] was a human trauma that screams for recognition.'[11]

So-called 'corrective rape' is a tactic of homophobic and transphobic violence that acquired its tools from colonial practices; ones which have systemically pathologised Black and non-European sexualities.[12] It is no coincidence that accounts of Baret's rape were projected onto Bougainville's coloniser narratives of Tahiti, or lyrically softened in the accounts of the sole medical professional on board the ship. Colonial rhetorics of sexuality, the 'noble savage' and human development of the kind purported by Denis Diderot in his *Supplément au voyage de Bougainville* displace the hidden violence of European colonialism onto a coercive fascination with the sexuality of Indigenous communities. The violence with which Baret's intermediate gender was met embodied the colonial violence of European expeditions.

Baret's willingness to shoulder the extreme physical risks of gender-crossing, and passing as a man, speaks to something else: a need not to be conditioned or controlled by the cultural expectations of gender, and a gritty determination to survive alongside the plants they collected and tended. This is why I address Baret as they/them: acknowledging the soft masculinity of their time aboard the *Étoile*. I don't just consider their cross-dressing as a form of self-protection and access to rights unaccorded to women – this was always a precarious decision in the face of little or no choice. There is something more to Baret's breast-binding and clothing and naming; something more-than-woman. Like Aotourou's ready acknowledgement of Baret's status as a *māhū*, I recognise Baret's shift across genders as a way of being in the world. I recognise them across the gulf of time as non-binary, in the terminologies most readily available to me now.

I say Baret's name to uphold them. To see them: herb-woman, botanist, carer, genderqueer explorer. Colonial collector, and lover of trees.

* * *

In the thick of the horrors of history, I want to make a place of safety for the spirit of the non-man, non-woman, who waits by the old forge lakes of Leonardslee.

They rest on fallen leaves between the knees of a bald cypress. Cheek to cheek with the mossy ground, they watch the waters of the lake move in slow eddies while autumn's insects dance a few inches above the surface. They attend to the sounds below ground, the tree's movements, its xylem and phloem, its mycorrhizae, its invertebrate companions. They listen, not to the anthropomorphic evolutionary bias of competition, but to the companionship of earth, water and animate life. For a while, the human world recedes and they lie with the time of trees. Alone-together, they witness one another. Tree-human. Human-tree.

I spin this yarn to make a cloak of fiction. A soft, mossy bed of safety to hold the tremendous weight of colonial violence that does violence to gender too.

I need to know that there is survival in this tale of horror.

The trees know.

The bald cypress, knees folded above ground, mycelial networks outstretched far into the forest, knows it too.

* * *

What do I know about genderqueer trees?

I know that trees have many sexualities and genders beyond the human binary. As Joan Roughgarden identifies, 'To a biologist, "male" means making small gametes, and "female" means making large gametes.'[13] Many plants produce both: monoecious plants have male and female gamete-producing flowers on the same individual; sometimes simultaneously, sometimes consecutively. Dioecious plants – like the Fortingall Yew – tend to produce only one type of gamete. Though of course this too can change over time. And bisexual plants will produce flowers containing both male and female gametes, and are therefore capable of self-pollination – like roses, lilies, hibiscus, mustard and sweet peas. The giant redwood of my tree dreams, thick bark stretched around its bole, is monoecious, capable of producing both sets of gametes across its long, long lifespan.

And what do I know about that long queer tree time?

If tree time can last for hundreds of years, what does the brush of human skin on bark feel like? If I stand there for a minute or two, fingers in the grooves, arms resting on the trunk, what does the tree feel? Is it the fallen-ash sensation of a sandfly, or the silence of a feeding mosquito? What is a minute in the xylem and phloem movements of a hundred, two hundred years? More? A millennium?

***

Time is fluid. Gender too. Neither Baret nor Commerson were disciplined for Baret's revealed gender, which was forbidden aboard ship. No-one on the Bougainville expedition was punished or disciplined for Baret's rape. Baret and Commerson did, however, leave the *Étoile* when it docked on the island of Mauritius in late 1768, where they remained, along with the ship's astronomer, Pierre-Antoine Véron. On Mauritius they were hosted by Pierre Poivre (the same Peter Piper who picked a peck of pickled pepper in the nursery rhyme), director of the botanical gardens. After Commerson died in 1773, Baret returned to France in 1775, with a state pension of 200 livres awarded to them in 1785 in recognition of their work aboard the *Étoile*.

Jean/ne Baret lived until 1807, two years before an Irish medical student, James Barry, began his studies at Edinburgh University. Barry became an army surgeon, working all over the British Empire as a public health reformer, working under colonial policy to develop regulations that would mitigate the spread of tropical diseases, improving living conditions in leper colonies, prisons and asylums. It was only after Barry's death from dysentery in 1865 that his assigned gender and name at birth were revealed: Margaret Ann Bulkley. He was, as his biographer Rachel Holmes describes it, not a woman in disguise, as more popular accounts have described him, but 'Betwixt-and-Between'. In other words, James Barry was non-binary, 'transgender before the term was invented'.[14]

A centuries-old oral history of herbalism unfurls its leaves towards queer trans colonial botany, which in turn extends its flowering vines toward queer trans imperial medicine. Queerness in the Straits of Magellan. Queerness in the straight. Queerness in the empire's asylums and prisons. Queer all over, entwined in the shivering bodies of plants and humans.

* * *

What is sensuality to a tree? Touch, sunlight, air. The co-symbiotic relationship of algae to fungus that forms lichen beards on branches.

Can you feel me, tree?

The answer to that latter question is both yes and no. Yes, in my biochemical intervention with the landscape – the oxygen I breathe in and the carbon dioxide I exhale and the microbial traces my feet leave on the land. Yes, in the vibrational pathways of my movement above root systems and the long threads of mycelial hyphae that make up the underground communications network of the forest.

No, because my human presence is irrelevant. My body components are of use when I die, but I am no more distinctive than any other ambulant lifeform. The tree's sense of the world exceeds mine. Its indifference and my attention coexist.

In Ursula K. Le Guin's short story 'Direction of the Road', a large oak tree bends space and time, and witnesses the death of a man whose car careens into them. Arboreal feelings are unlike human ones: electricity shimmers along that mortal connection. The oak of the story resents the human mythologies placed upon it: 'For I am not death. I am life … I will not act Eternity for them. Let them not turn to the trees for death. If that is what they want to see, let them look into one another's eyes and see it there.'[15]

I know what that tree means. Trees don't bleed haemoglobin. They don't eat living humans. They are not death; they only feed from the dead (as do all living things), and the dead have no use for the material constituencies of their mortal bodies. The competition model of Darwinist evolution – the popularised 'survival of the fittest' prototype that accompanies claims about the bloody brutality of nature – forgets about collaboration. Darwin's theories of evolutionary competition and dominance have largely overshadowed his interests in cooperation in processes of natural selection.[16] Cooperation, like kindness and empathy, is also considered a key psychological process in mammals – these are evolutionary traits, essential for our survival.[17]

Collaboration and mutual care exist within the tree world too.

Crown-shy trees in tropical climates pause their growth when sensing the light that reflects off their neighbours' leaves – they share the canopy, rather than compete. Underground, mycorrhizal forest networks act like brains, with neurotransmitters carried along hyphae strands, passing sugars and warning signals from one root system to another.[18] Above and below, life makes room for itself.

You might say this kind of collaboration was communitarian, though I have no idea if a tree has a self-concept of characteristic equivalence with the human version. But then again, human self-concept, in the European Enlightenment style, seems to have emerged before a deeper awareness of the human microbiome returned: the billions of bacteria that make up the human gut, the microflora that inhabit our skin, helping to protect and heal, guide and nurture, shape our emotions, feelings, even our thoughts.

We contain multitudes and together we are also multitude. It shouldn't come as a surprise, then, to learn that one of the largest single organisms in the world is the quaking aspen forest in Utah known as Pando, the Trembling Giant. Each individual tree is a clone, a single genotype drawing from a vast spread of root systems whose rhizomatic growth has supported the forest for at least 14,000 years.[19]

So why does the I-me stand before the I-tree, when we are more alike than we are different?

***

Hello to the tree, across tree times.

Jean/ne Baret was, according to Bougainville, an expert botanist, often taking on the collecting work when Commerson's failing health prevented him from travelling across demanding terrain. And Baret brought back with them a particular plant specimen – one of the 6,000 species collected by Commerson and Baret – that commemorates not Baret but the expedition's leader. The sturdy, brightly coloured, shrub-forming tropical tree Baret collected on an expedition in Rio de Janeiro is also known as the bougainvillea, now ubiquitous in gardens across the world.

Meanwhile, Baret's name is barely known.

Baret's gender-queering love, their love of plants, their complicit, colonising love, brought a shrub-tree into millions of gardens and yards across the world.

There were two attempts to name a plant after Baret: the first by Commerson himself, who attempted (and failed) to name a Malagasy plant genus, *Baretia*, with highly variably shaped leaves and 'doubtful sexual characteristics' after them.[20] The second was in 2012, when a new species of *Solanum* (the same genera of plants as the tomato, potato, aubergine and nightshade) from southern Ecuador and northern Peru was named *Solanum baretiae*, a year after Baret's biographer, Glynis Ridley, published her thoughtfully attuned book on Baret's hidden contributions to colonial botany and the emergence of botanical science.

I say Baret's name for their roots to grow.

Meanwhile in the arboretum, colonial acquisition and genderqueer botany entwine together like hybrid, enmeshed root systems.

* * *

A genderqueer tree-spirit lies between roots and canopy by the old forge lakes, ironworks long since decayed. How does the tree caress them, as they rest in the hollows between its knees? Do they smell the sap of the fallen needles, as chemical hormonal scents enter the limbic system and alter brain chemistry. A nurtured sensuality? An androgenic change?

What would it be like, to lie cradled in the knees of a tree, listening, emerging, cosexualising?

* * *

An arboretum is a curious space. A living tree museum, where specimens collected on colonial expeditions in the eighteenth and nineteenth centuries were brought back to the UK. Where they successfully took root and forged new relationships with the mycorrhizae of a very different land, these trees have outlived their planters many times over. How strange that wealthy British landowners irreversibly altered ecosystems, whose plant biodiversity outlived in many instances the patrilineal inheritance of landed country estates, as they shifted into public or charitable hands. How curious that the reach of wealthy white men should be outreached by the lifetime of trees.

The Himalayan expeditions seeking specimens of spruce and conifer, the import of rhododendrons from China, found in arboretums at Leonardslee and many other locations in Britain, were initiated by the growth of European Empire – first economic, then governmental. Trees, especially trees, can be orientalised, made exotic and glamorously other. They *were* orientalised, uprooted from the structures of their home habitats and transplanted into the Sussex Weald, for aesthetic arrangement into an arranged collection of tree-objects, in the place where once ancient trees grew.

The tree-collecting gardening trends of the nineteenth century continue to shape gardening practices now: the notion of the 'wild garden', developed by Irish garden designer William Robinson in the 1870s, among others, emphasised the naturalisation of non-native species from equivalently temperate parts of the world. It is to Robinson, and the wild gardening phenomenon, that is owed not only the invasive colonisation of Wealdland forests with rhododendron bushes, but also the hyperinvasive introduction of Japanese knotweed into Britain. This process was initiated by a single female plant imported into the UK from Utrecht in the 1840s, accelerated by the distribution of its rhizome fragments into watercourses *after* it had been chopped down, then redistributed by large-scale fertilisers, or unwitting neighbours mowing it and placing the cuttings in municipal composts – which only encouraged it to multiply.

Knotweed, a member of the mint family, is so fast-growing, so potentially disruptive of buildings whose foundations it can destabilise, that it is considered a biohazard. It can render properties valueless. What is wild is also unknown, and what is unknown is what is exotic. And what is exotic is – was – continues to be – attractive by virtue of its unfamiliarity, commoditised because of its apparent scarcity, then condemned in its abundance. Made hypervisible and then invisible.

I recognise this colonial strategy. It governs queerness, blackness, disability, femininity too. It is the background of Daphne du Maurier's novel *My Cousin Rachel*, where the protagonist Rachel's craft as a gardener is systematically undermined by her second husband, Ambrose. And then, after he dies suddenly, Ambrose's cousin Philip takes up the baton of misogyny, who at differing turns believes himself to be her lover and her husband. The import and planting of trees and other specimens form the backbone to the book, entwined with Rachel's apparently mysterious knowledge of herbs and tisanes, which murderous Philip mistakes for poison. The laburnum seeds, carefully transported from Florence to the Cornwall estate in which the novel is set, sadly outlive Rachel. I can only hope that the laburnums on the Cornwall estate also outlived the abusive Philip too, just as they did his psychotic cousin. Du Maurier knew misogyny so well, she mirrored it like a windless lake.

Indeed, the specimens collected and channelled into the man-made tree museum, the arboretum at Leonardslee, have outlasted all its owners. What Sir Edmund Loder had imported from the Americas, from China, from the Himalayan mountains, and what survived both the journey and the transplantation, stands across the estate – the same rhododendrons, azaleas and camellias that became the backdrop in 1947 for Michael Powell and Emeric Pressburger's decidedly queer and orientalising film *Black*

Narcissus. Meanwhile the knees of bald cypresses displace the mossy ground around Leonardslee's seven lakes, which once served the iron forges of medieval and Tudor Britain. The cypress has lived longer than the Loder family. It survived the ten years that the Leonardslee gardens were closed to the public, without people employed to care for the land. They remain when I visit one late November weekend, filled with the ripeness of autumn shifting into winter like knuckles clenched.

* * *

The trees I walk alongside in the Leonardslee arboretum and woodland garden exceeded the timeframe and lifetime of their garden architects and colonial collectors. They outlived the decolonial felling of British Empire that left collateral devastation in its wake just as it had devastated in its imposture on land and people. They survived the shifts in wealth and ownership that established notions of 'heritage' in place of 'Empire'; two concepts held within a breath of one another, one a direct cultural inheritor of the next. The inheritance of which is still at the heart of culture wars now, as the 2021–24 UK government and its constituents launched attacks on charitable organisations that illuminate the violence of Empire's own spent bonfires. On the sites of which, trees grow, and will continue to grow, and will outlive the culture wars, will outlive the government, will outlive me, as I sit between the mossy knees of a swamp cypress, looking out at a medieval lake, where ancient forests and ornamental trees meet, root-deep in iron-rich earth.

And I can't explain it, not yet, this feeling of immense loss and great vulnerability. The possibility of survival that can't be hoped for, because as soon as it is hoped for it will be gone, and then there will be nothing but death. And the trees who shelter the nymph and the genderqueer explorer, the yew and the cypress knees, the bougainvillea and silver birch, they witness all of this. The death and the joy, the lover's sensuality, the sexual power of the root, the desire for flight, community and mourning and vulnerability, the possibility of survival and the overwhelming likelihood of serious, life-altering dangers. What am I to a tree? I still don't know. But trees to me are the root of how I make sense of my queer body; how I understand what routes (and roots) took hold that transformed trees into colonial biocapital, and with them, the reinforcement of the wall that guards the binary. Wildlife or vermin. Man or woman. Native or invasive. Knife or breadbasket. Empire or heritage. I feel the ancient *animx* in the queerness of trees; the expansiveness of their intelligence, and all the ways I cannot know them.

The trees that make dark shapes in the sky. That is what a tree is also: a hole cut into the fabric of the night.

earth::radix::winter

4

hands in the mud (on labour, gesture and earth connection)

> To be queer and native and alive is to repeatedly bear witness to world being destroyed, over and over again
>
> Billy Ray Belcourt, 'Can the Other of Native Studies Speak?'

I am looking for the Q in the earth. An ecological act almost too intimate to bear, between climate emergency and global health crisis. I am looking for what feels like home, as if my life depended on it. Because it does.

In the midst of lockdown, I grieve my disconnection from land. One hour's exercise a day. Enough for a trip to the allotment and back, or a walk around the neighbourhood. Without my yearning hands in soil, I am ungrounded. My laptop streams films in the darkness, screen illuminating my face as I sit cross-legged on the bed. I am aching for elsewhere, but for now I am landlocked and without my land. And so I watch someone do what I most long to do. I am watching her hands deep in the mud.

***

She is bent double, arms submerged. Here in the landscape her gender is immaterial. She looks small against the wide grey frame. Her clothing is indistinct: she's too far away from the camera for her face to be visible. Her waders, dark trousers and white t-shirt might mean it is warm where she is, but that too is difficult to tell: the grey morning mist speaks to my British understanding of weather patterns. Perhaps the air is clammy, a touch cold. In the pre-dawn, the air is filled with noises. The hollers of crows and terns are familiar, but the call of a lone frog is definitely not what frogs sound like on my small island in the North Sea. For hundreds of metres, maybe even miles, there is a wide tidal mudflat, saturated. Maybe I can, maybe I can't see where the estuary waters begin further out. Maybe they are obscured by the mist.

As the figure bends down, her hands descend. She is searching for something with her fingers. There is a squelch; the satisfaction of skin against mud, silken, wooden, hollow and full. And then her body tenses for a second, her arm straightens, unsealed with a ringing knock. Her hands grip. With extraordinary economy of motion, she transfers the thing to her other hand, and then into a wide box with broad handles, which sits on the spongy surface.

She shifts weight to her other leg, planting her feet a pace or two in front. She repeats. Only it's not quite fair to say that, because each movement, each stance, is slightly different to the one before. Sometimes she bends fully from the waist. Or she plants one leg behind her in a lunge, then bows lightly, her body horizontal to the mud. Sometimes she is unsuccessful in her hand's quest; when this happens, she moves quickly to another spot, a few paces on. Sometimes there are many things in the mud, and three or four or maybe five times, her arms dive back into the thick silt, peeling away what she finds and placing items in the box.

She moves back and forth over the surface of the mud from one side of the frame to the other. Her body becomes smaller, more distant, and gradually so do the pleasing, sensuous sounds: the wooden-silken knock of shell against hand against mud against air. The faint catch of her breath. The work of bending and rooting and peeling and placing doesn't look easy; every so often she rises, stands, wipes the hair or sweat away from her face with the back of her arm. Her body is attuned to the task; she is practised at these movements. She is adept at judging the distances between her body, the box and her small boat. It too sits on the surface of the mud; weight evenly distributed so that it doesn't plunge the way her feet and hands do. But it is heavy enough: pulling the boat across the mudflats by the rope attached to its stern is clearly effortful. The way the woman's body leans forward as she does it says so.

As she goes about this patient, repetitive, laborious, skilled, sensuous, intuitively embodied task, something is happening to the light. The birds gradually reach a crescendo. What could be a mountain, a cragged hill in the far distance slowly becomes more nuanced in tone. What was one dark object becomes a range of shades; green canopy, tall fawn trees, the silvered line of a sandbank below them. The shining contour gradually transitions to pale gold, struck by the rays of the rising sun, whose gilded borders promise itself somewhere beyond the frame.

Maybe it's my memory that claims it, willing the sounds of the dawn chorus to climax at the moment the sun rises. I am not altogether sure that is how it went. I am, after all, writing this description from a sense-memory of the vision that this film, Sharon Lockhart's *Double Tide* (2009), inspires in me. What I remember is clear and unclear. My attention swerves and dives like a swallow overhead. When I lose concentration, and my eyes return to where the woman's bent-over body was, seconds or maybe minutes later she has shifted away, as if I am watching a stop-motion animation rather than the slow unfolding of dawn. Reading later about Lockhart's filming process, I learn that *Double Tide* was filmed on 16mm analogue film stock, each capable of recording about ten minutes of footage, and later transferred to high-definition digital video for editing. So the blurs in and out of focus; the stop motion, blink-and-you'll-miss-it quality are as much a part of the film as they are a part of my consciousness.

Once I have spent 45 minutes with this frame, and I have become so used to this woman, this mudflat, this low tide that I feel like I could watch forever, the sequence cuts to black.

It begins again, or appears to. Things are different. The sky is clearer, stratus clouds leaning across the frame. The estuary draws a mirrored curve across the rear distance. The woman pulls her little boat and her wide rectangular box into view as she places one foot after another through the mud. The boat slides to a familiar place, familiar to me, familiar to her, in the bottom right hand of the frame. Her collecting begins again – stooping, stopping, stepping, questing, reaching, rooting, rattling, pulling, passing, placing. All of it begins over again in the same place, but at a different time, and because it is a different time, it is therefore also a different place.

The mud between the woman and the living, moving beings she is collecting is not the same mud between the mist and the sky in the first sequence. The high tide in between the two parts of the film will have washed new silt into the estuary. The puddles of water are not the same silvered patterns present at that other time, and that other time must have been morning, must have been the dawn, because dawns grow brighter, not darker. In this frame, the light fades, slowly, almost on the scale of the imperceptible. Rose and coral shades enter the sky, appearing so subtly that at one moment they are not there and then they are and it feels as if there is no trace differential between these two states of pink and no-pink. That too fades, and light begins to rim the edges of the not-quite-visible puddles. Just as the line of sight also doesn't let you see the woman's face, or her expression, or the living, moving things she seeks as she plunges her hands into the mud.

There is much that watching the woman on the mudflats allows me to see; a great deal that it does not. I can hear her breath, and occasionally her almost-voice, when she coughs (has a particle of sand or a fly become lodged in her throat? Did she accidentally breathe when she should have swallowed? Is she nervous? She doesn't look nervous, only practised at this skilled labour of stooping and searching). I don't know anything about her speaking-voice, only the practised way she stoops and stops, bends and roots, rises to look outward toward the estuary. Maybe she is watching the tide rise; maybe she is resting between bouts of effort.

Towards the end of this second sequence, she returns with the boat towards the camera. The gradually, almost imperceptibly fading light makes it difficult to see the surface of the mud, but close by she finds a convenient pool of water. The wide rectangular box must have open slats, because she submerges the box, shaking it, releasing the mud particles from the living beings inside. She places the box next to the boat, and then moves between pools, washing down her waders, then her arms, then the sides of the little boat. The mud clings to her; it sediments easily on waders and boats. This, like everything, requires regular maintenance. And it is easier to do a bit of regular maintenance each time than to let things build up and up, till the boat becomes unusable, or the waders too caked and heavy to put on. Washing is the ritual activity that signals the end of labour. And it's true: she pulls the boat and her box out of the frame, to the shore and solid ground that I imagine is the same ground on which the camera rests.

This film is not a portrait of the woman in the mudflats. It is a landscape of her. She is a landscape. She is also *in* a landscape, shaped not only by millions of years of continental drift but by centuries of (mostly) European painters. The familiar rectangular ratio of the screen through which I watch her was also shaped by centuries of art history. The audio-visual technologies that produced it mimic the canvas of painters and the photographic plates from which cinematic technologies developed. And I know from years of teaching film that the sounds I hear, the complex whir of cicadas or the yelp of frogs, the caw of crows or the wheel of terns, the swallows and the boat horns, the cars and the children, and the slow, silk-and-wood sound of mollusc pulled from mud, of boot withdrawn from mud and placed down in mud; all of these sounds are real sounds, in that they originate in the landscape being filmed. But they are also unreal sounds, in that they were recorded by a microphone that must have been placed close to the woman's body, and processed post-production in what is still to me a magical, alchemical process of editing layers of sound. The sounds of the landscape are unreally real, hyper-real, transformed into sounds of great synchrony, and intensity, by the sound recordists and sound editors and sound artists working with this film.

This is what I love about watching film, especially slow, experimental films like *Double Tide*. Observing in obsessive detail what skilled labour looks like, what their full absorption in the natural environment feels like. To scrutinise this closely in real life would be called staring. Voyeurism. And my attention would be unlikely to hold. But watching film I have implicit permission. I love the way my attention shifts, striates, scatters across the moving images. I love the way that my slow, ponderous attention to *Double Tide* brings to my attention my slow, ponderous attention: where it fades, where it returns and what it returns to. Whether my gaze shifts to the woman in the mudflats, or the cicadas who I can't see, or the sound of the woman's hands plunging into the mud, knocking out silken-wooden rhythms with nothing but the fruits of the estuarine mud and air, I am also returning to my own consciousness. Slow, sleepy, observant, lifting the veil between waking and dreaming, midwinter.

All this save the latter part is known to people who watch slow films. It is also known to people who observe their breath, who watch clouds, who listen to the dawn chorus. I am not saying anything new about attention. Perhaps what is new (or simply a new reformulation of the previous century's pandemics) is watching *Double Tide* during a national lockdown while cross-legged on my bed with laptop and headphones, streaming from Cample Line, the independent gallery and arts centre based in Dumfriesshire, Galloway in the Scottish Highlands. I have never visited the gallery, tucked away in its former mill-workers' cottages in a village north of Dumfries, east of the Galloway forest, overlooking a railway viaduct. But I have befriended its slow methods of travel, and its screening of films connected to land, which soothe my own land-disconnection.

I connect to the intimacy of this woman with her hands in the mud because of my own disconnection from the wider circulating world. Disconnected twice, in fact: once by lockdown, and again by the seasonal depression that I submit to, burrowing down in the darkness. I connect to her hands through my hands, because I am thinking about the feeling of hands in mud, soil, sand, earth, clay, what keeps me grounded in the dark times. Hands in the mud, seeking something. My hands in the earth, seeking out roots, or making room for roots. The naked touch of a nature connection so fundamental that it feels as intimate as sex, only to call it sexual feels inadequate, because sexualities themselves have been mainly prescribed by their relationships to humans, between humans. I would call it erotic, in the sense that Audre Lorde describes it: a rich, feeling–touching groundswell of desire that is the bridge between the sensing world and the thinking world. Between my body and a body of land, a body of water. It's an erotics that calls on the self – my self – in communion with the more-than-human world. The mud that seals itself under my fingernails, that rubs itself into the grooves and whorls of my fingerprints, is a different sort of substance entirely to the sandy mud of the estuary in *Double Tide*, no doubt different again to the soil of Dumfries and Galloway, the earthly location of Cample Line's film at home series. But the gesture of bending over, down towards and into the earth; that is like a ritual of prayer.

This is ecological intimacy. It is spiritual and sexual, and there is no other way I can call it than queer.

For a long time, I felt cut off from my own spirituality. Prayer is not a familiar substrate. My rigorously, ruthlessly atheist upbringing is laced with the strict utilitarian Protestantism that preceded it. My knowledge of prayer is laced with an egoistic, muscular denial of the sacred, and a Protestant investment in prayer as begging, self-excoriation. Neither of these are positive starting grounds for an understanding of devotional practice.

Nonetheless, what I am coming to feel is my own coming-into-feeling, in the erotic extension of my contact with the earth, which is also sacred. The sense of wellbeing, of quiet, ritual pleasure and of gratitude; I am coming to understand these feelings, sensations, imaginations, as prayer. Prayer comes from a place of plenitude. I am following Robin Wall Kimmerer's description of an economy and an ecology based on abundance, rather than scarcity; that prayer is a sense of gratitude for the abundance of what is already there, and not an appeal to the Master Builder to throw down some scraps. As Audre Lorde taught me, the Master's tools will never dismantle the Master's house anyway.[1]

* * *

In *Braiding Sweetgrass: Indigenous Wisdom, Scientific Knowledge, and the Teachings of Plants*, North American Indigenous plant scientist Robin Wall Kimmerer writes: 'For all of us, becoming indigenous to a place means living as if your children's future mattered, to take care of the land as if our lives, both material and spiritual, depended on it.'[2] But she is also curious, doubting, suspicious even, about the capacity of settler-nations and coloniser-nations to truly embody that kind of materially embedded but not materialist, future-oriented but not futurist approach to land. In a gorgeous retelling of Indigenous cosmology and European Enlightenment biography, Kimmerer imagines the Anishinabek First Man, Nanabozho, on a walk with Carolus Linnaeus, the Swedish botanist most commonly credited with the development of Latinate binomial classifications for plants, as well as the structuring of plant sexuality into binary male and female systems, which would later go on to influence constructions of human sexuality too. Try as she might, Wall Kimmerer cannot create a beautiful synthesis of these two forms of knowledge: Traditional Ecological Knowledge from Indigenous communities on the one hand, and botany, ecology and plant science from Euro-Western models on the other.[3]

The two might learn from each other, but they are not the same; and one continues to be used to denigrate the other. Richard Dawkins' vociferous rejection of Traditional Ecological Knowledge in a letter to the New Zealand Royal Society in December 2021 is one example. Dawkins' short missive denouncing the introduction of traditional Māori knowledge systems into university curricula was informed third-hand by fellow hyper-rationalist Jerry A. Coyne's blog post, rather than a diligent analysis of the University of Auckland's curricula. Dawkins states bluntly that 'Creationism is still bollocks even if it is indigenous bollocks.'[4] Naturally his letter does not pursue the scientific method which it purports to uphold, nor does it hold a particularly well-defined remit for science. Dawkins excludes systems of knowledge (including sociology, anthropology, history and philosophy of science) from 'true science', despite the fact that 'science' in many contexts outside the English-speaking one encompasses the arts, humanities and social sciences, and that European research funding councils define 'science' as all of the disciplines contributing to knowledge.

Instead, Dawkins casts aside empirical evidence and rational analysis, using the guise of 'plain speaking' to diminish any contextual, historical or culturally specific understanding of science. 'Indigenous bollocks' is just one small example of a much wider structure of violence used for centuries to suppress and condemn Indigenous thought. And of course this reveals more about Dawkins' obliviousness to the evidence that Euro-Western science has historically constructed models of race and gender that upheld systems of imperial and patriarchal power[5] than it does about the introduction of Mātauranga Māori, Indigenous knowledge systems, into university curricula. Old racisms arise in new guises.

The dismissal of knowledge systems as truth or bollocks along racialised lines shows that humanity has not moved much further from the time when the body of Khoikhoi South African Saartjie (Sara) Baartman, derogatively named the 'Hottentot Venus', was preserved without her permission after her death in 1815. Displayed continuously at the Musée de l'Homme in Paris until the 1970s, her body was used without her permission nor that of her community to provide an 'evidence base' that linked her enlarged buttocks and labia to racist scientific claims for the diminished intelligence of racialised Africans. I feel my own sap rising: the old anger in me that returns when I see, smell, hear patriarchal and racialised violence in motion, in Dawkins' abusive attacks, clothed in claims of impartiality. Science has its own history of racist bollocks.[6]

Complex emotions arise then, when I read Robin Wall Kimmerer's respectful, empirical and spiritual efforts to bring together Traditional Ecological Knowledge and Euro-Western ecological knowledge. Her capacious writing style accommodates these conflicted emotions in her books – they put out their own tendrils of feeling. For the first ten chapters or so of *Braiding Sweetgrass*, that pure, painful sense of truth and joy and grief welled up in me, a non-Indigenous person with an ambivalent and tenuously connected relationship to the land I live on and with. Indigeneity cannot be built or taken or appropriated in a lifetime: it is not to be assimilated. As Wall Kimmerer writes, '*Indigenous* is a birthright word. No amount of time or caring changes history or substitutes for soul-deep fusion with the land.'[7]

How is it to be a white person – a settler-colonial person – and a queer person invested in the future of the earth? Is there a way for such a person to be entwined with the land, the locality, the micro-ecology of place? Instead of *Indigenous*, Wall Kimmerer settles upon a different sort of a name: *naturalised*.[8] Fused with nature. Aligned with it. Naturalisation in place: a fusion with the land, cooperation with land, where land (and sea, and estuary) are cared for, and care for us. For me.

How can I find the intimacy of the Q in the intimacy of place?

In other words: how can I show you the knowing I have in my bones, with my hands in the mud, that ecological intimacy is also queer?

* * *

When I talk with my friend A about *Double Tide* on the phone, after we have both watched it simultaneously but apart from one another, she points out how easily we both slip into a romanticised way of talking about manual labour. Since neither of us exert ourselves through physical toil as a way of making our living, and nor would our bodies likely be able to withstand it, it is easy for us to yearn for satisfying, strong, manageable bodily exhaustion, as an antidote to the intellectual and emotional work we perform in front of screens each day. Despite the awareness that this kind of repeated physical effort would just as likely destroy my body as heal it, there is a kind of arrogance that hovers at the edges of this romantic view of work. A kind of omission.

A particularly white, European, middle-class condescension runs the gamut from Jean-Jacques Rousseau's racist tropes of the noble savage to the romanticisation of the rural working class in the novels of Thomas Hardy. It's a risk: looking at the body of a woman performing highly skilled and dexterous, yet also demanding and repetitive physical labour, and thinking that, somehow, she leads a more perfect or more beautiful or simpler life because of it. This was the subject of Millet's painting *Les Glaneuses* (1857), where a group of three women, bent double in the landscape of a freshly harvested field, stoop to pick blades of wheat left behind by the threshers. At the turn of the millennium, the filmmaker, artist and activist Agnès Varda made *The Gleaners and I*, a digital documentary about gleaning and subsistence living. In its making Varda took a road trip around France to speak with people who live on the edge of capitalism, and fell in love with a heart-shaped potato. Her aim was to amplify the voices of the women in Millet's painting, who are not historical but many-gendered and present and living below the line of capital in the French landscape. As she did so, she also gave voice to her own ageing body.

The act of placing a woman before a camera lens, of transforming her from the subject of her own professional labour to an object; this is tender territory. The woman in the landscape that A and I look at, on our separate screens, in our separate lockdown homes, for 90 minutes of slow, detailed, unhurried clam-digging: this is also the long tail of Romantic thought. The sublime that the Romantic poets found in nature, and in landscape painting. Seductive and reductive, finding the sacred in the bent-double gesture of hands in the mud. It's easy to fall in love with labour as a source of transcendence when you aren't doing it. But that is not the film's fault. Rather this is something my white, European body carries with me, informed by the centuries of looking that have come before. And there are other bodies in the mud whose memory has been recorded and obliterated on film: Isaac Julien's multi-channel installation *Ten Thousand Waves* (2010) remembers and memorialises the deaths of 23 illegally trafficked Chinese migrant cockle-pickers, trapped by fast rising tides in Morecambe Bay, Lancashire in 2004. Hands in the mud are not a romantic escape. Prayer will not save the dead.

In her biography of twentieth-century social political commentator, novelist and essayist George Orwell, Rebecca Solnit notes how Orwell's critics tore apart his love of nature and gardening. They saw it as simultaneously crassly overindulgent, and aping a rural working class to which he did not belong, despite his own experiences of poverty. Solnit notes 'the desire to garden, to be in the country, to rusticate, is culturally determined and rooted in class, or at least the forms it takes are.'[9] This is both true and not true – a rural landscape looks very different to a middle-class writer slowly dying of tuberculosis; to a clam-digger who has worked in the same place their whole life; to a gleaner gathering potatoes from a pile of discarded produce considered too irregular in shape to be marketable; to a fruit-picker whose nomadic life trails the harvest across thousands of miles and many different nations; to a slave, modern or historical, whose short life is condemned to work and work and work on contaminated or crop-sprayed or tidally unstable land. All these relationships are to do with class and citizenship, but they are also to do with the land itself.

Still, it is difficult not to elevate the woman on the mudflats along lines of class and economic status, as a paragon of nature connection; a more fruitful life than the ones my friend and I spend locked into our computers to make a living. And we both know that this dividing line is artificial. Jen Casad, the clammer in *Double Tide*, is also an artist. Her work is not subsistence harvest; it is part of a richer and more complex set of relationships to the natural and human world. The clams that Casad harvests from the tidal estuary in Maine might well end up on the plates of weekend visitors from the cities nearby, who even after the financial crash of 2008 can probably afford the high prices that hand-dug clams might command in high-end seafood restaurants. The clams she pulls from the mud could be the soft-shelled kind that are currently in decline, or the hard-shelled kind, whose numbers have increased, along with eels and oysters, as the coastal waters around Maine have warmed. Artisanal, hand-picked work also has a commodity value – harvested soft-shelled clams from Maine were valued at US$15.5 million in 2024,[10] while between 2004 and 2018, the value of the Maine hard-shelled clam harvest rose from US$10,000 to US$2.6 million.[11]

The bigger the field of perception becomes, the wider the circulation of capital, the harder it is to distinguish without fetishising what is special about watching Casad go about her work, which she does without showiness, and without verbal explanation.

Is there something sullied about the act of watching? Cinema has its own histories of voyeurism. Watching in a darkened room, while the light of the screen conjures action and narrative: it's hardly surprising that the cinema has been compared to a peep show. Not surprising at all that the cinema has also historically been a place for masturbation, cruising and furtive sexual encounters. Sex and the cinema are as interlinked as cinema's dark exhibitionism. And there is something sexual about the noises of the mud as Casad's hand plunges, pulls and releases clams from the estuary bed. Something sexual in the feminine and non-binary, something queer, something about fingering and fisting and pleasure from a lover's hands.

My intuition is pulling at me now, asking for my attention. My intuition wants to say that there are ways that *Double Tide* is conscious of the voyeuristic risks of watching, but continues nonetheless. Because I never see Casad's face in close-up, I do not have access to her facial expressions – they are not mine to own in the act of looking. She is a woman in the land, no more or less important than the multi-species landscapes of plants and animals that surround her. In the first 45-minute-long take of *Double Tide*, she even disappears a little *into* the landscape; her body nearly melting into the mist. And because Casad never speaks in the 99 minutes of the film, I also do not have access to her thoughts, or the way she talks about herself. This isn't what *Double Tide* is about. I get the sense that, by not requiring Casad to verbalise what she does, how she does it, why and for whom, the banker with the weekend home in Maine who eats Casad's clams at the fancy seafood restaurant with a glass wall overlooking the bay is left behind. Even though A and I can see his ghost. There is nothing but Casad, and the mudflats, and the land. Everything is illuminated: her labour, the clams, the estuary, the mud, the treeline. Everything falls into darkness, too. And while there is intimacy in staying with Casad as she works, it feels intuitively like this has less to do with voyeuristic power than it does with witnessing, or allowing time, weather, daylight, tide, land, mud to unfold, in all its erotic, compelling repetition.

Hello, Q. I did not expect to see you there, in the mud-flats, in the long stretch of time. In those hands in the mud.

There is something important about remembering the land, its contours and instabilities, recalling the places where water meets mud, shorelines, estuaries, beaches. The land remains and renews, and comfort comes from that regularity of connection to land and place, but remaining and renewing are also shaped by human footprints. There is always a risk that the land will not be renewed if the data-driven society upon which we are largely dependent for labour and leisure does not find carbon-free energy sources; if we do not curb and resist the capitalist consumption machine; if we do not learn to reciprocate with land. Land renewal is dependent on a renewed respect for and contact with land and the materiality of all things. It relies on ecological intimacy as much as environmental policy.

***

I am by no means an expert on climate change: like many people, I worry about what a future world will look like if the worst predictions of global warming were to take place. And unfortunately, those worst-case scenarios may in many cases become the actuality: the 'Production Gap' that the Stockholm Environment Institute identifies is the difference between global projections of fossil fuel production (coal, oil and gas) and the estimated level of reduction required to keep global warming to 1.5 or 2° centigrade. As the 2025 report states, 'Countries are now collectively planning even more fossil fuel production than two years ago, with projected 2030 production exceeding levels consistent with limiting warming to 1.5°C by more than 120%.'[12] From this perspective, our collective responsibilities for pollution via fossil fuel production mean we are well and truly fucked.

How can I live with this knowledge – that the planet I was born into is being destroyed? How can I hold these truths without becoming paralysed by their sadness? And: where is the Q in climate crisis? What does thinking about the queerness I feel emanating from Jen Casad's body in *Double Tide* give me? In Casad's slow, processual, whole-body engagement with the land, I find what gives form to other kinds of knowledge: older, quieter ones built in the slow temperate relationship of nature connection. Ecological intimacy is queer, interspecies love. The Q in climate crisis is about learning again to see myself in the landscape, to see and feel, with hands in the mud, what an intimate, personal relationship with land might be. Embracing queer intimacy with our ecological world is nothing new, of course: it is the basis of the Traditional Ecological Knowledge built over time by generations of ancestral Indigenous thought.

I learned a long time ago about the shifting of the Gulf Stream, which might make Britain a much colder and less temperate place to live – and that is the least of its concerns, compared to the massive increase in tornadoes, typhoons, tsunamis and tropical storms that its shift will – has already – unleashed on more vulnerable shores. I reflect on my carbon footprint; how my decisions not to have children, or to minimise long-haul air travel (which was not exactly difficult during the early part of the 2020s), or choose green energy suppliers, or to minimise my plastic waste, or reduce the air miles of my food and eat organically and seasonally, or try in general to consume less stuff, contribute in their own tiny ways to the picture of reducing carbon emissions. I grow vegetables and berries on the allotment, though as many of them go to the birds and insects and slugs as they do to me. I stopped eating land-based meat a few years ago, though I am still complicit in the cruelty of dairy farming by eating cheese and yoghurt and cream. And yet, I know that each of these minor lifestyle changes is not nearly enough to avoid climate crisis. It is not enough.

What do I do, hands in the mud, or hands on my keyboard? What can I do to love the land the way it loves me?

Queer is not just who you sleep with. It's how you love.

And ecological intimacy is queer land love in its quietest, smallest form. The hands in the mud, whose tiny acts of life are both insignificant and world-changing. How differently we all might live if ecological intimacy was a vivid reality, to every person, in their own private, land-loving way.

* * *

I would eat the clams that Jen Casad pulls from the silt. I have eaten them, in fact – not the wide, kidney-shaped ones from *Double Tide*, but narrow razor clams at the Company Shed, a small seafood restaurant on Mersea Island in Essex that has been selling and cooking locally caught seafood since the 1980s. The island itself is estuarine, connected to the mainland by a causeway called The Strood, which can be flooded at high tide. I once visited on a crystalline winter's day, all frost and wide blue skies. That was over 15 years ago, when there had been a consecutive series of cold winters, snow and ice turning pavements into uneven skating rinks where I wished I had crampons on my feet. Snow from November to March.

I know I may not see a winter like that again; maybe not in my lifetime. When I place my own hands in the mud on my allotment, filled with earth-warmth, I'm also communicating with an earlier time whose memory the mud holds. Between the roots and the scraps of plastic and the insect life, there is the memory of the winters that were once cold and, for now at least, are tepid. Casad's hands in the mud from 2009 bridges the time between my clam-eating on Mersea Island in 2009 and the winters of lockdown in 2020 and neo-lockdown in 2021, and 2022, and beyond. Hands in the mud that reveal my own filthy contact with environmental crisis, and my own yearning for a connection to the earth that feeds me. Both, and.

In learning to love the land through hands in the mud, there is no either/or. Only both, and. Here and there. Past and present. Laptops and salt flats. Traditional Ecological Knowledge and the colonial impact of climate crisis. Ecological intimacy is about love, land, despair – and queerness before it was called queer.

And time flows backwards and forwards like tides, melding past to present through the accretions of mud. Time is oceanic, estuarine. Seasons bleed. One into another, they become *like* one another. The rains of autumn are echoed in winter and spring. The saturated mud of an estuary in Essex, in Maine, looks similar in November to how it does in March. In this small island corner of the northern hemisphere, ends look like beginnings, and beginnings look like ends.

5

compost (on medium, matter, mutter, mother)

> Planting seeds requires, medium, soil, matter, mutter, mother.
> Donna Haraway, *Staying with the Trouble*

A compost heap is an ecosystem and a process. Made of matter at the end of life, it becomes life-sustaining. Matter feeds matter, enriched by the waste products of invertebrates and bacteria. Compost is both doing and being. It is an exercise in patience, resilience, sustenance, and shit.

* * *

Margaret Elphinstone's beautiful, frosty otherworld of a novel *The Incomer* contains a whole scene devoted to a muck heap. Two siblings, a brother and a sister, spend dawn to dusk constructing it carefully, adding layers of dung and kitchen waste, animal urine and hay, patting it down, checking the symmetry. In the malleable descent from autumn into winter they craft a giant layer cake of waste, adding leaf litter, food scraps, cut-down plants, mouldering wood. The heap becomes an architecture rising between the two of them as they wordlessly go about their work, silent because they have no real need for verbal communication.

The whole process takes a day, and at dusk they mount its summit. Steam rises from the muck heap's sides, as they watch the sunset, till the last of the heat has shaken from their bones.

Their heap is a dense, precarious combination of organic matter and skilful orchestration. They build their tower of waste products, not so that it remains as testament to their labour but so that it breaks down. It is an investment in impermanence.

It is the most beautiful description of compost I have ever read.

Like the muck heap of *The Incomer*, I am telling this story by accretions, by retelling. There is no linear route; only layers and repetitions. This, and that, and this. And, And, And.

* * *

Our compost heap sits between four wide posts pounded into the ground, shored up by planks on all four sides. It is a makeshift structure, erected in a few hours by bodies stronger than mine, an electric drill and a rubber mallet. It is sturdy enough to hold in the pile of matter; loose enough to let it breathe. The heap and the structure that holds it sit in the corner of our allotment – a 50-by-10-metre plot of land leased from the local council and allocated to us by the volunteer-run allotment society.

We waited nearly three years for this plot. This is brief in allotment time. The past two decades have seen a huge uptick in allotment seekers, while urban plots have reduced substantially in number and sites have disappeared under new residential developments. Land, especially in London, is valuable. Valuable for building small flats with no outdoor growing space at prices so vastly exceeding the average living wage that most are unlikely ever to afford one. It isn't surprising that the shrinking availability of gardens and the rise in land values leads to an imbalance in the supply and demand of allotments. Friends of ours are on the waiting list in their local area. The average wait time is ten years.

A decade to wait to grow vegetables! Insane. And yet in lockdown gardens and allotments became two of the most valuable resources available to anyone. People need land to live on and with, to link their lives to land, to bond with it.

Before you have a muck heap, there must also be muck. *No mud, no lotus*, is the Buddhist saying.

For there to be muck, there must also be space to grow. And though this should be available to everyone, there are many layers of material advantage that come before this basic right.

* * *

Compost, which could not be more resilient or sustaining, is entirely made up of breaking down.

I loathe the word resilience. Rather: I loathe how it is used. Resilience training. Building resilience. Resilience as a resource to extract and then inject into those who are lacking. Transactional supplements to stave off the hunger of injustice.

What an inventive way to blame people for not coping with the world around them. If only you could be more resilient, then you wouldn't find it so hard. If only you were more resilient, then you wouldn't complain about the distressing things that happen to you. We'll train you how to put up with more and more shit, pile it on till it's over the top of your head. Blame you when you can't breathe. If you are resilient, able to withstand the social forces that tell you that your body, your mind, your gender (dis)orientation, your ways of living and loving are wrong, then you are described as 'brave'. What a load of shit to layer on.

Resilience that is about what I lack, about getting tough, is of no interest to me. But it is of great use to the labour-spinning machine of capitalism.

Hard resilience is a way of building perfect robots. Little workers who never get ill, who can withstand precarious employment, the erosion of pensions and healthcare and citizenship, the struggle to find meaningful work in communities that they love, the difficulties of raising a family when distance from the extended village, and the astronomical costs of childcare, make it hard to do anything other than work, and work, and work, and work, and work.

If resilience is about tolerating the intolerable, I'll have no part of it.

Fuck resilience.

* * *

What can compost teach me about my own resilience, where it comes from? Where I come from?

On a bland, drizzle-laden day in midwinter, mid-lockdown, I am watching YouTube videos of the Jim Henson Company's children's show *Fraggle Rock* while wrapped in a blanket. I was a child of the 1980s, pacified by TV for extended periods, and *Fraggle Rock* was one of my favourites. I identified closely with the Fraggle characters, particularly melancholy, hyper-cautious Mokey and impulsive, intemperate Red, who seemed to represent the two parts of me. I also implicitly understood the middle-ground that the Fraggles occupied: living beneath the garden of the humanoid Gorgs, who inspired fear but whose luscious garden provided some of the most tempting foodstuffs the Fraggles could find (radishes!). The Fraggles also lived alongside, and sometimes above, the Doozers, whose pragmatic, determined, constant, unchanging industriousness was a source of wonder, frustration and disregard. The adult world existed above and below, as a garden of earthly delights and a material substructure of boring, repetitive, incomprehensible labour. I loved radishes too.

The Fraggles' emotional openness and willingness to work together to problem-solve fascinated me. And when their moral dilemmas exceeded the frame of what they could work through themselves, they would visit Marjory the Trash Heap.

In the Fraggles' world, Marjory is wise, old, expansive, nurturing, confusing and messy. She often encourages the Fraggles to look inward, rather than towards her, for moral direction. Sometimes she provides pearls of wisdom; but often she is distracted and indirect, poking gentle fun at the Fraggle pilgrims for their indecision, or their egotism. She contains everything: all the scraps, waste and putridity, all the hope, song and joy. She sounds like a cross between a Jewish Brooklyn mamma and an English grandmother, and she sings the blues, as well as calypso. Her puppet frame rises from a rumpled underbelly of fabric; and then, when she is finished speaking, she returns to the textile-earth again. And though she does not smell good, this bothers neither the Fraggles, nor the rats, Philo and Gunge, who live with her and provide her with her life-source. If or when they leave, she starts to die.

Marjory fascinated me as much as she also gave me the creeps: I found it compelling that something, someone, could exist who was made completely of detritus, who rose up from waste and returned to it. Wittingly or unwittingly, she triggered my elevated childhood sense of disgust. Children often talk of disliking an adult for their overpowering smell or physical flaws in close proximity: I wonder whether this is a displacement, or a way of talking about the way an adult may transgress the boundaries of a child, unaware that they have done it. If an adult gets too close, and has not sought permission, then a child is going to struggle to articulate their consent or their boundaries. But they may be able to articulate what is disgusting. Disgust is a complex masking emotion: it does important work to disentangle where you end and I begin.

* * *

I am telling this muck heap story by accretions; a layer cake of retelling.

I have a recurring nightmare – or used to have it; it's not nearly so frequent now. It was at its most pervasive in 2014, just before I had my first of a series of world-curtailing bouts of depression. It returned, again, when I became ill in 2017. And again, viciously, compulsively, in 2019. I have a feeling that this vision waits in the shadows. When I am no longer nourishing myself, my body turns inwards against its own material.

In this bad, bad dream, I am a trash-eating robot, mechanised, senseless and unfeeling. It's my job, as this trash-robot, to consume everything that is broken, rotten, putrid. All the detritus, all the festering waste: give it to me. All the shit, all the mould, all the unspeakable end-products of a digestive system: give it me. In my dream, I swallow it all down, feel it entering my belly, groaning with distended horror at the contents inside that I know would make me very sick if I were human or an animal. But I am not human, not alive, I am simply a robot, consuming and compacting everything. The more trash I eat, the more robotic I become. The human parts of me shrink, smaller and smaller, and further away. Till the part of me that is human eventually winks out, like a light. And all that is left is robot.

I wish that were the end of the dream; I wish I woke up in fright at that point, but I don't. It goes on, and on, till eventually I fight myself out of sleep, paralysis deepening as I rise to the surface of consciousness.

It took me a long time to give this dream language. This, and the transitory sense of horror in the dreamworld, which became a much more enduring one once I opened my eyes each morning. Giving these experiences something with form took time, and effort, walking through burning shame to get there.

If I ask my heart, it tells me this was not a dream at all, but a reality. It took me a long time to speak about it aloud. Longer to write.

Now my dream has form I don't dream it nearly so often.

Another writer once said to me about my writing, meshed in guts and microvilli: 'It's a great metaphor. But where is the story?'

To which I replied: 'It's not a metaphor.'

The soft animal of my body refuses metaphors that only exist in the abstract.

Compost is not a metaphor. It is what we live in. Medium, matter, mutter, mother.

* * *

Marjory might be one of my earliest queer icons. I know my sense of fascination-revulsion is right on the money when it comes to the erotic charge of felt self-knowledge, where internalised homophobia (when does that begin? Early, so early) clashes with recognition. I am not the only one to feel this, my friend S affirms: Marjory circulates in the queer imaginary. She was picked up by performance artist Dustin Bradley Goltz in the ghostly queer accretions of his one-person show, *Fred Astaire's Dancing Lessons* (2019). She is the subject of academic scholarship on the Muppets and their relationships to social and environmental justice.[1]

It's no coincidence that trauma-revulsion and queer self-aversion might begin in the same place. If it is true that queer people often (but not always) have difficult early childhood experiences, then there is a relationship of both, and. It's not causation, but it is correlation. And though my sense memory can access the feelings I held in my body while I watched Marjory then, and watch her now, I can't extricate the entanglements of pleasure and pain, trauma and safety. When Eli Clare writes in his memoir *Exile and Pride* about the stones in his pockets, stones in his heart, those stones are entangled with the pleasures of erotic connection, the yearning for the rural landscape from his earliest childhood and the brutality of his father, and all of these wind through his identity as queer, disabled, trans. He writes beautifully about his earliest moments as a collector of stones:

> Only here did I have a sense of body. Those stones warm in my pockets, I knew them to be the steadiest, only untouched parts of myself. I wanted to be a hermit, to live alone with my stones and trees, neither a boy nor girl. And now 20 years later, how do I reach beneath the skin to write. Not about the stones, but the body that warmed them, the heat itself?[2]

For me, it is not stones (though I hold them in my heart too) but compost-matter that mutters the things I cannot make into a language I can call my mother tongue.

***

My father says to me, 'What you lack is resilience.'

Resilience is the psychological concept reflecting the capacity to move through emotional difficulty and to continue. From physics, it is the ability to be compressed, or stressed, or deformed in some way by a force or a blow, and to have the elasticity to return to one's usual shape.

The capacity to experience emotional difficulty and pass through it is developed when humans are very small and very young. If a child feels secure to express their pain and sorrow, feels held and loved and nourished while they express it, then that child will also learn how to self-soothe. They can experience pain and regroup afterwards. Eventually, they will learn how to ease their own burden. They won't stop feeling the pain, but they will understand that the pain is temporary, and that there is a place of love to feel that pain safely. When that loving security isn't there, or when the parent rejects the pain that the child feels, the adult that the child becomes finds it much more difficult to take hold of this tricky, painful environment, to allow it to pass through them, and find ways to care for themselves.

This kind of intestinal, composting resilience is linked to self-compassion. It is soft and pliable and elastic, and it needs communities of love to hold it and hear it. Oceans of love. And it doesn't shy away from the shit.

That isn't the popular face of resilience. My father's resilience is the much more commonly held one: it is about toughness, being impervious to life's arrows. It is about *not feeling*, not allowing pain to penetrate the hard carapace. Neither disclosing nor revealing it to others.

Informed by generations brutalised by war and empire, and the violence of public schools that acted as training grounds for both, popular resilience is impervious, unfeeling, sadistic. The bully is often seen as the paragon of resilience. Brutalised and brutalising, the bully refuses to accept or acknowledge pain and instead deflects it onto others. Paradoxically, when confronted the bully will also claim that they are the one who is forever hurting, the one who is in pain and fear. The narcissistic wound that never heals.

The dependence of popular resilience on outward appearance means never processing, never digesting, never composting pain. There is another term for this: emotional dumping. *Take care of my shit. I don't want it.* But deflecting pain onto others only works for as long as there are others upon whom to deflect. At the heart of the image of individualistic, hard resilience, is interdependence. And yet, hard resilience has to deny this in order to buy into its own impervious sadism.

What a human response to pain. Plant-beings know interdependent resilience far better.

Oak trees are tough: a storm can uproot them, razing to the ground hundreds of years of growth. But a tree is never alone: it is always connected to the plant life around it. If a tree is blown over in a storm, it might not die; instead it might develop regrowth from the fallen trunk, while the remainder slowly decays or forms habitat and homes for other plant, fungal and animal life. A tree will not deflect pain, either. In fact, dying or severely stressed trees fling out resources – sugar, water, carbon – to other trees around them, regardless of species. When a tree is unable to sustain its own resilience, it invests in the resilience of the ecosystem around it.[3] Soft resilience, even in the face of death.

* * *

Another accretion. Another retelling.

By the time our allotment arrived, the invisible thing waiting to fling me into the mud was already circling. By the time I was lying in my metaphorical pit, unable to feel my fingers, we had already begun work clearing the plot.

When I try to describe dissociation, I run out of words. It is, to me at least, the opposite of being human. When it happens, I no longer recognise my own body, or my place in it. I no longer have access to an emotional vocabulary where I am present to the words I am speaking. A robot takes my place. Where there was feeling, instead there is nothing.

Hard, isn't it? Because to write words that carry meaning, there has to be a bodymind from which those words emerge. No matter if they are words from the chorus of the muse, or from your own unique spirit.

Words need a body, and a mind in that body. No body, no words. No feeling, no words. No world, no words.

Have I managed it yet? Have I conveyed to you the

no-place that I cannot really write about, because it is where language cannot penetrate? The flimsy otherworldliness of writing about this place-with-no-words sends me into a tailspin. Spiralling down, into the earth.

All through the first winter of our allotment, my bodymind was broken. It did not know, really, how to be a body – how to sleep or rest, how to read, how to eat. But it did know how to dig. That is how I became reacquainted with the soil and the earth. It is also how the compost heap began.

Down to the earth to begin again.

* * *

I don't know what sits in the compost of my childhood, but there is something in it that speaks to disgust, consent and boundaries; all three tied together. Some memories don't rise to the surface, especially if they come from very early in a life. I only catch glimpses of what they are or might be: the sudden slug of tension, pressure or pain in my body.

For a long time I thought that, if I have no visual recall of an event, then nothing bad could have happened. But that isn't how memory works. It's not how trauma works either. Trauma is such a big word; it doesn't do justice to the myriad and complex ways in which an experience can override mental-emotional-physical wiring, leaving its sticky residues behind that secrete unpleasant chemicals at unexpected times, dispensing flashes of unbidden sensation.

Trauma to a child does not have to mean abuse, or the worst possible stretches of imagination. To a child, events of a traumatic kind don't have to be the cataclysmic disasters that an adult might fold into the realm of trauma. It can mean a repeated failure to have one's emotional or physical needs met. Or a regular transgression of boundaries.

I don't know more than that. I only know the layer of feeling without words. Knowing the particular shapes and language of trauma is the work of an adult brain: child brains do not know in this way. Knowing what happened is not always the point. I am learning how to live with the unknowing part of me, as well as the one that knows.

* * *

Feminist eco-theorist Donna Haraway gives form to things that are ideas, and because they are ideas, they become things. Her first book was made of crystals: how their material structures became scientific models, metaphors to think with. She has written on cyborgs and feminist transformation, and companion species, about her kin-relationships with dogs. And now, rather than claiming to be a humanist, she describes herself as a *compostist*: allied with, but not exclusively tied to humanity. Her 2016 book, *Staying with the Trouble*, has compost at its seams, in its matter. Compost is another model for thinking and being and telling stories. But this is where I wonder: how much compost is metaphorical, and how much of it is a real, material muck heap?

I want both. I often find myself frustrated when I look for the material in the metaphor. I know that good writing makes openings and beginnings, not closed loops. Layers. And I have learned from compost-building that this is also mostly what you need: combinations of materials layered on top of one another with enough water to bind, enough air for useful creatures who respire aerobically, enough new decay to encourage mycelial blooms, enough slow, old decay to encourage the anaerobic bacteria, enough warmth to keep all these processes going. It's delicate work, composting.

And while I read *Staying with the Trouble* about Haraway's compostism, I find myself asking: where *is* that compost? Where's the matter in the metaphor? Where are the accretions, and what form do they take?

For example: Haraway writes about *humus* – as in soil, earth, decay, not the chickpea-and-tahini dip – and its relation to the *human*. Earth-beings that we are, we are formed of the same etymologies, at least in English. But humus is also a very particular kind of decomposition: one more to do with the lifecycles and ecologies of places relatively undisturbed by human labour. Humus is the form of compost without direct human intervention.

What I most want to know is: where is the compost, in Haraway's compost-thinking?

Even she acknowledges her compost is a joke and more-than-a-joke. Compost is a thing to think with. Reading an interview with Haraway about her own actual compost piles, I feel kinship: she talks about the heaps that have failed in her life, and acknowledges the accretions of class, race and settler-colonialism that enable her and her partner to have their compost piles and bins, their hens and their American 'yard'.[4]

I feel my skin settle when I read this: I am at home in other people's conversations about cultivation and its failures, its accretions and muck heaps.

***

The hard resilience of my father's generation and socio-economic demographic is a remnant of empire; part of an obsolete colonial model that still shapes a social group most likely to occupy top positions in government. The public school-educated, white, upper-middle- and upper-class, masculine milieu, brought up during the decolonial era of the British Empire, was taught emotional cauterisation, disconnection and isolation. The fortress stands alone on the top of the hill, with no notion of the teeming life that withstands its weight below the surface of the soil.

It is not where I come from, but I bear its scars all the same.

Blended with the dialect of neoliberalism, where all people are individuals, and not powerfully and unconsciously linked to others, hard resilience forms like a calcified residue. It glazes over the social, environmental and political violence of capitalism and colonialism, rendering it palatable, smooth and even.

Resilience isn't about feeling nothing. It isn't about rejecting suffering. It isn't about accepting the unacceptable either, although that seems to be part of its popular meaning too: if you are suffering, you are not resilient enough. Your suffering is your fault because of what you lack. This claim conveniently bypasses any consideration that what you are suffering might be caused by socio-economic conditions that it is possible to change collectively. 'Resilience training' is a sticking-plaster solution to a pervasive problem; at worst it places blame on individuals who are suffering, rather than challenging the source of the issue. If your workforce is experiencing endemic levels of work-related stress and sickness, the problem is not their resilience. The problem is the work.

Breaking down is not a sign of weakness. It is a sign of truth.

Where is the truth in this for me? Why am I saying these things? More importantly, what can my compost heap teach me about resilience?

I say 'my' compost heap, but it isn't mine, not in any reasonable way.

* * *

Another nutrient-rich layer for the muck heap:

At around the same time that I became ill again in late 2019, my name came to the top of the waiting list for an allotment. The demand for a space to grow in London has never been higher. We were lucky, very lucky, to be contacted. And we took up the opportunity immediately.

The plot itself was overgrown, as handed-over plots usually are. The reasons people let go of their allotment are predictable: the demands of a young family, or a new job, or ill health, or old age, or a move to a new city or country. There is – or should be – no shame in this. Time turns: some things are possible, some too difficult.

What was to become our plot was covered in inch-thick bramble vines and three-foot high tuffets of couch grass, with a small, sad-looking trellis of abandoned runner beans in the middle.

All through the winter of 2019, when I could do nothing else, I dug. I remember digging a vegetable plot in 2014 too, in the large garden of the rented flat we lived in at the time. Then, turning over the soil and observing the creatures beneath was what had sustained me.

I knew that illness, which crashed back into my plane of being shortly after we were given the allotment, was an end-point in some way. I couldn't go back to the working environment that had made me so unwell. But there was also no way forward. How could I leave paid work with no paid work to go to? I was stuck in a bind, and the trash-robot nightmares returned. Horror in dreams, horror in waking. Clearing the allotment's detritus was neither cause nor effect; simply a fact of being that expected nothing more of me than to begin, and begin again, and again.

My imagination used to head skywards, toward treetops and cloud formations, atmosphere and cosmos. Digging turned my inner gaze downwards, into the stories that the earth encloses.

* * *

On 17 May 2008, in a ceremony in the redwood forest of the University of California in Santa Cruz, in front of a collected audience of over 300 human and more-than-human animals, artist and sex worker Annie Sprinkle and environmental ecologist Beth Stephens married the earth. Their *Green Wedding to the Earth* – part performance, part protest, full of love, was a two-hour extravaganza of performances, readings and dances by an assembled cast of over 150 of Sprinkle and Stephens' collaborators.[5]

In 2011 they did it again, in their documentary *Goodbye Gauley Mountain – An Ecosexual Love Story* (2013), where they married the Appalachian mountaintop in West Virginia, close to Stephens' hometown, that was being devastated by Mountain Top Removal: a form of strip coal mining that 'literally blasts the top of the mountains to smithereens, leaving dead trees, plants, animals (including hibernating bears), soil, and rocks strewn about in piles of debris'.[6]

They spent time in the rural communities, unearthing the rural queerness that has been part of the fabric of settler communities in the Appalachians for a long, long time. Their film is a combination of ecological and social justice, love, sex and ribaldry.

They did it again, and again, and again, marrying the Adriatic Sea in Venice, the coal in Gijon, Spain, Lake Kallavesi in Finland, the soil in Krems, Austria, the moon, the sun. As part of their Love Art Laboratory, they coined the term *ecosexual*:

> ecosexual \ ˈɛːkəʊ ˈsɛkʃ(əw)əl: eco from ancient Greek *oikos*; sexual from Latin, *sexuales*. 1. A person who finds nature romantic, sensual, erotic, or sexy, which can include humans or not. 2. A new sexual identity (self-identified). 3. A person who takes the Earth as their lover. 4. A term used in dating advertisements. 5. An environmental activist strategy. 6. A grassroots movement. 7. A person who has a more expanded concept of what sex and orgasm are beyond mainstream definitions. 8. A person who imagines sex as an ecology that extends beyond the physical body. 9. Other definitions as yet to be determined.[7]

Of all of the definitions of ecosexual, the one I love the best is the one yet to be determined.

* * *

Here is another deposit for my compost investment.

Throughout the autumn and winter of 2019 and 2020, once we had cleared the plot of its major detritus, we started to dig out, section by section, the roots and weeds that had grown horizontally across the plot, matted into the root-resisting membrane that had been set down years ago. This is the arduous, difficult route: I have since learned that many, if not most, allotmenteers put down cardboard and tarpaulins over stretches of a plot, leaving them for months until the weeds have died down and the cardboard has disintegrated, before digging in plentiful amounts of compost and soil improver. This minimal-dig approach would have been much easier. But then I would not have learned so much about compost, or soil composition, or what it feels like to have my hands in the earth, every day.

When it wasn't raining, I'd be there, slowly, hour by hour, lifting and sifting couch grass roots and torn agricultural membrane from the soil. Because I had nowhere else to be. Because there was nothing else to do except go home and stare at the wall.

Unexpectedly, slowly, sifting the soil brings new skills with it. We gradually learned about techniques of digging; how to be more careful about separating root from soil to protect the structure of the earth. Bucket by bucket, piles of pale tangles filled up the rectangular frame of the compost heap.

Each of the plotholders has different advice to give about couch grass roots. One suggests burning; the other removal to the municipal garden waste scheme. Yet another puts all of his in a small plastic compost bin and lets them rot down. Another plot holder tells me that in France couch grass roots are eaten, boiled up in a soup. They are highly nutritious, too. I'm reminded of the many ways that what is considered edible is also bordered and bound by culture. Britons don't tend to eat chickweed either, and yet it too is ubiquitous and palatable.

* * *

Over the months, the abandoned garlic cloves and onions in one bed of our allotment became a harvest of their own. With gratitude we planted tulips, dahlias and gladioli, discover overgrown artichokes, lovage and lavender, two clematises and a rose bush whose blooms are a delicious hot pink. Our summer harvest, mostly grown from seed – tomatoes and beans, chillies and peppers, salads, summer squashes and sweetcorn – came good, with a smallish but tasty crop of early potatoes, despite unexpected frosts in May.

It is easy to forget what the passage of time does, what it means.

* * *

This winter's job has been to move the compost heap three feet further into our plot, making room for a path at the end that was once there but had, over time, become overgrown and invaded by brambles and the incursions of our plot.

Moving the heap, with its five-foot-high entanglements of roots, plants, discarded potatoes gone bad, bindweed and bramble offshoots, takes its own time. The heap had lain in wait all year, growing higher as we pulled up the sturdy stems of spent maize and thick heads of gone-over artichoke. It is hard work forking out, and then forking in again, a few tonnes of semi-rotting organic matter. The earth does not yield easily to a spade or a fork: digging is durable, muscle-demanding effort.

Over the course of weeks, I saw, once again, the roots and grasses I had carefully pulled out of the soil a year previously. I saw them differently: in the slow process of decay, they had fallen away from their matted clumps, gradually softening into a different structure entirely. I saw where the compost, dampened by rain, had kept on breaking down into smaller components. And where the compost was dry, I saw roots in arrested form, some sprouting weak new shoots in the dark. I also saw the teeming wildlife of the heap – centipedes, woodlice and worms, moulds and networks of fungi.

The compost heap communicates to me through a kind of Bartleby refusal – Bartleby of Herman Melville's short story 'Bartleby the Scrivener' who gently, persistently refuses to work, refuses to leave, refuses to quit, saying 'I would prefer not to'.[8] Compost would prefer not to yield usable substrate when its conditions for creation have not been honoured. The compost heap speaks to me in gentle no's. I understand that. My first word was no. I entered into language through negation.

The layers of compost are also layers of time, but not of the linear kind. Forking out the compost, then forking it back in again, I see my memories of illness come in like tides, crumbled into thick composted soil, with undecomposed roots running through them. And instead of hard, angry failure, I feel softness, for what has decayed, and what remains.

* * *

In their ecosexual glossary, Sprinkle and Stephens reappropriate the term biodegrading, to mean 'getting excited by being called filthy compost'.[9] At their first *Green Wedding to the Earth*, each member of the audience was given a bag of soil to open and smell during the ceremony. At the culmination of their performance, *Dirty Sexecology*, which they have performed alongside other pioneers in performance art at festivals in Switzerland and Spain, they had sex on stage with a mound of soil and with each other, their ageing queer bodies messing with public perceptions of who can acceptably be sexual and with whom (or what). When they married the soil at the multimedia arts festival Donaufest in 2014, the musician Peaches spontaneously wrote a song called dirt, whose final line is 'dirt is the shit.'[10] In their collaborative performances of *Dirt Bed*, Sprinkle and Stephens and other participants got naked and squelchy in a giant bed of soil, complete with elaborate headboard and lovely dark compost.

By accretions, in layers of the years, Sprinkle and Stephens' multimedia performances, films, manifestos, actions, walks and parades are joyful acts of love and pleasure, wrestling with the darkness of environmental and social injustice. Their work is almost always collaborative, and they have built communities of artists and activists with them – weird kinships that extend across place and time. They are close friends of Donna Haraway, and even made bumper stickers for her with slogans like 'Composting is so hot!' and 'Making kin in the Chthulucene'.

But they also know that their ecosexual manifesto is not without its problems, particularly in its appropriative relationship to Indigenous knowledge, and the predominance of white bodies in ecosexual spaces. As Kim TallBear writes, 'There are no easy, literal translations between indigenous ontologies and ecosexuality, at least among the indigenous people I run with. Rather, there are careful conversations with much careful thought to be had.'[11]

I think about this often: how to have careful conversations about Indigenous practices and traditional knowledge without appropriating. My suffering will never compare to centuries of colonial oppression or decades of political erasure. How to acknowledge the structural whiteness of my social being, as I build the compost of my life – its complicities as well as its struggle? The *both, and* of the muck heap.

* * *

My compost heap doesn't sing to me or give me guidance of the verbal sort. But it has allowed me to see time in a different way. My human time and the time of compost are different, but interconnected. The material of the compost container has its own temporal matrix. The plastic bins that contain piles of roots and grass cuttings on the edges of the plot will yield fine, granular compost much faster than the wide, open frame of the larger heap. My heap once had a coat of old carpet to cover it, keep it warm in the cold months and prevent it from drying out during the warmer ones – but old carpet leaches chemicals and now I have disposed of it. Compost building is a skilled practice: it is like making an entity of many parts. Our unskilled assemblage of the heap 18 months ago will continue to reflect its pace of decomposition and recomposition another year from now. Layers of illness, learning, recovery leave their imprints in the muck heap.

Compost decomposes at varying rates, according to the conditions that are supplied for it. You can speed up the composting process by applying heat and anaerobic conditions, which then generates more heat and faster decomposing. I've listened with joy to expert composters speak about cooking their dinner slowly in the middle of their heaps. Heat made in the making of waste, that nourishes and warms the food on the table. Layerings of fast and slow, nourishment and decomposition.

* * *

In my worst times, I dream of trash. More than this: I dream I *am* trash. I am a trash-eating robot, consuming everyone else's detritus.

My trash-robot takes things away for others, removes their unwanted emotional and physical waste. I take it all in with no outlet. I am an all-receiving vessel for other people's shit.

When I dream these dreams, I am not capable of regulating what goes in nor what comes out. And nothing comes out. Nothing at all. When those worst times come, in my waking life I watch the placid slowness of a compost heap coming into being.

The magical alchemy of compost requires time, patience and presence. Compost isn't a rubbish dump; it isn't made of any old thing. It is slow and it is multiple; soft resilience and metamorphosis.

Composting, not trash-eating. Transforming, not consuming. A slow, boundaried settling, not an infinite acceptance of the unacceptable.

I have still so much to learn from compost, about resilience. Multiplicity. Sexuality. Time.

6

roots and radicals (on recovery dreams, radical politics and rebuilding)

Fifteen years ago, I trained as a Samaritan to sit by the phone, waiting for it to ring. 'Samaritans, can I help you?' was the first line of the conversation that might or might not happen. I might sit for hours listening to someone thinking about, or in the middle of, taking their own life. Someone who saw nothing left in life but its end. They might say something, or nothing. I was trained to listen with kindness, and without judgement; simply to be there for someone who in all likelihood I would never meet.

The Samaritans are the largest organisation for suicide prevention in the UK, whose secular mission is to listen, with empathy, without judgement, in the presence of another human being in distress, respecting each person's right to personal agency and, ultimately, self-determination. Part of my training was to understand the difference between sympathy and empathy. The analogy was relatively simple: sympathy was *feeling for* another person. If someone is sitting at the bottom of a pit, unreachable by daylight, sympathy would look down and feel the sadness, the heartache, the pity even, for the fallen one. Sympathy might fall into the pit too. Sympathy, I was taught, while commendable as an emotion, is also pretty useless for the person in the pit.

Sympathy takes the light further away. No-one wants to be pitied. No pit-dweller wants to haul others down with them.

Empathy, on the other hand, is *feeling with*. Empathy takes a ladder down to sit with the pit-dweller, in the dark, in the cold. Empathy asks questions about what the pit looks like, feels like. Empathy doesn't seek to change the shape of the pit, doesn't try to move the person stuck there. Empathy accepts, and asks gentle questions, and when empathy is ready, it leaves. The hope is that, by illuminating the pit floor, the pit-dweller might not feel so wordless, so alone. Maybe one day the pit-dweller might see a way to stop living in the pit and start to climb out, for themselves. Maybe one day the pit is not a pit but a landscape of cold light.

Words can help bring light to the dark places. Empathy is their vehicle.

What follows is pit-writing. Deep in the earth, waiting for the light.

* * *

I am concentrating on the handful of earth between my gloves. An inch of pliable foam padding between my knees and the damp ground, I stare at the narrow trench in front of me, six inches wide, six inches deep. The soil between my hands looks dense and sticky, but when I tease it apart, it crumbles. It is full of matter. In any handful, there might be: half a plastic spoon, an unidentified plant bulb, shards of glass and ceramic broken by their time underground, round pebbles, fragments of flint, a corner of brick, a scrap of foil from an old crisp packet, a pen lid, a hundred half-germinated seeds, worms, woodlice, slugs, ants, centipedes, beetles. And roots, thousands of roots; some so fine they break as soon as I pull the clod apart; some sturdy, cream-coloured, with junctions and nodules that snap easily. Some of the roots are fragrant; some bright orange beneath their brown coating.

The roots are the source of my focus, as I tease the loam away so that they come out whole, shifting, piece by piece, the horizontal strands of couch grass roots from the plot.

In the dark times, language comes apart. What is left are no longer layers for the muck heap, but fragments; roots in a bucket. In my terrifying robot dreams, all I am is unfeeling, inhuman robot. By day, all I can do is mechanical tasks: rhythmic repetitions of things that work my body out of its unending cycles of darkness.

I spend hours like this, bent, kneeling, investigating the soil. During those hours, my focus, my energy, my thoughts are consumed by roots. All I can see is roots. In my sleep, I dream of roots coiled in a bucket.

These root dreams are safe. They are a recourse from the dark places. Recourse from the hasp and the tarpaulin that snag at my memory. All the times, all the places where I was not human enough. Where to be queer, or strange, or different, was not to be at all. If I cannot see the light, at least I can go down into the earth. I can hide, retracted in my snail shell, brittle, broken and waiting.

Dreaming of roots in a bucket saved my life.

***

What's radical in a root?

Radical (adj.)

1 Relating to, consisting of, or going to the root or fundament; necessitating, entailing, or favouring fundamental social, economic, or political change. *N.*
2 A group of atoms that is unstable in the free state but when bound together in a molecule behaves as a single unit, such as the acetyl group $-COCH_3$. See also free radical.

[From Latin *radix* a root + *-icalis* of, relating to, or resembling][1]

radical

Applied to a *leaf that arises from a *rhizome or from the base of a stem.[2]

Root and rhizome. Rage and root. Root and radical. What was my process of taking root? Of radicalisation?

There goes the etymology again.

*wrād-

Proto-Indo-European root meaning 'branch, root.'

It forms all or part of: deracinate; eradicate; eradication; irradicable; licorice; radical; radicant; radicle; radicular; radish; ramada; ramify; ramus; rhizoid; rhizome; rhizophagous; root; rutabaga; wort.

It is the hypothetical source of/evidence for its existence is provided by: Greek *rhiza*, Lesbian *brisda* 'root,' Greek *hradamnos* 'branch;' Latin *radix* 'root, radish;' Gothic *waurts*, Old English *wyrt*; Welsh *gwraidd*, Old Irish *fren* 'root.'[3]

Lesbian?

Lesbian is a language. The language of Lesvos/Lesbos. Sappho's island.

Brisda.

I want to know more about this word. Brisda. Like *Bris*. Jewish ritual of welcoming and circumcision. Do these things have anything that holds them together? Like Robin Wall Kimmerer's association between the *yawe*, the animate verb that describes being of all kinds in the Indigenous Potawatomi language, and *YAHWEH*, the *god-name* of the Old Testament, or the unpronounceable tetragrammaton of the Torah.[4]

Brisda, the root. *Rhiza*, the root. *Radix*, the root. All these words that circulate.

Radical is one of them.

* * *

When I dream of roots, endless roots, knotty, creamy pale roots, following their lines, their routes in and out of the soil, the dreams soothe me. And my quiet root dreams start to ease my violent, robot dreams. My inner robot recedes, leaving space for my inner human to return.

Roots take me down into the earth, but also laterally beneath an abandoned plot. I note how the chair of the allotment association repeatedly tells me that the plots I identify as overgrown, windblown, seeded with grasses, bushy sage leaves just peeking through the tall blades, are not abandoned. They have custodians, but many of the plotholders were unable to access the allotment over the course of the pandemic. Many became ill, or needed to self-isolate, or were unable to care for their plot because of caring responsibilities or sudden work demands, or were immunologically vulnerable and therefore shielding themselves at home. Some were stranded abroad, burying relatives, unable to return. And so the plots really are not abandoned, but temporarily let fallow. He is correct in correcting me, though I guess what I mean by abandonment is not the same. *Abandon* doesn't necessarily mean to leave forever. It can mean to temporarily withdraw, surrender. To yield. Reflexively (to abandon oneself), it can mean quite the opposite of abandonment – to devote oneself utterly. Sometimes the act of retraction, of turning inwards, is safest. Surrendering to what is: the pain and the grief. Abandoning oneself to what is also: composting, rematerialising. Finding one's roots. This is not just about not being visible in the world. Being visible can be tough at times for anyone, not least those who do not inhabit a body readily aligned with the matrices of the binary world. Straight/gay. Man/woman. Able-bodied/disabled. Being visible takes an extraordinary amount of energy, because visibility involves the effort of trying to pass (or refusing to pass), to fit into a cultural world that has precious little room for the fitting. No wonder that in dark times there is a need to retreat, to abandon to what remains of self. Sometimes being is already enough. Sometimes being is already too much.

Still, the chair of the allotment association is not looking to play word games with me; he's simply identifying the fact that some plots may look wild, but custodianship, and the intent to care, remain, and are to be respected. The roots of the desire to plant seed, to cultivate, are still there in the ground. It's the routes back towards them that look different. Sometimes the routes don't even look like routes at all: they might be a forest path that dwindles to nothing.

I feel the call to woodland while I kneel six inches from the ground, under conditions of lockdown. Wide, thick woodland; acres of it to walk through. That forest path might suddenly be broken by a fallen trunk, or a vast sprawl of brambles, threatening to cut, scratch, hold. A route might not be a route at all; might narrow and dwindle to a slippery matting of leaves beneath saplings too tight-grown to pass. In which case the route splinters, returns, rounds and rewinds.

And yet ... routes and roots. My routes are different, though I recognise familiar patterns in them, even in the earth. A route can be meandering, winding. This is how I think of my route to writing, but also my routes towards and around gardening, cultivating, nature connection, queer community, feminist and interspecies kinship. Routes that meander between Donna Haraway, whose explorations in interspecies community, influenced by the writing of Ursula K. Le Guin and Octavia E. Butler, all influence me. Gutsy, earthy writing on soil and earth, compost and seed, growth and decay, violence and survival, mycorrhizal networks and interstellar travel. I see a familiarity and a home in all their writing. Something speaks to me through the thicket of their prose. I see a network of ghost women and queers travelling on the routes I pass, winding in and through and between trees and thickets. I am not standing on the shoulders of giants; I am walking with those who live with me as my own arrested journey unfolds.

* * *

When was I radicalised? *In all times.*

How was I radicalised?

By planting my garden. By recognising that I am not the robot to be buried in the ground. By acknowledging that I am part of a larger whole, that my pain is not simply my pain, that screaming into the abyss creates no change, that my depression is my anger swallowed, that what I feel is not an island but a bridge.

What was I radicalised with?

A return to roots.

* * *

Brisda is a Celtic name also. Related to 'Bridget'. The bridge. The late moment of turning toward change.

The root and the bridge. Radicalisation is the bridge between the root cause and the shared cause.

Radicalisation is a forbidden word. But it is what happens to every one of us. A return to one's roots. It just depends on when and where and how you found them.

I found my roots in the soil of a small allotment plot in South East London. I found my roots in my experiences of sexual harassment and abuse (who, who is exempt from this?) I found my roots in my attractions to women, to men, to beings in between. I found my roots in my love of reading, dreaming, digging, planting. I found my roots in my desire to dance. I found my roots in humiliation and abasement. I found my roots in my own, particular story of harm which is both like and unlike other people's stories, of roots, and rage, and radicals.

* * *

Here is a root, winding laterally beneath the soil of my thinking. Roots breed radicals. There was a queer woman, a radical woman who in the early twentieth century challenged the legal claims of the Church of England to the earnings of farmers and agricultural labourers; a woman named derogatively as a 'mystic' in her time, who, like the Kewriosities, wore breeches and men's shoes and cut her hair short, and smoked and drank gin, and co-wrote crime novels under a pseudonym, and played jazz in a trio in the local pub. The first woman in Britain to compare organic farming methods with high-yield chemical agriculture, she demonstrated how and why organic farming was better at sustaining life. The Haughley Experiment, as it was named, ran from 1939 to 1970, providing a substantial body of evidence that established the signal importance of healthy, thriving soil for healthy life – plant, non-human animal and human animal too.

Her name was Eve Balfour. She was the co-founder of the Soil Association, which developed the first organic standards for farming in the 1960s and is now an organisation powerful enough to influence food and agricultural policy in the UK and Europe, and which owns one of the largest certification programmes for organic products in the world.

This radical queer person whose life lay at the heart of organic farming wrote a book about it, mystically entitled *The Living Soil* – and her queer spirals between land, spirituality and sexuality I would not have chanced upon, had it not been for a conversation with Guy Baxter, Associate Director of the University Museums and Special Collections Service at the University of Reading.

Reading has a curious assemblage of collections, drawn partly from its rural origins as an agricultural college outside Oxford. The Museum of English Rural Life is a Victorian redbrick building beside a garden cared for by experts and volunteers. Years out from my winter in the pit, the autumn day I visited was framed by a red-leaved maple across the MERL's entrance to its garden. Rain shed itself like silvered skin between bursts of sunshine that turned the maple into a glowing giant. A barn-like extension housed the permanent exhibitions: tools, films, tractors, carts, seed catalogues and a board game about artificial insemination and cattle breeding that was staple entertainment in the lives of many English farming families.

The MERL's archive includes the assorted records of the Women's Land Army, many of Gertrude Jekyll's publications on gardens and shelf upon shelf of agricultural newspapers and journals. There is an original photograph of Balfour from *Farmer's Weekly* in 1936, taken from behind a sea of straw boaters in the crowd below. She stands with her mouth open, mid-word, dressed in a pale Peter Pan collar, boxy jacket and stripy peaked cap. As she delivers her speech to the crowd of five thousand farmers assembled in Hyde Park, behind her sit a bank of men in suits and ties, hats and pipes, watching. She addresses the crowd with her hands held behind her back. Her boyish pose, sun-baked skin and queer androgyny are hiding in plain sight, one pale figure in an ocean of dark-suited figures.

What is queer in the rural is not just who you sleep with. It is about an intimate relationship to land, labour, speech. To communities that may be both hostile and attentive. To hands held in pockets, behind the back, holding in, holding forth.

* * *

In the time of my internal darkness, I spend several hours a week pulling cream-coloured roots from claggy soil. I learn that turning soil when wet is a bad idea. Not only is it almost impossible to separate out useful, life-giving earth from invasive roots; digging wet soil also damages the soil structure, which is difficult to repair once that happens, and can only be resolved over time with the intervention of earthworms and microbial life that help restore its aerated density, stability and moisture retention. Waiting to dig for periods in between the rain becomes something of a game: spontaneously taking the chance to go out to kneel next to the brown loam and pull out more weeds and creamy, horizontal couch grass roots.

The hours staring intently at the ground make green after-images of roots behind my eyelids. My root dreams protrude through the topsoil, waiting for me at night. The mechanical repetitions of digging, kneeling, root-sorting become a part of the me that is not made of metal or trash. They give me a body to come home to, even when I try to escape it, dissociating into the ether with my hands in the soil, brown crescents under my fingernails. And the trash robot, whose consumption haunts me nightly, paralyses and mutes me, it gradually slides away from my subconscious, to be replaced by knobbly couch grass roots, waiting to be plucked and sorted, uprooted and loaded into the compost.

* * *

Do not stay in the pit with me. You can turn to the light, with her.

According to Rose Collis, historian of lesbians, Eve Balfour became a vegetarian aged 7 after witnessing the shooting of a pheasant, and at 12 decided to become a farmer.[5] Her family, who included her uncle, former Conservative Prime Minister Alfred Balfour (unmarried, possibly queer, certainly enjoyed BDSM relationships with women according to *Closet Queens*, Michael Bloch's queer history of MPs),[6] known to the young Eve as 'Nunkie', supported this decision and she trained at Reading, which at that point was an outpost college of the University of Oxford. Collis identifies Eve as the 'Compost Queen', and compost is indeed mentioned 419 times in *The Living Soil*. Balfour also wrote about mycorrhizal networks and the relationships between soil fungi, root systems and compost in enriching tree growth. She demonstrated how the roots of the Lodgepole Pine (*Pinus contorta*) developed so much faster and more richly when assisted by humus-rich compost, and cited studies that indicated how naturally occurring soil fungi were capable of voraciously consuming nematode worms that could infect cattle and horses. She sang the praises of earthworms, too, borrowing from Darwin's writing on the subject to demonstrate how essential worms are to the retention of nutrients in the soil, the production of pH-neutral humus, the fixing of nitrogen in the earth as nitrates that plants are capable of consuming for their growth.

Eve Balfour consulted with botanists, plant scientists and agriculturalists all over the world. She wrote in a sustained, careful, scientifically validated way about the almost incalculable value of soil to all forms of life, and particularly those devoted to food production (which is, in essence, also *for* all forms of life, and death, and the transitions in between). To do this, she wove a tissue of quotations through *The Living Soil*, acknowledging her relationships to global voices who were also advocating for soil care as a means of providing natural health protections for pasture animals, for microbial and mycorrhizal life as a vital component in crop and plant health, and for proper nutrition as a means of combatting the exponential rise of tuberculosis in working-class urban populations. She saw all of these things as interlinked: 'the earthly habitat of man's spirit is his body, and the roots of his physical and mental well-being spring from the soil itself, whether the individual be town or country dweller.'[7]

Balfour also drew from anthropological examples of Indigenous cultures where good health and longevity had been staple factors for centuries. And though she does not herself point out the relationship between colonisation and nutritional impoverishment, it is difficult not to note in her accounts the upswing in ill health experienced by, for example, Faroe Islanders when Danish boats docked at their shores. Even so, the sweeping generalisations made by the scholars she cites about the health of rural Chinese populations or Indigenous North American communities are firmly rooted in imperialist assumptions of superiority.

When Balfour writes about the knowledge practices she is most interested in – the processing of waste, composting, retaining nutrients for sustainable agriculture – the return to the soil remains the key factor. That she sees prudence in this return feels to me like more than a glimmer of acknowledgement that Euro-Western chemical-intensive farming techniques did not hold the answer to sustaining human health; that millennia of Indigenous agricultures hold wisdom in communion with the soil. I will not excuse the colonial or Christological sentiment in *The Living Soil*, but I recognise the mysticism contained within it.

* * *

When was I radicalised?

How was I radicalised?

When did the idea that I was to blame, my internalised shame, my sense that I was the bad object, in all senses of that phrase; when did that begin to change?

With my hands in the earth, that began to change. It began before then too, when I swallowed my rage, shovelling it down. It began when my rage wasn't quelled, no matter how much mindfulness I practised, no matter how warmly I tried to think of others who had hurt me, no matter how much evidence I gathered about how, perhaps, I was not hateable, when all those networks of things started to come together in such a way that I began to doubt not my sanity but my madness.

When I began to see that what I experienced was also part of a larger pattern of things occurring, large and small.

When I began to see that larger pattern of things was not personal in the sense that I could have been any queer person, any person struggling with pain, exhaustion, mental illness. Except that I also wasn't any queer person, any person struggling with mental illness, I was *this queer person struggling with mental illness*.

When what took root was not a seed but a sense of roots themselves. That my connectedness to others was not through being acceptable but through embracing what was considered unacceptable – what *I* could not accept about myself.

* * *

Balfour's politics were neither totally aligned with the nineteenth-century pity-philanthropy of her Victorian predecessors nor with the imperialist logic of her early twentieth-century compatriots. She was aware of the alliances between the fascist politics of her contemporary world in 1943 and Euro-Western assumptions based on the 'conquest' of nature, and forthrightly calls this out in the first pages of *The Living Soil*: 'When man preys upon man it is a form of cannibalism. When man sets out to "conquer" nature by exploitation, it is no less a form of cannibalism, for man is a part of nature.'[8] And tucked beneath the copiously cited scientific literature is a political-spiritual manifesto for working with the soil, born out of Balfour's many years working on the land:

> for it seems to me that of the many attributes that man needs in life, four of the most important are: (1) sufficient humility to recognize that a higher authority exists than himself; (2) sufficient self-confidence and purpose to undertake great enterprise; (3) sufficient patience to take a long-term view, and (4) the will to fight.
>
> All four qualities are in the gift of the land.
> [...] This gift of the soil; this health of spirit, mind, and body which a farm life can bring, should be made available to all, in the new Britain of equal opportunity.[9]

In 1943, at one of the darkest points in the twentieth century (and there are so many to choose from), Eve Balfour spoke of the hope and gifts of the soil. Soil is spiritual matter as well as the stuff of life, death and everything in between. Hands in the earth, there is transcendence too.

* * *

Roots and robots. How could I not have noticed, until my friend and mentor M mentions it to me, that they are only one letter apart? Take the b out of robot and you have root. Take the bullshit out of the robot and you have, again, root.

Take the bastards and the brutality and barbaric Britishness and Brexit and bitterness and boredom of successive lockdowns out of the robot, and there is the root. Creamy-white, nodules dangling.

Rip the motherboard out of the robot and you have the fine interconnecting wires, hanging free.

I don't want to brutalise this robot; I want to take the brutal, and the brute, away. All the things I feel are inhuman about the robot in my robot dream are actually its most human qualities – just as they are also the ones that make me feel less than real.

What if I buried my robot in the ground, let her rest, let her feet grow roots underground? Let a leaf unfold from her left eyebrow. What then?

* * *

Although Balfour's postscript to *The Living Soil* expresses a Christian ethic, I hear echoes of other radical voices. An awareness of the animacy and sacredness of all life, microbes included. The tremblings of Quaker business ethics where privately owned companies serve the community before the individual. There is an anti-materialist, worker-led sentiment that sounds a little like the original anarchist Peter Kropotkin's social ecologies – and he too was concerned about the connection between capitalist monocultural agriculture and the vast damage this was doing to soil fertility in *Fields, Factories, and Workshops Tomorrow* (1899).[10] And echoes in the dimensions of Darwin's theories of evolution that demonstrated cooperation and collaboration, rather than competition and survival (*Mutual Aid: A Factor of Evolution*, 1902).[11] There is even – whether Balfour was aware of this or not – a powerful parallel to the moral philosophy of Mahatma Gandhi, particularly on the importance of a sense of internalised obligation and duty towards others, which at times surpasses our own, more self-interested desires. Balfour's soil-based radicalism sings in this short paragraph from her postscript:

> Human ecology demands that we should think less of our 'rights' and more of our duties to all other living things, including each other. We must start again, with a new and better attitude towards life. Indeed we must in some cases relearn that life exists.[12]

Relearning that life exists. Relearning what life exists. Relearning what is life. I hear these things. The soil, and the roots in the ground, taught me them. With my hands in the earth, I learn about responsibility. The web of mutual enfoldment that leads me to tend to this land, which, months from now, holds the promise of a reward: food. I don't have a right to this land, to this soil; it does not have a right to me either. Rights-based thinking is important, but it is not the ground from which a better world can grow. To be consumed with rights is also to be consumed with wrongs: and there are so many. So many wrongs to be righted, so many battles to be fought. This is exhausting. What if you lose a battle? More importantly, what if the metaphor of the battlefield destroyed the delicate ecologies of the soil on which you build your life? And if you win – if there ever can be such a thing as winning – what is left?

Rights-based thinking is binary. And it is needed: the absolute no that rises up in times of civil unrest, in trade union disputes, in social and cultural refusals to continue any longer with legislation that fails to hold the civic contract. Disdain for human rights is one of the 14 early warning signs of fascism, as outlined by researcher Laurence W. Britt, whose poster was for a time sold in the shop of the United States Holocaust Memorial Museum in Washington DC, and whose original article in the humanist journal *Free Inquiry* in 2003 has become one of the most widely cited defining resources about fascism. Rights are necessary, important, and they are certainly asserted as inviolable, though in truth human rights violations take place on a daily basis around the world.

Responsibilities-based thinking is wide, reciprocal, mutually interdependent. I can't live according to my rights, which can be granted as quickly as they are taken away.

But I can care according to my responsibilities to the land I live on, the beings I live alongside. I can expect that responsibility to be shared, because care is not a choice: it is a matter of co-survival. Self-actualisation is community actualisation. I cannot be free until we all are free. All flourishing is mutual.

* * *

Put the robot in the soil. Put her in the trench I've made. It's not a grave: she isn't dead. She's a robot, and robots don't die. Place her, gently, in the earth.

Why is she a she? Because she is mine. My binary being.

Let the electrode plates of her feet fizzle with the mud's electrolytes. Let her arms rest, dislocate from their screws and sockets. Let the wires that power her melt with the earth.

Let her rest. Let her decay.

Let the spores of earth-dwelling fungi fill her chest cavity with new growth. She does not breathe; she does not need the air.

Let her rest. Let her not move.

Let her batteries lose their charge let her logic be corrupted let the endless error message play until her screen goes blank. Let the chard in the compost set seed in her right ear. Let the worms make nests in her elbow. Let her chemicals be broken down by anaerobic bacteria and organisms less than a millimetre long. In her hip crease let wild carrots grow. In her knees let ants build windmills.

Let her rest. Let her be. Let her grow.

Let the b of *benign* breathe through her.

Let her build breath.

Not hers, but the life that comes through when she rests.

Let the robot become roots, and the roots become life, and
the life become breath, and the breath become ease,
there, in the soil, resting.

* * *

As Angela Davis puts it, as it has been repeated so many times by grassroots communities, 'radical simply means "grasping things at the root."'[13] My radicalisation; my return to roots; the emergence and evolution of my awareness that I have roots, rhizomes, buried underground structures that connect me to others, arose through my experiences of pain, of shame. And they arose through the speaking of that shame out loud. And in speaking the shame, I heard other voices listening, and other voices recognising, and I was not alone. I realised that I had roots of connection to other broken bodies, other bodies' pain.

What is radical for some – radical in the negative, radical in the opposite sense of the word in fact, radical as in *uprooting of tradition* – is simply a shift in perspective for others. This is what sociologists describe as the Overton window: the fluctuations of public political perception over time. What is extreme for some – and radicalism is often used interchangeably with extremism, though some of the most violent political acts are in fact conservative, populist, ultranationalist – is for others simply a result of the shared consequences of living. Prison abolitionism is only seen as 'radical' for those who have not also witnessed the networked archive of feeling, seeing, knowing, hurting, dying and surviving that sits beneath it. Grassroots are what grow from the radical, reaching into the ground, observing the conditions of what already is, not what might be in theory or law. Radicalism begins with its hands in the earth.

In a way, calling out the radical as *dangerous*, regardless of its root, is oblivious to the *type* of root we are talking about. Attempting to destroy the radical is a monocultural world-making project. It fails to understand the interconnectedness of all beings. It is a surface-dwelling framework, neglecting what roots are shared in the dense material mat of life, living in the soil beneath.

The UK government's Prevent strategy, established in 2006 as part of a wider counter-terrorism strategy and expanded to include 'non-violent extremism' in 2013, is an attempt to uproot radicalisation, which does not recognise its own complicity in root-building resistance. As the United Nations Special Rapporteur on the rights to freedom of peaceful assembly and of association stated at the conclusion of his visit in 2016: 'It appears that Prevent is having the opposite of its intended effect: by dividing, stigmatising and alienating segments of the population, Prevent could end up promoting extremism, rather than countering it.'[14]

The Met Police's attempt to break up the vigil for Sarah Everard in Clapham Common on Saturday 13 March 2021 was an attempt to suppress the networked roots of organisations countering violence against women, an attempt that does not recognise its own complicity in the violence that produced those roots to begin with.

The Nationality and Borders Act, which, as scholar Gurminder Bhambra identifies, is the second phase of a governmental project to 'unravel the citizenship rights of those within Britain who came from [its] colonies and Commonwealth',[15] uses the subtext of controlled migration to deny citizens their rights – any citizens, it seems, who the government deems it to be appropriate to strip of their human rights. Where there is a precedent – Shamima

Begum, who was born in the UK, whose citizenship was stripped from her by the UK government – there will be others; have already been others.[16] What term might be used to justify this irrevocable violation of the universal human right to recognition as a person before the law – article 6 of the Universal Declaration of Human Rights? *Radicalisation.*

Root-finding, returning to roots, finding strength in the grassroots of community is what human beings do. Humans search for their roots like unturfed plants, longing to find a home embedded in human-earth connection.

Eradicating radicalisation is an oxymoron, a futile restraint that will result only in more violence.

The more you suppress, the more egregiously you flout the basic human rights of every person on earth, the more there is a return, a reaction. The more you chop up bindweed or couch grass or Japanese knotweed, the more the rhizomes grow. And wherever you scatter the remains, more grows. You cannot suppress forever. If you commit to that, you commit to ever more ludicrous levels of violence, not just to one person, but to all.

A radical is the first leaf. A radical thought necessitates fundamental social economic or political change.

To deradicalise is to remove the first leaf of a rhizome. To deradicalise is to cause someone to adopt a more moderate position. But what if the more moderate position also allows people to die? To starve? To be brutally murdered by uniformed policemen? What then?

What is moderate about state-sanctioned brutality?

* * *

I buried my binary robot in the ground and roots grew through her. I unearthed the roots from the soil to make room for new planting. In the process, I grew new ground. The roots I can still see in reverse imprint behind my eyelids are the reminder of the bottomlessness where nothing could touch me except thousands of nubbly, cream-coloured strings. And while those rhizomes, tubers and threads gradually decay in the compost heap or in the plastic power-composters, what has happened to the roots I might call my own?

What part of me regrew once the robot was laid to rest?

* * *

How do Eve Balfour's radical ecological politics relate to her sexuality? Why should it matter who Balfour slept with anyway? Her companion, Kathleen Carnley, with whom she lived for 50 years, was initialised as KC throughout her lifetime, just as Derek Jarman's partner and platonic lover Kevin 'Keith' Collins became initialised as HB in *Modern Nature*, Jarman's garden diaries of Prospect Cottage, and in the credits for his last long-form film, *Blue* (1993). Queer love includes many flavours of partnership, family and kin. The Q is not just who you sleep with, but how you love. How you tend the land you love and live with it, and those who tend that land with you. Eve Balfour lived to the age of 91, and died on 15 January 1990, on the same day that the UK government announced for the first time that it would allocate funding to organic farming.

* * *

Roots, and rage. Most of my rage has been confined to journals, to the shame of covering over. I remember once asking my mother if she had any chipped crockery I could smash at the bottom of the garden – somewhere to bury my shame. Though she was surprised, she helped, which surprised me too. Offered me some old, whole mugs to try it out with. The problem was, things don't tend to smash against soft London clay. So I was left with my shame and my rage, embarrassed that the feeblest attempt at self-expression had failed.

* * *

This is what I have learned from allotment gardening. My agreement with the soil lasts only as long as you remain. If I turn away for too long, nature with its long roots will reassert itself. Field will become grassland. Grassland becomes heath. Heath eventually becomes forest. In these parts of the world, anyway.

This is not a battle, but a relationship. Measures that violently suppress that natural ecological rhythm, or try to eradicate the passage of time without being in relationship with ecological life, only require more toxic approaches to the land. That toxicity will eventually poison me: my attempts to control and determine instead control and determine me.

My roots are the roots on the compost heap. My roots are the places where I find and seek nourishment and in return can give it. Root building is not a crime. It is an embedded human endeavour that comes from connection. I understand this even when I do not accept it.

When, for instance, 'gender critical' feminists renounce the term TERF (Trans-Exclusionary Radical Feminist) as a slur, they also abandon their relationship to the radical feminisms which have always existed on the margins of feminist debate; with it too their marginal outgrowth of a particular relationship to biological essentialism. Instead, fear of displacement or erasure, because of precarity in times of scarcity, poisons everything.

By *forgetting* their radical, marginal roots, 'gender critical' feminists are then able to claim the mainstream for their own. By denying their place on the margins, they can then make the case instead that some new and sinister species of marginal thought, 'trans ideology', has appeared overnight. By rewriting the history of gender, feminism, women's rights activism and sexuality, the ecological sensitivities of these relationships are trampled. What is set in place is a monocultural, scarcity-modelled fear of 'silencing', rather than an acknowledgement of the many-rooted, ecologically diverse forms of gender and sexuality, the histories that include transgender bodies and those that have erased them.

This matters, because it effaces history, and responsibility. A common war-cry of 'gender critical' feminists is that their rights are being taken away. They claim they are being silenced, cancelled, made unsafe by an encroaching and 'dangerous' radicalism that is gender diversity. There is no contract of responsibility, no framework of mutual care.

When there are no human responsibilities, only rights, there is no space to live otherwise. When there is no mutual accountability, there is no space for doubt, for self-abandon, for retraction. Only acts of violence which force bodies who do not fit the binary back into the shape of the robot. Back into constantly passing for what you are not. Back inside the prison walls. Back into a living death. Or death itself.

There have been many, many attempts to force people who live between or beyond binaries to conform to them.

Look at the histories of Indigenous nations in North America, Australia, Aotearoa New Zealand. Look at the genocides of fascist and communist dictatorships.

Actually: don't look. You do not need to see in order to know.

***

Roots, rage and radicals.

I am radicalised by my earliest and most painful childhood experiences, which make me no different from the millions of women and queers to whom these, and much worse, also happened.

I am radicalised by my early experiences of body-shaming – my body which was deemed too fat, too large, too tall, too clumsy, too cumbersome.

I am radicalised by my experiences of bullying, which began young. Which I was helpless to stop because I had been trained to believe that my anger was unacceptable, and I had internalised that anger and that shame so that I was unable to respond or intervene.

I am radicalised by my experiences of abuse, some of which took place while I was unable to articulate words like coercive control because there was no social language that I knew to discuss them. Because consent was an issue a long way from anyone's lips.

I am radicalised by my experiences of misogyny and ableism and homophobia, in the various forms they emerged, in the various times they emerged.

I am radicalised by the racist colonial patterns baked into British culture, root to tip. By the violence of whiteness that makes me, too, complicit in it.

Each time I have experienced violence, and witnessed violence, I have come closer to my own fury. The fury which I was told I must not have. And each time I have come closer to the fury, what I have seen is not that I am a victim, nor simply that I am the descendant of colonial perpetrators, nor that I am only a sole individual, but that what I have experienced is connected to the experiences of others. And also that my own pain, fury and shame can and should exist in relation to the experiences of others, for whom it has been worse, for whom it has been better. Modulation does not erase or deny. It creates a chorus.

What roots have I let go in order to regain others? The roots I was told to have, the socially sanctioned ones: the nuclear family, the model of 'straight' coupledom, the sense of an 'able' bodymind, of normalcy. A sense of excess moderation: that to react with anger is always an overreaction. The comfort of my whiteness, the charade of it that enables me to walk through the world with fewer impediments and dangers than my Black and brown friends, colleagues and kin.

Radicalisation is a deracination of sorts. An uprooting.
Deracination is a radicalisation of sorts. A re-earthing.

And I am lost in this. A root yearning through the earth, seeking and meeting with connections of water, mineral, animal, fungal, vegetal.

air::change::spring

7

seed/lings in space (on seeds, science fiction, speculation)

When your heart is broken, you plant seeds in the cracks and pray for rain.

Andrea Gibson, 'Dive', *Pole Dancing to Gospel Hymns*

Perhaps change is commonly like that, a buried star oscillating between near and far

Rebecca Solnit, *A Field Guide to Getting Lost*

In a moment of transition, there is no distinction between what is dead and what is living. Change takes place in the dark. You need the darkness for the change to happen, as much as you need the hope.

Seed planting is an act of hope with nothing to show for it. The changes are barely discernible, if they happen at all. In the seed there may be life. There may not. Life may founder. From the inert stone comes a living plant. Not always. But still, it comes.

As winter shifted into spring, I grasped the dark candle of the night and let it rest in me. In the midst of a global pandemic where unvaccinated proximity to other people was dangerous, and in midwinter, I observed the slow extension of the daylight hours. A few minutes each morning. By the end of January, it was no longer twilight at four in the afternoon; nor pre-dawn at seven in the morning. I weathered the storm of winter, when nothing else is possible but to shut down all ancillary functions until the light returns. And I did return.

Once my root-dreams and rooting hands had done their constant, undemonstrative work of putting my robot-self to rest, I began to write about seeds. Hope. The cycle between writing and doing feeds the cyclical intuition. Writing with, not against, the microclimates of South London, the spirals of my own circadian time. Hands in the soil. Composting. Roots, robots and radicals. Seeds, space. Speculation.

I sowed seeds last year, and this year, again. The pattern of the season grieves for what has gone before. Seeds need soil and nurture; but their requirements for community bring about garden rituals of sowing, pricking, planting. Each one hands me back my memory of what has passed between cycles of viral times.

In spring 2020, during the early, eerie silence of Lockdown Number One, I bought seeds. Plenty of them, selected from an organic, biodynamic seed cooperative. The company's website stated that stocks were limited: farms and food growers were the priority. I felt guilty about my amateurish seed-purchasing, when other smallholders might need them more: tomatoes, beans and squashes; chillies and sweet peppers, salads and lettuces, herbs and wildflowers. Friends with whom we share our allotment plot brought seed potatoes and little squash plants, dahlia tubers for cut flowers, and sweetcorn from an old spare packet in the communal shed. I sowed, early and copiously, in tiny seed trays lining the bathroom window and our small cold frame, and ended up with too many of one thing (squashes and courgettes) and not enough of another (narrow-leafed herbs like chamomile, with tiny, fragile seedlings that perished easily). Some seeds never germinated, rotting in their soil-filled divots. Others thrived, pressing against condensation under plastic roofs.

Within weeks, seedlings clamoured for space. Transferring each one to its own pot was painstaking, back-aching work. The chronic joint pain that returned during those months made it too painful to stand for the time it took to prick out and plant. So I sat in a chair, planting and potting. Sometimes, I failed – my hyssop seedlings ran out of room before I pricked them out. Thriving and failure were the two poles of seedling labour, between me and the plants, the bathroom windowsill and the cold frame.

Sorting the tiny grains of this book into manageable sentences, I sow them in pots of earth, covering them in their incubators next to a sunny bathroom window. I watch each one germinate and develop its true leaves, before transplanting into larger paragraphs. I rear these tender marks, hardening them off slowly. Then I plant them out, and watch them grow.

Climate crisis feels more palpable when you track the change of seasons in writing. Lunar cycles are more reliable: so is the six-weekly shift from winter solstice to Imbolc, spring equinox to Beltane. Whatever the season in this temperate zone of the planet, six-week intervals mark change. Weather meets climate crisis, even in this protected part of the globe: my small suburban garden and allotment in South London.

Words are seeds that sow something, between a bundle of proteins and carbohydrates and the rich earth. Words like hope. Seed. Recovery

From 2020 until 2023 words washed over me, with meanings that held common currency for a brief while before disappearing into cultural amnesia. R-number. Curve. Variant. Bubble. Shielding. Though their impact structured every daily movement for nearly three years, they have become distant words. They never took up residence in my heart. There are words that do: *seed. Season*. And one I reject: *seminal*.

A few years ago, I stopped using the term *seminal* in my writing. The world feels already too awash with fertilising fluids. I don't see why semen should indicate a beginning any more than an egg or a seed, or in the case of some kinds of plant life, a polygendered, primordial green slime. Foundational, yes. Seminal, no. Sperm does nothing on its own.

Germinal might be a better word – but only just, since big or little, a seed is a spark at the earliest moment of development. Seed to plant, zygote to being. Germinal shifts from the seed itself to its ways of being in the ground, on the ground.

Breaking ground is the moment of turning the earth to plant a seed. But also the way a germinating seed breaks through the hard carapace of its shell, first shoot mounting the surface of the soil, rearing its head through layers of compost. Robin Wall Kimmerer speaks of *puhpowee*: a word in the language of the Potawatomi Nation that feels and sounds to me a little like tumescence, but specifically refers to the power of a mushroom to push its fruiting body through the surface of the soil.[1] There is something strange, uncanny, *queer* about the erotic growing power of *puhpowee*. Growing, erect, upward. Burgeoning big dick energy, for anyone, anything, with swagger and swing.

Another word. Pivot – an engineered shift from one time to another. From underground root time to overground seed/ling time.

Germinate.
Break ground.
Pivot.

In the centre of this book is this chapter, pivoting from time deep in the earth, to the slow, uncertain, impossible shift towards change. Sowing to grow new life. Sowing to speculate.

Much as I would prefer to rest with *puhpowee*, my Indo-European origins mean I can't extricate myself completely from the seminal season. Spring, the time of growing from source. *Semen* as an etymological root also means seed. The Proto-Indo-European root, sē, means to sow. I just wish it wasn't so often framed in the masculine. Eggs are seeds too. Big gametes, little gametes.

* * *

Seeds taught me how to live with the maybe and the not-yet; science fiction taught me how to imagine them. There is speculation about what is, and what might become. Science fiction, the Ur-genre of speculation, has been telling me this for years.

I grew up on spaceship films. In the 1980s, the decade of my childhood, space travel was on the brink of its own adolescence. By the time of my birth the moon landing was a 12-year-old technological phenomenon. Science fiction and fantasy raised me: bookshelves of Ray Bradbury and Isaac Asimov, Philip K. Dick and Terry Pratchett. Films too. Regretfully, Ursula K. Le Guin and Octavia E. Butler only entered my life later.

The softest part of Claire Denis' space film, *High Life* (2018), is its garden. The garden is essential to the biorhythms of the spaceship inhabited by Monte (played by an uneasy Robert Pattinson) and his daughter Willow (Jessie Ross). Their space garden processes human waste into soil, which then nourishes vegetables and maintains the oxygen levels essential for their survival. Meanwhile there are bodies – Black bodies – buried in the abundant garden. It is impossible to be casual about the presence of Black bodies beneath the composted shit reprocessed in a spaceship that is the undermatter of *High Life*. Black lives are the substrata of nutritional plenitude – this much is clear in capitalism and empire's giant forays into food. But Denis' films walk a fine line between parody and affirmation on matters of colonial violence. I cannot tell whether the body of Tscherny, the Black inmate of the spaceship played by actor and musician André 3000, is a sacrificial vessel or an extractive source of harvest – for the white protagonists and for Denis. Maybe it's both.

In Denis' space-garden the labour of cultivation goes largely unacknowledged after the death of Tscherny the Black gardener. The dogged labour of maintenance is there. But care is an act of weary obligation, not a flourishing of love. And *High Life* is casual about the body count that builds up. It is a violently, splenetically heterosexual film, obsessed with semen and blood and milk and women as receptacles of all three.

Semen is the goopy, slick material around which *High Life* orbits. It is what Juliette Binoche's resident scientist–inmate, Dibs, eventually (non-consensually) extracts from Monte and (non-consensually) inseminates another inmate, Boyse, who, after giving birth to the first healthy child on the ship, projects herself into a black hole, where she explodes into long strings of matter. Life is futile; there is only violence, sex, death and maintenance. And very occasional reproduction.

The film has nothing positive to say about maternity, and precious little to say about women. I struggle to lift the veil of films like this: *High Life*'s sticky, miasmic presentation of misogyny and white colonialism is finely aligned, exquisitely presented, cruel. I notice the hair's breadth between scrutiny and affirmation. When does critique become glorifying totem?

It is so easy for critique to fetishise the things it claims to abhor; for the artist-critic to be absolved of the moral weight of being a person. I am tired of the endless repetitions of satire. The abandonment of hope in *High Life* is what leads me to turn away from Denis' splenetic obsessions with spunk and violent patriarchy. Space is not the inferno, nor are all importunate humans channelled into hell.

I need new seeds to sow. New speculation, visions of space and earth. I can't uphold the vision of Claire Denis, critical darling of the arthouse world, in seamless radiance. And I no longer want to justify complexity by releasing Denis, or me, from ongoing doubt and hope for how things might be otherwise.

Because holding up a darkened mirror does not feel like nearly enough. Writing on culture – or cultural critique if you'll have it that way round – asserts answers far more often than it asks questions. The binaries of yes–no, good–bad, left–right fling themselves into the void as if answers were enough. As if questions about why humans do terrible things to one another could be resolved in one science fiction epic. As if questions about why and how humans can or cannot care for one another, for their environment, could be satisfied in one comfortable epithet.

It is not enough. I am not looking for absolution, but I need to live in the possibility of a future. I want to plant the seeds of doubt about endless misery. Q is for questioning as much as it is for queer. All of us have different relationships to nature. All of us have the potential to reserve judgement. There is no should, no ought and no demand that can be made by critique alone. We cannot argue ourselves out of climate crisis or gender wars.

When you sow a seed you ask a question of the earth. Sometimes there is no response. You cannot demand something of the earth beyond its capacity to give. It will starve you. And you will know it is your own responsibility. No demands. Only questions.

Some questions hurt; some questions mean turning away from answers that scream in the dark, towards ones that whisper themselves into possibility.

And yes, I am talking about what it is to be queer. But I am also talking about what it is to live in a time of crisis. Both, and.

* * *

You watch and watch the soil, and scrutinise it for any sign of life. You dare not peek below, because to do so would risk the slow unfolding of root and shoot, and the delicate chemical–hormonal and rhizomatic actions that transform the emergence of plant from seed. So you wait, watching every day for signs. Sometimes there will be disappointments: sometimes the seed tray will go a little green from the moisture, but won't summon the emerald shoots of pleasure for you. And yet, the watching itself feels miraculous.

On occasion a little disturbance in the soil will indicate that first flourishing of the monocotyledon or the dicotyledon, the embryonic leaf or leaflets that are part of the code within the seed, but that don't resemble the plant. The same dicotyledon formation that is part of the plant emoji. Or represented in the animated film *Wall-E* (2008) as the source of ecological life.

I have spent a lot of time watching the soil intently. I know that the force of my will or my gaze or my love won't make the seeds germinate any faster. But still I watch. Because my life depends on it too.

* * *

The sowing of queer seeds in the dark requires stories of survival, as well as doubt.

In my early twenties, black peat was the soil in which one of my queer seeds was planted. I had moved to a small village about 15 miles south of Norwich, the East of England's only major city, along the only dual carriageway that existed in Norfolk at that time. There was nothing wrong with the village beyond the typical whiteness of rural England. It was well served by roads and a railway station. A squat flint Norman church dominated the main village road, alongside a supermarket, a small gym and a pub, a community centre, doctor's surgery, shops selling bits and bobs, and a small hotel with a restaurant attached. Decent amenities that my current self would have appreciated more than my 21-year-old one. The village wasn't the problem.

I had recently moved with my then-boyfriend to this small village in south Norfolk. This after a year in Paris that had left me with a powerful sense of my own expansiveness, and a desire for cosmopolitan urban life, not small rural community.

Talking about this time in my life makes my skin itch. I feel shame and guilt crowding in, interrupting the flow of the story. Shame for the ways I betrayed myself. Shame at how my queerness was ingested greedily as the object of my ex's overloaded, porn-fuelled desire – no doubt fed hungrily by the same early 2000s raunch culture whose horror is, a full 25 years later, in the process of being revealed. Guilt for my complicity in allowing that tender Q to be seized; in what I was willing to endure for the price of its non-exposure. Two decades later and I still feel it. Perhaps that is why the memory of soil is so important to me.

My twice-daily commute involved either a 50-minute drive through the fens and pine forests that signal the transition from rolling, open Norfolk skies to Cambridgeshire fenland, or a 45-minute train journey and accompanying cycle-ride to the other side of Cambridge. At that hopeful time in the early new millennium, the train line between Norwich and Cambridge had recently reopened, after the Beeching Act cuts of the 1960s had closed it for nearly half a century. There was money to invest in public services (how novel that seems, two decades later). Despite the looming threat of the dotcom era's boom-bust cycles, the risks of the millennium computer bug had passed uneventfully. Post-9/11, pre-financial crash, for a few this was a brief window of relative wealth, economic growth and a Blair government that had begun another war.

Still, trains on the Norwich–Cambridge line were relatively infrequent. I recall the station in the icy morning cold, where I am the only person on the platform awaiting the 7:21am two-carriage diesel train. I fold myself into a window seat, radiators against my feet, and drowse.

The warmth is blessed: sleep is a rare, interrupted prize in my bleak, damp, vicious homelife. For that year, this early-morning corner of a train carriage is my dreaming space; a place to journal, to read, alone.

Somewhere in the fens near Ely, the train slows at a signal point. My cheek is warm and I wake to weak morning sunshine skirting the fields. Wide, barely undulating, morning mists framed by hedgerows and ditches. From time to time they are flooded, flashing gold in the rising sun. On higher ground, the ploughed fields are rimed with silver frost. Beneath, the soil is velvet black. Peat-black. A cold sun shining on light's absence. The deep black of space. Its soft appeal rests my eyes from my warm seat.

Fenland peat gave me my first sense of soil as a direction, as geographical spread. Different from the claggy London mud I grew up with; different again from the iron-rich, red mud of the West Country, or the pale yellow sandstone, chalk and granite of southern France, where I have travelled for spiritual adventures. Something that might, one day, give me a feeling of home. Not now, but *soon*. And I think now that I can only make a home when I also feel with all my senses the palette, the darkness, the spaciousness of earth.

Plant me in that earth and I will grow.

***

The ritual of sowing is a recipe for building community. Sorting the seeds (finding, identifying) and giving them a warm, light, well-watered, nurturing place. Providing an incubating medium, a rich but undominating compost in which to nurture the spaces of connection. Offering just the right combination of light, water, air and nourishment to allow those connections to flourish. Shift the dialogue towards the community's needs.

adrienne maree brown talks about this process of nurturing, sowing, growing in her book *Emergent Strategy*. For brown and her chorus of interlocutors, emergent strategy is an intensely ecological process of small, collective, adaptive social change. A life's work. brown's communities adopt patterns of biomimicry (imitating models of nature to solve complex human problems) and permaculture (agricultural and social design centred on stimulating patterns observed in natural ecosystems) to create meaningful, soulful social change.[2] Her thought is fed by and seeded from the writing of science fiction writer Octavia E. Butler.

Earthseed is the binding principle of Butler's trilogy of speculative fiction novels: the name she gives to humankind. Flourishing under the most difficult and violent of conditions, and finding, and failing, and finding again a reasonably benign space to do so, is part of the enduring logic of her books. The trilogy's main protagonist, Lauren Oya Olamina, is 18 when the first cataclysm destroys the community in which she has grown up. She is an empath; as a result of her mother's drug addiction, she is born and grows with the ability to feel others' pain, to bleed when others bleed. This forces her to develop strategies for survival, and ethics for living that are quite different to the biblical ethics that frame her early existence.

The concepts of Earthseed are what Butler's Olamina develops in her journals and diaries in *Parable of the Sower*: axiomatic precepts similar in truth and flavour to the ruminative poetry of Rumi, or Lall Ded, also known as Lalla or Lalleshwari, the fourteenth-century Kashmiri saint and mystic.

All successful life is
Adaptable,
Opportunistic,
Tenacious,
Interconnected, and
Fecund.
Understand this.
Use it.
Shape God.[3]

Rather than considering the internal world as a place of self and unselfing, Olamina's precepts are about the survival of humanity. The stakes are high. In the Earthseed trilogy, humans are capable of survival on earth only if they understand, accept and shape the singular truth that change is the only constant of all existence. God is change. Shape god.

Change is what is most resisted. Change disrupts the psyche. It destabilises the ground that might once have been firm, unyielding. But ungrounding is what allows for seeds to be sown and new life to emerge. Change is the precondition for what is to come.

Anyone who has experienced a major life transition will know its accompanying sense of lostness. It is not comfortable to shift the ground you walk on. But it is necessary for the continuation of life. And this is what is less often talked about in the midst of culture wars about gender and sexuality. It takes a long time to walk away from firm binaries, and to accept – no, surrender to – the inevitability of change. The process of capitulation to what already is, namely a changing, fluid world where binaries are short-lived phenomena, is difficult for anyone. Change and transformation are painful, but resisting them is so much harder. Lonelier. Sharing change with others though: that makes a harvest.

The Earthseed trilogy is so far from Claire Denis' *High Life*'s splenetic visions of humanity's crushing horror, so distant in its aspirations to take root among the stars rather than await the inevitability of death, that I feel myself shifting imperceptibly towards Earthseed's light in the darkness. Both the bleakness of human cruelty, and the possibility of forces that might one day coalesce into something beyond our wildest imagining.

* * *

Imagining a garden takes time. Imagining yourself within that garden, as part of the world that makes it, takes longer.

The house I lived in for a year in my early twenties, in that small village in Norfolk, had a garden – two in fact. A front garden with a hedge of damsons, protecting the house from the road and the nearby dual carriageway. From the damsons I made jam, and slowly infused gin for my mother. The rear garden contained no edibles, and instead was lush with conifers and shrubs and lawn.

I wasn't a gardener then, not in my adult form. I left early for work, returned late and, for reasons that aren't reasons, household labour fell to me. Building a picture of the past is delicate. It is easy to dwell on the things that kept me trapped in that house, rather than freeing me onto the land. They are painful memories, and I have rehearsed them so often in therapy that I'm unsure what value it holds to repeat them again here. In any case, garden-making for me has always required a sense of safety. If the ground cannot hold me, I cannot tend it.

A few years after my experiences of fenland peat and damson jam, I was loosed from the terrain of that soured relationship, and writing my doctoral thesis, whose admission onto the programme felt like an honour I thought I could never match. In the first home I moved to with a garden I cherished – a home I shared with two other women; a home in which I felt safe for the first time in my life – I bought tomato plants. I wasn't very successful: the tomatoes needed much more growing medium than the little pots in which they'd been sold. I did not have the energy to find and then carry heavy bags of the stuff on the back of a bicycle, and I wasn't invested enough to try. I often felt very tired back then; tired and guilty, in debt and with little money. I did not yet understand what long-term stress does to a body. Things like compost and growbags felt like unwarranted luxury – a luxury to give myself what I needed. And I did not, could not yet ask for help.

During the two years I lived in that house next to a busy intersection, protected by another yew hedge that shielded my ground floor bedroom from the cars beyond, the summers were bewilderingly hot. In the heat, I forgot everything: my purse at the market stall, how to sleep, how to write, how to water plants. Ripening tomatoes burst quickly after exposure to drought and ample drenching as I forgot and then made penance.

In that house, in the spring before those heated summers, I met my first girlfriend. It was a beautiful, intense, short-lived relationship where my own senses burst open after long years of drought, revealing new landscapes in me, and a lasting tenderness that took years to heal. I wasn't able to sustain my tender planting while also supporting hers. The end still puzzles me. When the relationship crumbled, I did too. Wide open, engulfed by the abyss. And so I left again, to Paris.

* * *

Earthseed is a sign of hope and possibility, in a world that is desolate and violent. The series – a trilogy, though the third book was not completed before Butler's death in 2006 – depicts a hypercapitalist extension of a future USA, where water costs more than gold, and looting, rape and arson are commonplace. My realisation while I read *Parable of the Sower*, as for so many people, is that it describes not so much a dystopian future but a dystopian present. The privileged ones – myself included – often fail to see this present, because the walls we build around our little gardens blind us to it. Fortress Europe, which ignores the deaths of refugees in the Mediterranean Sea, in the English Channel. The Calais camps. The prison barge that the UK government acquired to detain refugees off the coast of Dorset. It is hard to see what is hard to see.

And yet, Earthseed creates hope in the dark, whose seed germinates in the horrors of the present. Acknowledging the truth of the matter gives room to create an alternative. Butler's writing appears often and regularly in activist and cultural communities of queer and intersectional feminism. In the New Suns festival of contemporary literature at the Barbican in March 2021, the keynote conversation was entitled 'The Parables of Octavia Butler', between adrienne maree brown and Ama Josephine Budge, both artists and pleasure activists. Butler was a soothsayer, a truth teller unafraid to reach into the horror of racist, misogynist, homophobic violence; equally unafraid to seek new ways of building community between otherwise unreachable people. She is also conjoined with many other stories of hopeful change, which adrienne maree brown names in *Emergent Strategy*: 'being in right relationship with the natural world, learning from the ways change and resilience happen throughout this entire interconnected complex system.'[4]

* * *

Seedlings need time. Time and land, nurture and waiting. Waiting needs security, the safety of remaining. The alternative is to cast seeds randomly across the earth. But even then, to cast a seed you have to have a sense that you will return to see it grow. Maybe.

The sense of return is what I have been battling with, naivety shedding like the papery skins of physalis fruit. Having spent every chance I could living abroad, in Paris and elsewhere in Europe on and off for years, I thought I was a cosmopolitan citizen of everywhere: that my coming and going was not dependent on wealth, and my ability to study and work and travel across Europe meant that I would remain free to do so indefinitely. Until 2016 I was a European, secure in the identity that had formed me in that most formative time: childhood. I thought I was someone free to live and work in 28 member states. I thought my life – which began with language and grew through learning languages – was cosmopolitan, moveable, free, filled with art and delight and as rich in community resourcefulness as it was poor in money. Freedom of movement, study and employment was, for me, connected to freedom of thought, and freedom of being. I did not have to live in the straight, almost exclusively white enclave of my Section 28 childhood. I did not have to model the narrow frames of existence to which I had been exposed. I knew from an early age that there was life across the water, and I longed for it. I knew from an early age that I was queer too, written in code in my diaries – like, I later found out, Victorian lesbian Anne Lister's millions of words in encrypted journals. To find a new path away from the narrow walls of straightness, and whiteness, and Britishness, I fled as soon as I could – but I returned because I thought I could live in a perpetually fluid state of movement. Neither one nor the other, living without borders. How I lived, how I loved, could be fluid. I could walk away from one place and find a multitude of others. Always coming home, or making home a field of open possibility.

My life is not this, or was this only for a short time. It is the invisible substrate, that combination of structural advantage, education, health and political climate which allowed me to grow in this way. It's not just the case that my life stopped being cosmopolitan when the UK referendum on Brexit found in favour of leaving the EU or when it finally did leave in 2020; or that my life stopped being cosmopolitan when my health collapsed again, and again, and again, from 2014; or that my life stopped being cosmopolitan when Coronavirus and successive lockdowns shut down most of the planet.

My life stopped being cosmopolitan when I began to realise that to have *both* – a sense of connectedness, of rootboundness, a secure anchoring home, *and* a cosmopolitan life of movement – requires a level of health and wealth and status and structural advantage that is and was always tenuously built on the structural disadvantage of others. My freedom was not freedom for all. The citizens of nowhere in the past did not have both. Migrants and exiles built homes elsewhere, not from choice but survival, away from pogroms and genocide and violence, and fundamentalist, ultranationalist governments that wanted them dead.

And that's not all: the history of imperial slavery is also its own history of land-stealing and statelessness. Slaves all over the British Empire lived and died with whatever they could hide from the slavers to call home and land and oral history. Zakiya McKenzie's beautiful pamphlet *Testimonies on the History of Jamaica Vol. 1* puts those oral histories of land back in, imaginatively reconstructing traces of land-relationship. Rooted in extracts from the colonial and state papers of the West Indies, McKenzie summons an alternative natural history of the ancient island. Cosmological ancestors are called forth, embodied as trees in pre-colonised Xaymaca, alongside syncretic KwaZulu and Yoruba gods and spirits. McKenzie writes the echoes of the Indigenous *Taíno* people in the Jamaican mountains and forests, who taught tactics of survival to rebel slave runaways and Spanish maroons left behind after Britain's occupation. They are stories with roots, winding through history.

One of McKenzie's embodied spirits is Tansy, the slave who walked twice up and down the mountain called Catherine's Peak ahead of white slave-owner Catherine Moore (née Long) after whom it was named. Tansy describes the gardens grown by her slave grandmother, cultivated where no plantation owner might notice, communing with what remains of the family around her; the place where Tansy's umbilical cord was cut and buried in the earth. Tansy's last wish is to decouple her spirit from her embodied life as a slave, and to return to the natural world: 'This is the last time you see Tansy, forget about me like this. Look for me again, maybe in a storm or a whirlwind.'[5]

I am looking for her, in the storms that race across my garden in these early spring months. I have the joy of a garden, and I do not have to hide it. I have citizenship and land, and my white body carries the complicity in colonial history that European white bodies carry. As a well-educated homeowner in London, as a white body with a British passport, my layers of structural advantage are already significant.

To truly live between, as I had for decades hoped to do, in this contemporary age of hypercapitalism, massively inflated property prices and insecure tenancies, I would need access to the kind of wealth I can only dream of. And I have questions about these cosmopolitan urges. To be two different eras of plant life, taking root and setting seed, to be freely mobile and to have land to return to, to what end is that? Whose land, whose home would I trample over, in order to achieve that dual state? The bar of inequity draws higher. I can continue to chase after it, or I can stop and ask why the bar exists in the first place. I can sit with the communities of human and more-than-human lives around me, and listen. I can play my part in enriching and amplifying those who have upheld me for centuries. A safe home is a basic and fundamental need afforded to relatively few.

It is time to listen. Listening is the substrate of change.

* * *

For queer seeds to grow, you need to remain with them. And I was always leaving. Fleeing my own queerness, because I did not realise what community might lie waiting for me.

Allied to Roxane Gay's bad feminist, I am a bad queer. I have said this in queer book groups and queer writing groups. I am a bad queer. Not queer enough for gay. Too queer for straight. Bisexual, pansexual, in-between. Unaffiliated with a fixed gender position, but still retaining the traces of the femme I once was, or tried to be. Whatever the name, I live in the in-between, passing and failing and fleeing and returning.

For a long time my queer seeds were untended. They lay in a brown envelope, gnawed by mice in the back of a shed. Planting, tending and nurturing them so that they become plants that flower wasn't something I considered to be safe, or desirable, or even needed, until the time came when

I couldn't deflect or defer the knowing any longer. Not so much a coming-out as an out-pouring of myself into the world. And out I pour. Still flowering, still seeding.

Does it make sense to say that writing is also about coming into being? That while there are many parts of my queer body and my queer soul that do not need language to flourish, that instead need soil and seed and sun and rain and time, language is also part of the observing and feeding and watering, the sunshine and the warmth, the canes and twines, the mulch and the manure, that feed my queer garden?

***

On a dry, cold, grey Sunday afternoon, my partner and I sowed:

peppers and chillies, two types of tomato, hyssop, thyme, chives, French beans, sweetcorn, courgettes, sunflowers, sweet peas; and other things which I now forget.

Some of them waited on the bathroom windowsill – the sunniest and warmest in the flat. Already the tiny grains of thyme sprouted into tiny green seedlings, barely a millimetre high. Easily crushable by finger and thumb, they stayed put until they had a chance to grow. Every year I sow, I am struck by the wonder of the seed to plant to seed cycle: that a tiny granule, sometimes less than half a millimetre wide, can become a sturdy plant, with swathes of fruit, flower or seed, that by the end of the year becomes material for the compost. It is part of the plain ordinariness of plant cycles that is neither plain nor ordinary.

When I plant organic, open-pollinated seed, which hasn't (yet) been made infertile by contemporary high-yield manufacturing processes, I'm also planting histories of cultivation that mean *just this* variety of tomato will, with some luck and the right conditions, grow into small, yellow, pear-shaped, super sweet fruits. *Just that* one will become large, round trusses of red tomatoes streaked with green tiger stripes. And not a single one will be the same. Last year I excitably over-sowed, leaving reams of plantlings stranded without enough soil or pots to put them in, or neighbours and community members willing to harbour them. I tried to avoid the same disaster this year, to nurture a smaller number from grain to ground. The snow outside suggests the time for breaking ground is a while off. Our young potato plants were crushed by a late May frost in 2020: leaves burned black by the cold. They recovered, and the tubers were fresh and delicious. But still. Prudence.

Recovery is tender. It requires doubt and love in equal measure. You have to do it in the dark, covered over in earth, and you have to believe that change happens even when you cannot see it, because doubt confides in you that things will not remain the same. You have to hope that one day the force of your own love will break the surface and the light will come. Because even when it doesn't, the darkness changes.

I am trying to get the timing right: to bring this knowledge of doubting and hoping and loving and growing into my intuitive body memory; so that instead of thinking about recovery, sowing, speculation, my body knows how to break and begin again. I want this to become intuitively part of the life that I lead, so that change and hope and doubt are as familiar and normal as getting out of bed, or washing my face, or going for a walk, or any of the things that become impossible in the darkness. As normal as celebrating Samhain and Imbolc and Beltane and Lughnasadh, the

Gaelic seasonal festivals that also mark the tides of imperceptible change. I want the ordinary-extraordinary normality of change to fill my life, so that I stay in this place, so that I have a reason to keep living, to watch the cycles of plant life that I sustain and that sustain me.

Queer seeds of queer life. Or just life, that can be queer or not. To borrow Mary Oliver's poem *Wild Geese*, the queer soft animal of my body, bringing out the Q that is there, but sometimes silent. The queer soft plant-animal of my body, loving what it loves, knowing what it knows, sowing what it sows.

8

magnolia, fern (on prehistory, polygenderedness, erotics and shame)

By late March, the *Magnolia stellata,* which sits in the centre of the narrow garden strip sheltering our flat from the street, is in full bloom. On these unseasonally warm blue days, the little tree has unfurled its early flowers, ivory white, with long delicate fingers open like a starburst. A few furry buds remain, but it is gratifying – oh so gratifying – to see the difference a year makes. A year of taking root and growing, unobtrusively, slowly, in the brick circle of the raised bed. The repetitions of each season, which in fact aren't repetitions at all, but growths, year on year – at the pace of plant time – are reasons why I stay in place. When the heavy anchoring of COVID lockdowns and episodes of chronic pain forced me into immobility, the growth of plants was always an invitation to stay. When flight is not an option, remaining finds its own uneasy pleasures.

The magnolia – a tree genus older than honeybees – evolved around 95 million years ago in the regions of the world that would become North America and Asia.[1] Though bees can and do pollinate magnolias, their primary pollinators are thought to be tiny Nitidulidae beetles.

By contrast the oldest bee specimen preserved in amber dates from 80 million years ago (mya). Social bees are prodigies of gendered uncertainty: gender is subsidiary to role, hormones and collective communication. Community bioregulation (the collective ability to stay alive) is as important as sexual reproduction and rearing of young, which is also a communal effort. Bumblebees arrived 30–40 mya;[2] honeybees 12 mya.[3] Long after the first magnolias opened their flowers to their invertebrate companions.

To think over this deep time is impossible, and yet representations of it are always accelerated at unimaginable speed, like time-lapse photography of a shoot unfurling, or the fruiting body of a mushroom erupting through the earth. By means of scale, it was only around 7 mya that apes began their slow journeys towards humanoid forms.

Put me in the frame of deep time, and I am a speck of life, rising and falling faster than the rhythm of a sandfly piercing human skin. Faster than the time it takes a tiny flightless weevil, the kind upon which magnolias are dependent, to slide down the long petal gradients and gorge on a nutritionally complete meal of protein-rich pollen and sugary nectar at the heart of the magnolia's sexual organs. The beetle eats their fill, and then tracks onward, carapace showered in the pollen that will transfer to the stigma of the next flower, and the next. The flowers of some magnolia species are warmer at peak sexual maturity. This rare thermogenic capacity transmits scent and provides a welcome resting place for a beetle-pause. Beetle jaws are adapted for eating, not collecting, and so the petal's waxy, thick textures protect the magnolia from the worst of the beetle's gnawing habits. This cosexual interdependency accommodates beetle and magnolia millions of years before bees evolved their sophisticated flower-love mechanisms: a proboscis and honey stomach, and hairs on their rear tibia to collect and distribute pollen.

As the days start to lengthen and the sky deepens on cloudless days, the *Magnolia soulangeana* at the end of my road flowers pink and huge and saucer-like, 20 feet in the air. Each morning the sun sweeps in through the narrow gap between Victorian terraces and remains for the longest part of the day, as if the tree knew where to place itself most perfectly. In early spring, it blazes with pale pink glory, obscene tongues opening out to the sky to take their fill of beetles. How could I not see the sexual, labial qualities of this display? Hot flowers, weeping scent. What feels like a short, late bloom in my street is the tail end of a relationship that has been going on for tens of millions of years without me.

But still … something catches. Something stays.

* * *

In her book about the polygenderedness of nature and people, *Evolution's Rainbow*, Joan Roughgarden writes that 'to a biologist, "male" means making small gametes and "female" means making large gametes […] Beyond gamete size, biologists don't recognize any other universal difference between male and female.'[4] In the plant, animal, bacterial, algal and fungal kingdoms this small difference in biological sex translates into a polyphony of gender, sliding between many types of male, female, both and neither. As Roughgarden puts it, 'gender, unlike gamete size, is not limited to two.'[5]

Roughgarden is a transgender ecologist – her journey of transition and process of enquiry are both addressed in *Evolution's Rainbow*. Life-process and creative process are the beating hearts of curiosity, always entwined. Quietly building the evidential basis for the many-genderedness of nature, human life included, Roughgarden seeds her own garden of gender diversity in plant, non-human animal and human realms. She notes how scientific disciplines – biological and medical, sociological and anthropological – have guarded what sorts of Euro-Westernised knowledge can be acceptably grown in them. Despite the resonances and resemblances, Roughgarden also cautions against lazy equivalence between human cultures and non-human animal biology. What is queer in one sphere is not the same queer in another. I remember this as I observe the creamy extremities of my small *Magnolia stellata*, its sexual exploits at my fingertips.

* * *

March is usually a month of rain, and yet this year, the soil is parched. On the last day of the month, unusually sunny, the *Magnolia stellata*, the large box planter on the pavement, the palms, the French *Lavandula*, the bowl of tulips and narcissi have all taken on that near-imperceptible shift from green luscious growth to greying thirst. I open the gauge to the water butt beneath the drainpipe to fill my watering can. It barely contains enough for one can-load; the rest comes from the indoor tap.

As I come close to the magnolia, I notice for the first time its blossom perfume – somewhere between jasmine and narcissus. Citrus, saffron, sweet.

Can a scent be queer? I feel that it could.

It's more about the relation than the essence.

Sweet, high, fresh, enticing, intimate – move your nose more than a few inches away and you won't smell it so much as feel it. I wonder whether the natural uplift in my mood that I feel in spring is directly related to the scent of the flowers that I feel in my body before I recognise them in my nose.

And yet, something doesn't feel right.

The scent of magnolia.

There is a tune there. An uneasy song.

***

Charles Darwin's theory of sexual selection comes under fire in Roughgarden's book, and not for the first time. Scholars like Evelleen Richards have shown how Darwin's key work on sexology, *The Descent of Man*, was powerfully influenced, even curtailed by the sexual, political and legal strictures of Victorian Britain. This too shaped the evidence for his theory that human racial and sexual differences, mental and moral, could be accounted for through the evolutionary mechanisms of sexual selection.[6] *The Descent of Man* spiked the interest of renowned sexologists like Sigmund Freud and Magnus Hirschfeld. It also inspired the model of social Darwinism pioneered by Darwin's cousin Francis Galton, widely recognised as the inventor of eugenics and racial biology, models that later underwrote some of the most unforgivable abuses of power in modernity.

Despite these constraints, scholars like Ross Brooks have shown that Darwin's writing is threaded with terms that hint at sexual and gender diversity, all the while couched in Victorian opprobrium.[7] Bruce Bagemihl's *Biological Exuberance* documents the extraordinary interpretive contortions nineteenth-century naturalists made to explain away sex-change, polyamory, same-sex cohabitation and non-reproductive sexual behaviour across species.[8] Evidence of multiform sexuality has always been present; what changed was who was permitted to see it.

Curiously, the figure of the primordial hermaphrodite, imagined as an originary dual-sexed ancestor of humans, inhabits Darwin's early writing just as it does Indigenous cosmologies, theological texts and early medical treatises. And though celebrated by sexologists like Hirschfeld, the hermaphrodite was also co-opted by eugenicists and racial biologists. For Cesare Lombroso and others, hermaphroditism signified degeneracy: a slide into criminality and pathology. Degeneracy theory pathologised racial, socio-economic and sexual difference, and prepared the ideological ground for segregation, the criminalisation of Indigenous communities and the incarceration and euthanasia of disabled people. It also metastasised into the Nazi category *entartet* – the word that fused sexuality, race, disability and cultural difference into a single target of annihilation. *Entartet*, as So Mayer points out in their book *A Nazi Word for a Nazi Thing*, 'stops the mouth, takes away the words you have for yourself, and then uses them to destroy you.'[9]

Degeneracy theory has been universally discredited, and yet ideas do not disappear when disproven: instead they pass through medicine, law, bureaucracy and care. The unlawful DNACPR orders placed on disabled people during the first COVID wave – without consultation or consent – belong to the same lineage.[10] So did the UK's so-called ban on gay conversion therapy 2022, which still permits certain coercive practices under the guise of adult consent or religious exception.

Old ideas die hard.

* * *

The magnolia has medicinal and food uses that were known long before its larcenous arrival in Europe. Ground to a powder, the flowers of *Magnolia grandiflora* become a seasoning. The *Magnolia hypoleuca* and *Magnolia kobus* produce edible young leaves and flower buds.[11] Some contemporary medical trials suggest that magnolia essential oil has 'anti-cancer, anti-stress, anti-anxiety, anti-depressant, anti-oxidant, anti-inflammatory and hepatoprotective effects'.[12] Anti-everything.

The magnolia was named after the French botanist Pierre Magnol, even though it wasn't Magnol who 'discovered' (thieved?) the magnolia. It was Charles Plumier, whose expeditions to the Antilles with the collector Joseph Donat Surian resulted in thousands of drawings and illustrations, including the book *Nova Plantarum Americanarum Genera* (1703–4). I don't know if it is my queerness that reads homoerotic power into this exchange of names and places. Or if homoerotic power exchanges read queerness into me.

I know that my old friend Carolus Linnaeus picked up on Plumier's trail, and incorporated the magnolias into his classificatory compendiums. And in his complete works, Johann Wolfgang von Goethe elevates Plumier in the hierarchical order of travellers in order to mention the work of Maria Sibylla Merian: 'Sibylla Merian, probably inspired by the fame and reputation as a traveller of the highly deserving, much younger Charles Plumier, ventured to Suriname and in her depictions moved to and fro between art and science, between nature observation and artistic goals.'[13]

Merian's journey to Suriname, in South America, was facilitated by her ingenious escape from her husband some years earlier, when she took her children and joined a cult. The Labadists, acolytes of the mystic Protestant preacher Jean de Labadie, believed in absolute gender equality, self-reform, the priestliness of all members of the community, a personal and intimate connection with god, shared personal wealth and communal living, and the non-sanctity of marriage, which could reasonably be broken apart if a believer had an unconverted partner.[14]

Exploiting the desire lines of colonial exploitation, the Labadists also attempted to set up a colony in Dutch-ruled Suriname, to which Merian then travelled with her daughter to continue her lifelong practice of painting through knowing, and knowing through painting the relationships between plants and caterpillars, looking for the in-between. Through the intimate detail of her texts and illustrations, Merian observed metamorphosis: that mysterious state of transformation from one life form to another. She survived extremes of tropical heat and illness, returning to Amsterdam to publish *Metamorphosis Insectorum Surinamensium* in 1705.

Metamorphosis Insectorum Surinamensium influenced Linnaeus' and Goethe's pursuits of natural history, and Linnaeus used many of her watercolours and plates in his taxonomical endeavours. Merian's seventeenth-century botanical illustrations of insects, flowers and fruit were displayed at the 2022 Venice Art Biennale in the Giardini exhibition hall, which, without ever proclaiming itself as such, focused exclusively on women, trans and non-binary artists, many of whom history has conveniently forgotten.

Merian dedicated her life to transformation, and to patient, meticulous looking and drawing. She was one of the few imperial travellers to write about slavery and the appalling treatment of Indigenous people by her settler compatriots. She also observed Indigenous medicinal practices, describing the abortifacient seeds used by African and Amerindian slaves to avoid giving birth to enslaved children.[15]

Merian's knowledge of abortifacient plants such as the Peacock flower were not widely disseminated. As women's reproductive care at the turn of the eighteenth century in Europe was medicalised and shifted into the hands of men, knowledge of women's reproductive freedoms disappeared. Restricting birth rates would also limit the labour force, the growth of empire and the wealth of nations. And so there was instead a 'culturally cultivated ignorance' that removed the sources of knowledge about self-managed reproductive care.[16] Somewhere between the ships returning from South America and the bibliographical notes of Merian's report on the abortive qualities of the *flos pavonis*, the botanical knowledge of birth-givers to care for and protect themselves was lost.

* * *

Magnolia species have spread across the globe from West Sumatra to Haiti, from Peru to Mexico and the south east of the USA. It is the emblematic flower for cities in China and the US alike. The *Magnolia grandiflora*, indigenous to the south-eastern United States, grows ubiquitously in the green subtropical forests of the Gulf and South Atlantic coastal plain. Since 1952 the magnolia has been the state flower of Mississippi, and is more widely associated with the southern states of the US. The Deep South.

But.

And.

There is the chorus again.

The scent of magnolia.

The song that sends feeling off-kilter.

* * *

A few days pass, and March transitions into April. The globe-like stars of the magnolia's petals shed as quickly as they arrive, and though a few furry, unopened buds remain, most have become small seed pods – tiny green fruit standing proud from the tips of the branches. There are more furry buds, smaller and further down each branch; some of them reveal the tender chartreuse of new leaves. I don't know whether the blooms have fallen so fast because this is the nature of this magnolia or because the tree is thirsty. Guilt grabs me by the stomach. Not watering enough, not tending enough.

My outdoor plants are thirsty and my indoor plants are drowning. What is to be made of that? The last month has been worryingly dry – upending rhythms of rain and heat as I dream nervously about crops in the ground elsewhere that will be struggling. As I attempt, once again, to learn how to run through the parks that lie within the two square miles from which I have barely shifted in the past year, it has been weeks since the rain pattered on my shoulders. The world is off-kilter too.

* * *

In her letters to her friend, the queer gardener Christopher Lloyd, Beth Chatto wrote often about the table under her magnolia tree. To 'Christo', she described the guests and gardeners-in-training she receives at her table in the garden, at which her husband Andrew might sit, or not, as his health deteriorated. Sprigs of *Magnolia grandiflora* decorate the entrance to her home in winter to welcome guests. Returning to the light after a period of depressive illness, she describes 'watching the candle-smooth buds of *Magnolia x soulangeana* opening day by day'.[17]

Vita Sackville-West wrote about her magnolias too – especially the huge, impressive *Magnolia grandiflora* 'Goliath', which flowers in July and August, still at Sissinghurst. If ever there was a piece of erotic prose about a magnolia flower, this is it:

> I have just been looking into the heart of one. The texture of the petals is of a dense cream: they should not be called white; they are ivory, if you can imagine ivory and cream stirred into a thick paste, with all the softness and smoothness of youthful human flesh; and the scent, reminiscent of lemon, was overpowering.[18]

Magnolias are queerly sexual; the scent holds you close; the petals enfold you. Their pale cream petals gain flesh-characteristics of a certain kind. A whiteness that is sexual, creamy, reminiscent of body fluids.

They also speak of something else. The evolutionary theory of eugenics in one century that bore a sour crop in the next.

A dreadful phenomenon of human design built on racial biology and eugenics settles itself upon the scent-speech of the tiny *Magnolia stellata*. On all magnolias, big and small.

* * *

A prodigiously talented singer, civil rights activist and queer Black woman sang about the scent of magnolia – not once, but many times – at the end of each show. There would be no encore.

Interpreted, performed and recorded by Billie Holiday, written by Abel Meeropol under his pen name Lewis Allan, the seeping sweetness of magnolia is laced with the scent of burning flesh. 'Strange Fruit' is undoubtedly a protest song;

a song about the horrors of lynching; a song about the racialised brutality of the Deep South; a precursor to and instigator of the civil rights movement in the US. Neither folk nor jazz, it raises the hairs on the back of my neck. That is what it is intended to do. Black feminist thinker Angela Davis describes 'Strange Fruit' as an awakening; a step towards 'the rage of a potential community of resistance'.[19] It is a call to allyship, forged in the fury of injustice.

Davis also adds, 'art never achieves greatness through transcendence of sociohistorical reality'.[20] Art instead needs roots to grow. 'Strange Fruit' is a song that descends into the long history of racism, embedded in cultures of European colonialism, histories of evolutionary biology and racial eugenics. And equally, the political alliances of Black and white activists seeking to challenge racial, class and gender inequalities in 1930s America. The song, like Holiday herself, is a bridge between musical generations, political artmaking, and histories of racism and anti-racist activism.

A panoply of people line up to take credit for the song. Not Meeropol, who wrote the original lyrics, but the many (white, male) historians who have written about Holiday. Even Barney Josephson, the owner of the club Café Society in which Holiday first performed. They have all underplayed Holiday's intelligence, talent, determination and capacity to sing 'Strange Fruit'.

Beyond the horror contained in this song, the joy of sensation, the hope in queer storytelling feels futile. How to bear it, when, when so often, the end result of these intertwined stories is not just death, but murder? Expropriation, eugenics, genocide: always there, hiding in the wide scented bowl of the flower with its tiny beetles. It is there because I am here; because of the complicities of white Europeanness.

As Davis writes, '"Strange Fruit" publicly bore witness to the corporeal devastations occasioned by lynching, as well as to the terrible psychic damage it inflicted on its victims and perpetrators alike.'[21]

How to acknowledge the psychic damage of complicity that my white, European body carries across the generations? It must be – has to be – treated with care, not because white shame deserves care more than the racialised violence conducted in its name, but because it is easily passed over in the deflection and denial that the incredible anti-colonial thinker Franz Fanon noted in his second book, *The Wretched of the Earth*, was an intrinsic part of the psychological violence of colonialism.

'Strange Fruit' sees it, pierces it, calls it to action. Skewers my own private fantasy about the pale skin-scents of magnolias. Magnolia is a species; it is also a history.

White shame runs so deep it can feel like new wounds, not old agony. No wonder then that it can also bring about claims of white victimhood, accompanied by all the insidious perversions of language. It should neither be underestimated, nor should it exceed the truth of the racialised persecutions enacted in the name of European whiteness.

Horror in one direction, shame in another.

And in the air between the two, the scented magnolia, witnessing both.

* * *

The eighteenth-century artist Mary Delany, friend of Jonathan Swift, creator of a prodigious array of artworks ranging from needlepoint to collage, memoir to landscape drawing, painted queer magnolias. Not queer as in strange, or queer as in at odds with the world. Queer as in sexual, labial, pornographic.

Delany's *Magnolia Grandiflora* papercut illustration from 1776 is wide open, its folds and clefts waiting to be touched. Delany cultivated communities: she was a garden designer, as interested in the erotics of a garden as she was in the muted sexual pleasures of the plants she depicted. We know that she had relationships with men and women – though it's not my job to prove who slept with whom. Delany wrote copiously and excoriatingly about heterosexual marriage, calling it an 'irksome prison'.[22] And she designed and planted gardens.

Before she married her second husband, Patrick Delany, he had developed Delville, the garden surrounding his country estate outside Dublin. In numerous prose poems about the estate, Swift mocked his friend Delany's extravagant expenditure on his garden. By the time Mary came to it in 1743, Patrick had already been working on Delville for 24 years. Influenced by a wide range of styles, including Capability Brown's 'natural' garden design and the 'ribald garden' of Sir Francis Dashwood in West Wycombe, Oxfordshire, Mary installed a distinctly yonic scoop in a hillside, inside which a hermit's retreat was hidden, which she named 'ye Beggar's Hut'.[23] This was one of several vaginal grottos, caves and concealed porticos that Delany designed in her lifetime, both at Delville and at Bulstrode, the estate of Margaret Harley, Duchess of Portland, with whom she lived for half the year, every year, after Patrick's death in 1768.

Delany is best known as the creator of nearly a thousand paper cut botanical collages. She began these in the later part of her life, when, widowed for the second time, she took up cohabitation arrangements with Harley. Delany's illustrations are mostly of flowers, and particularly those newly arrived specimens from colonial voyages by botanical artists like Joseph Banks and Daniel Solander, who she met at Bulstrode. Faithfully replicating Carolus Linnaeus' sexual schemata for flowers, which gendered flower parts in strict binaries, Delany's work also inspired the writing of eco-poet Erasmus Darwin, father of Charles, who, as queer historian Lisa M. Moore points out, may have been one of the first to refer to 'inverted' plant homosexuality.[24]

Delany's botanical illustrations are uncompromisingly direct, adapting the cloaked vulval forms of the classical nude to petals, pistils and stamens. Moore calls Delany's *Magnolia Grandiflora* in particular, and her botanical flower mosaics in general, lush, vigorous 'images of feminine potency' with 'a vividness and frank sensual appeal that is unprecedented in eighteenth-century visual culture'.[25] By contrast to other botanical artists of the time, such as Pierre-Joseph Redouté, who often showed the back or sides of the flowers he depicted, Delany's images are full frontal. 150 years before Georgia O'Keeffe was painting her vast, intense flowers at the height of her emotionally intense affair with Frida Kahlo,[26] Delany was already building queer networks of female intimacy in careful, detailed, botanically accurate style. And of course, in that lineage of queer gardeners, O'Keeffe kept a walled garden in Abiquiú, New Mexico, where she lived from 1949 until her death in 1986, growing roses, fruit and vegetables with the assistance of the Lopez family.

And I can't, no I can't, fail to mention that both of these figures – Delany and O'Keeffe – were pioneers in all senses of the world. Pioneering as in outstanding, unique, ahead-of-the game. Pioneering as in powerfully invested in the settler-colonial histories that installed their white bodies on colonised land. Queerness is colonialism's dodder vine:

Figure 2 Mary Delany, *Magnolia Grandiflora*. Courtesy of The British Museum.

parasitic, thriving, outrageous, destabilising and yet also … complicit, vampiric, symbiotic.

Both, and.

* * *

A small magnolia bush in the front garden of a Victorian terrace. The bitter condiment made from crushed petals. The labial folds of a gigantic flower. The scent of magnolias. The call-to-arms of a protest song. The names, the endless names circling around European men who quested across the globe to give names to things to create certainty to invent knowledge. And that same knowledge used to support the most disgraceful and repulsive methods of human oppression.

What am I saying?

The purpose of essay writing is to find out what is there to be written. The *essai* in essay is about trying, attempting, figuring, exploring, speculating. Failing, too.

Can I hold the *both, and* above the waterline? The queer stories, and the shameful truth of white complicity in empire, colonial botany and racial violence.

I don't know if I can accommodate the expansiveness of these things. So I return to plants, to ask what they can tell me.

* * *

On a chilly, greyish morning in early April, I've opened the French doors in our bedroom. They lead out onto the steel staircase that drops down to a path laid with hexagonal tiles along the side of the house, and the cascading fern collection we planted alongside it. A small pocket of overcast sky is sandwiched between the window frame and the kitchen extension of the house next door. Propped up on pillows, I wait for my broken ankle to heal – a running misstep that stretched my hypermobile joints to breaking point. The ferns wait patiently, brown fists extending into long fingers outside my window.

While I was mobile I preferred another prehistoric plant; one that grew while hominids descended from trees and began to walk, shamble or crawl across the grasslands of the earth. One which carries the scent of shame and racial violence in its sweet unfolding.

Only when immobilised by temporary injury do I turn to the prehistories of plants that rest in permanent shade.

A shift also happens in that reorientation from magnolia to fern: from scented shame to remediation.

At some point in our peregrinations, my partner and I acquired a potted fern collection. Friends whose garden ends in cavernous woodland donated a handful of the self-spored brackens that erupt regularly through their lawn. Others followed.

The ferns travelled with us for so long that I didn't know when or if we would ever have a place to plant them in the ground. The removals van, when it came to transport our belongings from rented home to mortgaged one, was 50 per cent belongings, while the other half was filled with pots, plants, trees and pond. Pulling up the ivy-covered flowerbed at the back of the flat and replanting it with ferns and scylla, snowdrops, brunnera, hostas and thalictrum felt like making good on an unspoken contract. I had promised the ferns, one day, a place to put down roots. Now that compact was complete.

Ferns are much older than magnolias. Their prototypes first emerged from around 419.2 mya. Most ferns appeared around 145 mya, during the time of dinosaurs: likely why I associate them with giant reptiles in my childhood natural history picture books. The full diversity of the world's ferns is more recent – from around 70 mya. When I try researching the average age of an individual fern plant, the results are inconclusive: anecdotal accounts range from ten years to a hundred. The average age of trees is well recorded, but the lifetime of ferns is a subject of curiously little interest.

The furled fronds of a young fern are called fiddleheads. I rejoice at this description, thinking of the mystical fiddler in Margaret Elphinstone's Scottish speculative fiction tale *The Incomer*. Some fiddleheads are considered a delicacy in North America, even though they are responsible for stomach and bowel cancers. Rather the opposite of the magnolia in this regard. Why do I find that so often the plants I would never have considered eating can supply such bounty, if only I were to look for it? Plant-food-medicine knowledge feels like old language, forgotten under the layers of the new.

* * *

Eyes filled with green, I watch the naked backs of young men, trailing slowly into a frondular world. The first grasps the stipe of a pluming fern, taller than he is, whose blades arc splendidly over his head. Gently he pulls the frond down towards his upturned face. It falls gracefully over him and they kiss: again, again. Another stoops to gather the upright stems of a shorter fern towards him in a tender, sensual, body-length embrace. A few seconds of grace, in which screen-filling foliage is silvered, textured, feathered with fern and forest growth, before the next image reveals all five men, tiny in the rainforest masses, each pale-skinned, dark-haired, arranged in a yonic V-shape completed by moss-covered boulders leading from the centre of the shot towards its base. Each man moves slowly, delicately, with intent and sensuality, caressing and being caressed by the ferns with which he engages so intently. The sounds of the forest – birds and insects – fill the frame. And then jade letters appear in the centre: PTERIDOPHILIA.

Moments later, a close-up of a sunlit hand grasps and ungrasps (tenderly, sensuously) the fronds of different ferns: one pinnatid, the other bipinnate. Each fractal formation of the leaves becomes a different kind of hand, many hands, many fingers to caress. Human hands and fern hands clasp, not simply to hold or to touch, but to *be* touched; to revel in the sensation of leaf against skin. The ferns move tantalisingly in unknown breezes. As I watch, immobilised, my mouth fills with saliva: sensing, tasting, touching, *green*.

* * *

Ferns don't have predetermined sexualities: *their communities decide for them*. Baby fern plants are tiny single-layered gametophytes, heart-shaped clusters of green cells, capable of transforming into male, female or hermaphrodite. Imagine them, fronds waving gently across the wet basin of a forest floor, trees rising high above, canopy distributing dappled patterns of shadow and light across the fern community. The fern in question is *Lygodium japonicum*. Its leaves look like fractals: each pinna (the leafy protrusion off the main stalk) contains pinnules, themselves pleated like tiny fingers. And actually, it rises much like a tree; the vine-like rachises (main stems) climb other plants.

So to re-picture this forest vision, ferns populate not only the ground, but the air, following the lines of tree trunks

30 metres skywards. These mature ferns observe the growth of their community as their spores set on the forest floor below. They witness these new ferns taking shape, observing their sexual variety. The mature female ferns begin to secrete the pheromone gibberellin, adding a nifty volatile methyl ester chemical group that helps the younger emerging plants to take up this hormone, and then begin to grow male sex organs. This process of intergenerational cooperation helps to maintain genetic diversity, by enabling the ferns to reproduce with one another, rather than hermaphroditically alone.

Methyl esters are plant-based chemical compounds that often form the basis of essential oils. And so *Lygodium japonicum* ferns regulate sexual differentiation through the scents they offer one another. They waft this complex vocabulary of growth through the air, and in doing so they encourage the younger members of their community to take up specific sexual characteristics. Big gametes, little gametes. Female ferns regulate gender variance to maximise the whole community's flourishing.[27]

Difference is a matter of survival. And sex is not predetermined, but developed in community with others.

I want to know – would love to know – whether the baby ferns are able to choose how much gibberellin they take into their emerging bodies. Fern spores 'set' in humid soil, protected from light. It is some kind of magic to me to learn that, as they begin the process of multiplying and developing, the spores transform into a primordial hermaphroditic green slime, from which, eventually, fern leaves will start to appear. But before they do, this slime isn't just undifferentiated green mass. Ferns begin as tiny green heart-shaped gametophytes, busy multiplying to create organs like root systems and rhizomes.

I have heard it said that mammalian embryonic development begins from the rectum outwards. Humans begin life as a tube: all mouth and arsehole. But ferns begin from a heart-shaped mass of green.

***

Lying back under the fern that rises above him, a young man runs his hands across the full surface of the fronds that cover his graceful skin, eyes opening and closing gently with the felt rhythms of each rachis and stipe, sensing the midrib. The fern's sex organs are hidden on the underside of the leaf-like pinnules; he is right to seek sexual engagement from these most prominent parts. And breath enters the frame in the heaving abdomen of another man, who gently explores the tip of an unfurling fiddlehead by taking it into his mouth. Another plants his face at the base of a mass of shining, lime-green single-leafed blades, inhaling, submitting to the fern's emerging glory. Another embraces a bipinnate fern's crown so fully that fronds reach around his neck and back in sinuous multi-limbed encirclement, as if he has gained green-bladed wings. A lissom man-boy writhes on the forest floor, one single-bladed fern at his head, another with many-fingered, feathered leaves and a long dark stipe wrapped between his thighs.

The first part of Hong Kong-based ecosexual artist Zheng Bo's series *Pteridophilia* ends in the sound of orgasm: full, sensory, breath-squeezing. But the final shot is of a fiddlehead; the quivering, as-yet-unfurled extension of a young frond that will result in the fully mature, sexually equipped leaf. In every part of the film, the invitation is to gaze erotically on the naked skin of young men, and to extend that same erotic looking to the ferns of the forest floor, the scatter of light and shadow through leaves. Sexuality is sensual, sensory, girded by breath and birdsong, earth and frond.

* * *

After care comes healing – and ferns do this too. The *Pteris vittata* (brake fern) is used to absorb arsenic from the soil.[28] I have heard of phytoremediation before: that certain plants have cleansing properties, capable of extracting the good to release it into the atmosphere, or trapping toxins in their structures. The swathes of borage, which grow plentifully in my garden, and whose blue flowers taste deliciously of cucumber, are also phytoremediators. Used as a form of green manure, borage and ferns can extract heavy metals from polluted urban soils.[29] Phytoremediation and mycoremediation, the capacity of plants and fungi to heal human-manufactured toxicity, are two of the most hopeful futures I see.

Where I see the hope in environmental science, its counterweight to centuries of environmental damage, I also see the possibility of living otherwise than wedged between biological essentialism and centuries of colonial botany. Maybe there is also humour.

Speaking of science's humorous turn: a small genus of lipferns was named after Lady Gaga by biologists at Duke University in 2012.[30] There is a striking similarity between the shimmering Giorgio Armani emerald green costume that Stefani Germanotta, aka Lady Gaga, wore at the 2010 Grammy awards and the lipfern's bisexual heart-shaped gametophyte. And the genus of desert-dwelling ferns contains a characteristic DNA sequence, GAGA, which precedes the Lady by millions of years.

* * *

Sexing through scent, scenting through sex; the collective pattern of fern sexuality takes into account the whole not the one. Beyond the harms of magnolia history comes an even older history of sexual care, healing and remediation. And when, swollen ankle healing day on day, I observe the small fern collection along the passageway that leads to my back garden, fiddleheads bulging and tightly wadded, waiting to release themselves, I am relieved to see the occasional new fern plant rising between them. Erotics and cohabitation make them queer kin, their different species homed together because of my own haphazard, slow, accidental ways of knowing. They reassure, just as the scents of the *Magnolia stellata*'s finger-like flowers unnerve.

But there is always risk in writing about gardens and gardening, queer fern sex and queer scented magnolias. In writing myself into a story about them.

That risk is about individuality. Not just the anthropomorphising tendencies of humans to align individuality with a fern plant or a magnolia tree in the same way you would a human (and I love *Pteridophilia* for repeatedly transgressing these boundaries through acts of ecosex). The environments for ferns and magnolias are unique, but their relational being to other species, plant, animal and human, is fundamental.

In one way or another, when I am writing, or gardening, or watching ferns grow, I must not imagine for one minute that I am the sole person to have done this.

What I have learned about Jamaica Kincaid and Vita Sackville-West, the Kewriosities and Jean/ne Baret, Margaret Elphinstone and Marjory the Trash Heap, Donna Haraway, Robin Wall Kimmerer, Eve Balfour, Octavia E. Butler, adrienne maree brown, Billie Holiday, Mary Delany, shows me that I am not nearly the first, nor will I be the last to wind this path through gardens, growing, art, literature, sexuality, gender. My urbane 'discoveries' in the allotment and garden are knowledges that have been known before, more likely passed on by fork and wheelbarrow than in writing.

I am submerged in a chorus of beings who knew certain things about nature connection, and sexuality, and history, and botany. They send their methyl ester trails after me, shaping my queer being. These different times and types of knowing come together in the garden – in many places that were once gardens or might at some point become them. A London allotment, or the side passage of a Victorian terrace, or, as I make my small journeys on my healing ankle to the high street, a pocket of uneven concrete regularly filled with other people's trash at the boarded-up rear of a charity shop on the corner of a junction, with a fern dripping from the drainpipe.

There is a temptation to write about nature as if it were *my* wisdom to impart, as if I held some magical key to the truth kingdom that is natural embodiment. I just know what I know, and my soft, queer body loves what it loves. I add to that knowing, and that loving, one word in front of the other, cell by cell. As if I were a green gametophyte, waiting to be shown how to become a fiddlehead.

My gardening companions circulate in and between gardens and nature writing. Some are old: the Indigenous cosmologies of the skywoman who fell to earth and was rescued on the back of a turtle (thank you to Robin Wall Kimmerer for the telling of this tale), or the etymological root of the garden – enclosure, orchard, wall. Or the worms and bacteria whose voices I have yet to learn how to hear.

The writer David Whyte knows well the connection between land and water, and the tenuous bridge in between that a writer follows in pursuit of a voice. He calls it 'the line between speech and revelation, hearing and arrival'.[31] I am living and breathing that surface line. The boundary layer. The horizon.

9

hungry gap (on gardening, mortality and seasonal dearth)

A litany for my dead plants. For the grief of their falling:

The blue campanula I planted under a tree
and then failed to water, till the shade and drought had consumed it
The white camellia, pleached in a round,
that submitted to the harshest fenland hoarfrost known in 20 years
The salad leaves,
ruthlessly depleted by an army of snails
The tomatoes with burst fruits,
whose thirsty roots snapped the base of their small pot in two
The many small roses
gifted to me as housewarming presents
that caved to greenfly and starved in weak soil
The overwatered *Senecio peregrinus*
(I have failed succulents more than any other species)
The many African violets wilted under my care
The gorgeous bicoloured lobelia
whose leaves dropped and became twigs before flowers could flourish

The yellow suns of dahlias
grazed by earwigs
The money plant whose one shoot remains of a towering tree
The broken-stemmed snapdragons
kicked up by the foxes
The dark-headed tulips who, because I failed to lift them,
now only rise in spring as green
The primroses with red tongues and purple heads
disappeared without trace
The squashes dead in their beds from scorching
The pink geranium that flowered all winter
Only for slugs to gorge on its new green leaves.

This list grows longer every year. For every success there is failure. My neighbour R, who trained in horticulture at Kew, tells me not to get sentimental about plants. If they are lost, they are lost. If they need to be separated, I should do so ruthlessly, cutting through the entwined root stocks. As an amateur I am indecisive, uncertain when or if to prune and how, furiously searching for tips online. I often leave it to the wrong time of the year, nipping off buds when I should allow them to flourish. My garden is a journal of my errors, and forgiving of my mistakes.

Still, I feel the sadness of the lost beings. The pointless ends.

I don't know if it is blessing or curse to read that, even for Jamaica Kincaid, a supreme gardener, gardening is 'an act of utter futility'.[1]

The Hungry Gap is the space of loss and grief, palliation and illness. It is the shadow side of growth.

* * *

I am hungry. I have always been hungry. And to sate the hunger, I ate. I ate and I ate. I ate like it was breathing; I ate like it would fill the void. I ate to stifle the boredom; I ate to celebrate. I ate to control. I ate to abandon.

My hunger cannot be sated. It has nothing to do with food. My hunger is a way of being on earth; a survival mechanism of feeding unfelt feeling; a gorging desperation searching and reading and prying and listening and sensing. It is never enough. I am *hungry*; and I feed the starving monster inside me by watching and reading, growing and harvesting, living. And eating. I am not cured. But I live with my hunger in a different way. Robin Wall Kimmerer names the starving monster of consumption, of capitalism, after Indigenous tradition: the *Windigo*.[2] Its insatiable greed threatens to swallow whole cultures. If I call my hunger greed I disown it, yet it is a part of me.

The intensity of my hunger is desire, or near to it. The part of Ann Cvetkovich's *An Archive of Feelings* that touched me near the bone was her description of *femme* sexuality: the expansive, world-encompassing receptivity that is misread in heterosexual encounters as passive or submissive, reproved and controlled by a masculine fear of unmet desire.[3] Femme is an endless, inexhaustible hunger. I felt that, while I was one.

Eating can be a shared act of communal reciprocity though, a building of kin. adrienne maree brown's second book, *Pleasure Activism*, is all about the joy of pleasure as a radical act of resistance for women and femmes, even more so for women and femmes of colour.[4] Sexual pleasure and embodied self-knowledge take centre stage. In the chorus of people she invites, with whom she shares and disseminates knowledge, a recurring theme expands to include food in the repertoires of sensual and sexual pleasure. Eating and not-eating are also, for many of her interlocutors, a means to self-soothe in times of darkness.

Food is pleasure when it's done right. Eating is resistance, too.

* * *

Unearthing the Q feels like ground work. Inching my way along the surface of the soil, investigating each exposed root clump, parasitic shopping bag, smooth-edged glass shard, pottery fragment, oxidised coin, rusty screw, seed, rhizome, algal bloom, leaf mould, bark chip, lichen, moss. I search for clues with my hunger. My inclination towards the faintest whiff of something *queer*; it makes me wonder whether this is how pigs forage in the forest, for acorns and truffles. Truffling for queerness. My soft pig body scans ground and horizon for traces, pointers, hints and especially innuendoes.

I observe the perversity of the archaic term 'queer', used to mean odd, or set-apart: how often it appears in Radclyffe Hall's thinly veiled autofiction *The Well of Loneliness*, particularly during protagonist Stephen's childhood in an aristocratic household, and her powerful, tender, moving connections to the land and gardens that surround her childhood home.[5] For all its tender invocations of nature, Hall's book is knotty and overwritten; it is also brutally upper class and contains all the racism, antisemitism and jingoism one might expect of a Victorian-Edwardian aristocrat. It stands ambivalently as a queer document. 'Queer' in its archaic sense leads to queer in its contemporary sense: unstraight; non-heterosexual, joyously and melancholically other.

Famously, Victorian gardener Gertrude Jekyll was described by her father as a 'queer fish'. Her queerness was 'unnatural' this far out of the water.

***

What better time to think of these tender shoots of violence, grief and loss than the Hungry Gap? A phenomenon of the seasonal growing cycle in temperate oceanic climates – like the one on this island outcrop of Europe – it is a time of ferocious growth, but minimal harvest. This gap in food production necessitates a cycle of interdependency, where places like this small island are dependent either on their overwinter food stores of root vegetables, the security of which Britain has long exhausted, or on imports of food from warmer climates, dependent as it has been for hundreds of years on colonised and postcolonial labour.

For most of my life the Hungry Gap has meant little to me: no matter how it rises to my consciousness, I do not starve, unless I starve myself. My food security has only ever been challenged by a lack of money, not the absence of supply. I have never found myself in an urban food desert, unable to buy fresh vegetables for miles.

But I know these things to be true for many.

Denial of access to nutritious food is an act of violence. Deprivation of access to food choice – the right to choose what one puts in one's mouth and body, when and how – is an act of violence.

This was the choice the 2019–22 Conservative UK government made when it shifted payments to the families of children eligible for free school meals during the COVID-19 school closures to 'food boxes' outsourced to a private company.[6] Images flooded social media of the onion quarters and carrot fragments, a corner of plain cheese, tiny baggies of pasta that would more appropriately contain grams of recreational drugs than nutrition. This was not the first time that food poverty and exploitation over food insecurity raised its head during the pandemic: food boxes provided by private contractors to shielding and vulnerable people in the early stages of lockdown showed astonishingly poor regard for human health needs and nutrition, as well as poor value for money.[7]

The miserliness, the inefficiency, the denial of what even Abraham Maslow would acknowledge is the root basis of anyone's hierarchy of needs, left me slack-jawed. Playing on aged stereotypes of the undeserving poor, the whole structure of feeding a nation was shipped out to a company that expropriated a substantially larger portion for itself. Individual risk of fraud is replaced by wholesale capitalist exploitation.

Isn't the story always the same?

April is the cruellest month. So let me wallow in this cruelty. Let me scream and holler, with tears rolling down my cheeks. Let me grieve for the bodies malformed and undernourished. The ashes of what might once have been called justice.

And let me recognise the gardens that remain.

* * *

So Mayer's book *A Nazi Word for a Nazi Thing* is full of ashes.[8] The ashes of burning books, burned photographs, records, archives. It is a raging requiem for the records lost, the things not known about the past and the not-so-distant past of queerness, in all its forms, with and without the naming. Centred around Magnus Hirschfeld's *Institut für Sexualwissenschaft*, which was ransacked and razed to the ground by the Nazis in 1933, the book is also a volume of repair: recuperating and regenerating from the lost archive like the first green shoots after a forest fire.

I am not on fire, not now, but I am burning with the desire to know. To find. To seek. Whenever I speak the Q in queer gardens, I find willing interlocutors; people overjoyed to talk about their allotments and their art works, their seed banks and restoration projects, their community gardening and wildflowers. Not just this; I also find the connection of these projects to assemblages of people, communities, groups: people thirsty for knowledge about plant-life, herbalism, foraging, growing, making food on urban plots and rural smallholdings. People who are also often queer across the rainbow spectrum: non-binary, trans, intersex, bisexual, asexual, aromantic. My queer garden is both capacious and comforting, disquieting and sometimes erotic. In it the desire to know and to learn and to share combine: the ecocritic and the rewilder, the forager and the honourable harvester, the permaculturist and the composter, the walker and the wild swimmer.

Naming the Q in this assemblage of currents is tricky. To name is to know and to know is to own: colonial botany was very clear about that. But naming is also about calling into existence. Naming is an act of god. There is no story without a name, and stories are the basis of memories passed down the human chain of being. All the memories we can speak about, anyway.

And yet:

To remember, I need a name. Naming is a transformative act. I can't name a thing, a person, an action, a community as queer without changing something about the ways they are remembered. There was something queer before queer, just as there will be something after it. Queer is a word, powerful and old, but it is also just a word. Being came before naming. In the beginning was the beginning. Words came later, so much later.

How to live with this double-bind?

To answer, I must do what I always do in these moments, and sit with the trouble.

* * *

Sitting with the trouble of the Q in garden is where I began. Seeing the invisible in the visible. Finding the trace of scent in the air. Sometimes that scent is heavy, mossy, earthbound. I find this in Anne Lister's garden at Shibden Hall, which she landscaped and designed while she was courting Ann Walker, the woman whom she wed in a church ceremony in 1834, just two years after she had inherited the estate in Yorkshire. Not entirely dissimilar to the yonic landscapes of Mary Delany's garden at Delville, the moss-roofed hut in the garden of Shibden Hall was a place of sanctuary, intimacy, sexuality and sleep for Lister and Walker. This *chaumière* features heavily in Lister's diaries from this period – a collection of 5 million words, one sixth written in code, and considered so important for national heritage that it was listed by UNESCO's Memory of the World Programme in 2011. And Lister herself is more widely known care of the HBO series *Gentleman Jack* (2019–22), which adapts those words into television drama: a 'Jack' being Lister's own terms for her and her acquaintances' butch presentation.

The moss hut was an enigmatic place of 'cross-thinking' which, for Lister, was code for masturbation and/or orgasm.[9] It is only written about, pictured in words, since the hut itself no longer exists. It was a temporary structure, made of materials that return to the earth. In stark contrast to the impenetrable stone and granite obelisks erected in other masculine-owned gardens, the moss crumbles, the wood rots; what was built returns to ground. Stone returns too, but more slowly, over time we cannot see and will not live to experience. Jack's words do though: Lister has been described as 'the first modern lesbian', but even that category is not enough. Lister described her lovers as wives; herself as husband. Her masculinity was expressed in dress and land ownership, in her conservatism and her self-describing language.[10] While queer, butch, lesbian, trans might begin to describe Lister's relationships to land and lovers, the ultimate destination of the name is not as important as the journey of naming.

Words will be outlived. Sometimes words outlive us. We will be outlived by stone and moss. I will be outlived.

Outliving; living beyond, living out of sync. Gardens have outlived many of their inhabitants: Jean/ne Baret, Maria Sibylla Merian, Mary Delany, Anne Lister, Gertrude Jekyll, Edward Carpenter, Vita Sackville-West, Derek Jarman, Christopher Lloyd. Gardens remain of what love humans had for their gardens, lovers and kin. Gardens also remain of what theft, what labour illicitly stolen, demanded or forced, what imperial violence brought *this* plant to *this* space at *this* time. Gardens hold bloodshed: do not be deceived. Gardens also hold grief for this violence, for this loss.

* * *

I am writing as though my life depended on it. Maybe it does.

***

If there were ever to be a canon of queer gardening literature, Derek Jarman's *Modern Nature* would be somewhere at the top. And, much as I am suspicious of ecclesiastical or literary laws, I think Jarman would have delighted in the prospect of heading up the Q-list. He was, after all, canonised by the Sisters of Perpetual Indulgence on 22 September 1991. Terminal illness drove the making of the garden at Prospect Cottage: it was a retirement home of sorts, for Jarman and HB. As I write this, I feel the sticky sensation of writing the bleedingly obvious: the *point de repère* for every piece of queer garden writing. Derek Jarman's garden.

Gay white men, gay white male artists are the flowers of the queer ecosystem. Despite Mary Delany's feminising approaches to the botanical illustration of flowers in the eighteenth century, when the garden is already queer there are certain parts that gain the most visibility and (sometimes) notoriety. Gay rights campaigner Edward Carpenter's Derbyshire home, Millthorpe, was a hub for some of those flowers. A friend of Walt Whitman, Carpenter helped launch the career of E. M. Forster and was a lifelong advocate for simple rural living and a 'Uranian' lifestyle – including cohabiting with his partner, George Merrill, from 1898 until their deaths in 1928 and 1929. Carpenter, who was from an upper-class family, and Merrill, born in the slums of Sheffield, became the model protagonists of Forster's *Maurice*. Carpenter's circles of influence included the Bloomsbury Group, architects, artists and politicians: he was an activist for women's rights as well as gay rights, vegetarian with occasional lapses, and a sandal-maker. Carpenter is not particularly visible to a straight eye, but to the queer worlds of gardens, he is a blooming figure; a prototype for Jarman's utopian-dystopian gardens at Dungeness, filled with daffodils, poppies and viper's bugloss.

Jarman and Carpenter. Roger Fry, the queer Bloomsbury group painter and critic. Christopher Lloyd. Gay white cisgendered male gardeners are the first to be seen: it is not coincidental that male homosexuality was criminalised in the UK, while female homosexuality was not. Patriarchy makes some parts hypervisible and others not at all. Colourful, eye-catching, perfumed, elaborate, blowsy, ornate, gorgeous, flowers draw the eye and nose and mouth: that is what the sexual organs of plants are meant to do. They are a component part of the plant's structure – and botanically speaking of course, flowers often have more than one gender. But the gay flower, in whatever form, is always in communication with queer stems, stipes and rachises, roots, radicals and symbiosis rhizomes, insects, soil, mycorrhizae. This is an oblique way of saying that I have centred other voices in this book.

I spend three months of the year – every year – wallowing in the dirt. I owe my first allegiance to the soil. Jarman's beautiful flamboyance already radiates splendour, complexity, fire and anguish. Illness, transcendence and untimely death. If I elevate him again, who do I cast into the shadows?

And yet, beautiful he is. Jarman does not flinch from the soiled, the debased, the difficult, the painful and the ill-tempered. *Modern Nature* tracks Jarman's diaries from 1989 to 1990: AIDS-related illness did not claim him until 1994. There was a long road still to be travelled. In March 1989, Jarman could still heft sacks of manure to make beds for his roses.

I was a child at the time of the AIDS crisis and the public hysteria that surrounded it with mounting alacrity in the late 1980s and 1990s.

But it was only on a sunlit afternoon, while talking to the artist P. Staff about their work *Bathing* (2018), that a sudden memory rose like an electric shock. All of the drinking fountains abruptly turned off at primary school, during one of the hottest, dustiest summers of my childhood. Suddenly we all had to bring in our own water bottles, and our own water: mine were huge 2-litre bottles filled with frozen lemonade or fruit squash. This would have been 1990 or 1991. I am certain the words infection, cross-contamination, risk were uttered. Lead poisoning. Disease. I remember the fear about blood, too – entwined with other fears, other food scares about meat and eggs and milk.

In 1992 I was 11 years old, beginning secondary school. And I remember things from that time in the hazy, partial way that I have best seen captured in Carla Simón's semi-autobiographical film *Estiu 1993* (*Summer 1993*, 2017), about a young girl, Frida, newly orphaned after the death of both parents from AIDS-related illness. In Simón's film, the world talks about Frida, not to her. There is a feeling of hearing and seeing everything underwater, even though sounds and colours are perfectly clear and bright.

And though my life contexts are very different, I recognise and long for that quality of opacity in film. Because that is how I remember that time too.

In Olivia Laing's foreword to *Modern Nature*, they write, 'it's hard to explain how bleak and frightening those years were.'[11]

And they were strange and bleak times. But I was only partly there, living underwater, only queer on the inside, concealed and weighed down by the effects of Section 28 and all the other things that made me feel less than human. I was a child, after all. So was Laing: coming of age just as the first truly effective antiretroviral drugs began to reduce the viral load of HIV infection, creating a 'Lazarus effect' that was too late for the already dead.

Child time and adult time are made differently.

And what about illness time?

What about the time of outliving? The time of the Hungry Gap between death and life. The slow gradual turn toward the light in the wake of darkness. The recovery that is never fully recovered, only turned to a different path.

* * *

Derek Jarman's film *The Garden* (1990) begins with the void.

> I want to share this emptiness with you
> Not fill the silence with false notes
> Or put tracks through the void
> I want to share this wilderness of failure

The wilderness of failure is, to me, the perfect description of the Q in the garden. The *both, and* nature of it, the profusion and the desperation ring true. But the wilderness of failure is not exactly a promise that *The Garden* fulfils.

I'm not certain that Jarman's *Garden* and mine have much to do with one another. I don't know that I'm capable of a Garden with a capital G: my gardens are not flamboyant affairs. I am often looking for companionship between plants: places of profusion and cohabitation. The three sisters: beans, squash, corn. Oregano and *Erigeron karvinskianus*.

And though I share the sentiment of failure, wilderness, silence; the bleak, flat horizon of Jarman's Dungeness in *The*

Garden feels rich, vast, copious. The opposite of silence. The Christological *paradaiza* is where *The Garden* begins: an entwined naked man and woman crying as a moustachioed, leather-strapped Tom-of-Finland serpent-satyr grins wickedly and crawls away from them, bare buttocked and dildo-gloved, over the shingle.

Later, as Jesus and Judas unite in an extended, tender, even chaste celebration of their love, across Spanish widows' tables, in bathtubs on the shale, and in green-screened commercial interludes that invite me to Think Pink, what I want to return to is not the Garden of Eden but Jarman in his pebbled garden; Jarman's Super 8 footage of the poppies and salvia; grainy images of Dungeness power station and flowering sea kale; Tilda Swinton crouched in a purple sea of bluebells, a red admiral butterfly alighting from a butter-yellow clutch of flowering common ragwort (*Senecio jacobaea*). Those Super 8 sequences remind me for a moment or two of the experimental filmmakers Margaret Tait and Rose Lowder: women who dedicated themselves to their gardens, to filmmaking, to making a creative life out of the natural world directly in front of them.

* * *

I search for the void. Where is it?

I search for the garden too. Where has it gone?

Where has my garden gone, in this Hungry Gap, in my mobility-restricted form?

My garden is hungry. The fuchsia-pink tender pinnacles of the *Dicentra formosa* – now known as *Lamprocapnos spectabilis* – pour out in streams from ground that was bare only a few weeks ago. Each perfect heart-shaped flower is burst open with a white protruding aril, that in some lights looks phallic, in others clitoral. The two peonies, one much more vigorous than the other, slowly extend their reddened hands towards the light. The African daisies, *Osteospermum*, are already on the move across the flowerbed, following the new patterns of sunlight as the sun tracks from east to west, bathing the whole garden in morning sun before disappearing over the rooftops in the afternoon. The *Cornus alba* 'Sibirica', whose red stems gave me such pleasure through the winter, is now full of lime-green foliage and tiny pinprick clusters of white flowers. And the tadpoles filling the pond's edges with dark movement are ravenous, grabbing at the algae bite by bite.

It's a plentiful hunger, this. No-one is going to be tarred and feathered in my garden.

***

My broken ankle is far from mended, and Dungeness feels further away than ever. I am trying to write about a queer garden I cannot visit. Queerness has always been ingenious in its diversions and allusions and make-dos. So I return to film to continue this queer gardening journey.

There is an arresting sequence of transphobic violence sequestered in the middle of *The Garden*. Three cis-gendered women, each dressed in a ball gown befitting the cusp of the 1990s, pop out across the washed-out 16mm film. Teal, puce and apricot dresses chase across the screen, petticoats flying, while three men wearing black, the paparazzi who earlier relentlessly chased Tilda Swinton's Madonna and child across the shingle of Dungeness, carry flares that encircle the women. A trans woman, dressed in shimmering blue sequins, creeps her way along the grey sea barrier, incongruous in this landscape empty of care. When the three women reach her, they harangue, forcing her to bend double from their blows as they tear the wig from her head. They attack and attack, media apparatuses swirling, a riot of teal and puce and apricot, jewelled ears leering at the trans woman they have destroyed. In the final shot of the sequence, a man in black-tie attire looks on in the distance, surveying the scene, a quiet smile on his lips.

Derek Jarman knew what he was talking about.

***

What am I hungry for?

I am hungry for growth. I am hungry to plant. I am hungry to leave my laptop and my incessant typing and to go and stand in the wind, with cold hands, coaxing tender bedding plants into troughs and planters. I am hungry for change, for this garden to become what it is longing to become: grasses waving gently in the wind among purple scabious and *Verbena bonariensis*. I have *vision* for this garden that is still becoming, and every year is becoming something else. I want and I wish and I wait for things to grow. For tiny sweet pea shoots to become tall straggling plants bearing the sweetest and most delicate of all flowers, for me to pick and pick and stuff myself with their scent, of which, ravenous addict that I am, enough will never be enough. I am hungry for the true leaves of the tomatoes on my bathroom windowsill to become large and hairy-pungent, ready to prick out and harden off and transport to the allotment. I am hungry for this change, which when it comes will quickly overwhelm me and, like every year, I will fail some of my plants, and they will die from my laziness, my slowness, my neglect.

I am hungry to begin the annual pattern of stewardship. To learn more than I did last year, to avoid its mistakes. I look at the garden and I look at the dry sky that has barely rained, and I think ruefully about my enthusiastic planting, when the more I plant, the more my garden needs me, for watering and mulching, pruning and training. And the more I realise how much my stewardship needs a community of knowledge I can barely touch.

In the allotment I learned more in a year than I had in the previous decade of gardening. I learned because I was working in community with others, who generously shared their knowledge: garlic needs at least 10 months in the ground; the French make nutritious soup from couch grass roots; poached egg plant, whose gorgeous, sunny, daisy-like flowers with a bright yellow centre and white tips generously donate its name, is a useful form of green manure.

* * *

It takes a re-reading of Jarman's *Modern Nature* to identify the tall blue stems that waver along the green-screened video horizon in *The Garden*. *Viper's bugloss*. A curious name. I also find that the Garden Museum in London exhibited a simulacrum of Jarman's Prospect Cottage in 2020, as I was setting out to write this book. Of course – I think to myself. Always late to any party. 2020 was the same year the Art Fund launched its Crowdfunder to preserve the cottage itself.

Much richness that I … missed. For reasons of the void. In early 2020 I was in recovery from a depression so oceanic I didn't know if it would ever end, a thick grey pall that tasted sour and made everything, every gesture, every movement, utterly valueless. I still catch its flavour now and again, and its aftertaste is futility. While the Garden Museum exhibited Jarman, I was swimming in Brockwell lido, learning how to feel pleasure again. I was in my allotment, adding manure to the soil to plant tomatoes. I was pouring hot syrup over elderflowers and dripping their sweet-sour mixture into a bowl, leaving tiny white stars in the bottom. I was an inexpert, incomplete and amateur gardener, learning how to live. And so I failed – failed to see this exhibition, which experienced local and then national lockdowns to curtail it.

I failed and I failed and I failed and I failed. I failed to see, to read, to write, to watch. I saw failure, and lived my tiny one-inch square on the map like a snail tucked far into their shell, mucous lining sealed shut. From the outside I must have looked dead. I lived in a tiny calciate world sealed in by my own pain.

When there was nothing, there was the garden. The allotment. The tiny place of being that did not require reading, writing, thinking.

That is how I lived in the summer of 2020. Emergent and trepidatious, unable to process language and art. I feared central London and so I missed Jarman's cottage in the middle of the Garden Museum, founded in the abandoned church of St Mary's at Lambeth. My project failed before it even began.

And yet … I can't ignore Jarman now. I don't want to. There is a lot of bad writing about *The Garden*, strutting academic writing that claims this or that interpretation as fact; that makes the easy association between shame (public school), shame (gay male), shame (HIV positive) and the rampant symbolism of the fetish-geared snake in *The Garden*'s Garden of Eden. I feel nauseated, not by Jarman but by the way he has been territorialised as a martyred saint, transformed into a national treasure more than 30 years after his cruel death, when his work was always radical, critical, brutal, tender. Writing this all the while knowing that Jarman submitted to his own canonification on the shingle of Dungeness, witnessed by the London House of the Sisters of Perpetual Indulgence, an activist order of queer and trans nuns, on 22 September 1991.

There are saints and then there is sanctimony. And now that £3.5 million have been raised to preserve Prospect Cottage and its garden, there is also: monument.

Why do these contrary thoughts bring me out in hives? For the same reason that queer heritage is in a process of perpetual erasure and becoming in gardens and landscapes across the world, in tender vines that hold vast archives of colonial botany and queer history. Canonise one and erase all the others. Naturalise one and make it stand in for all the rest. Transform a thriving queer ecology into a monoculture.

It deadens the Q in garden to do this.

And.

What if Jarman were not the only bible for the modern queer naturalist? The more I research, in the ground and on the page, the more I find plenitude, not void. What happens to the stories of illness and gardens that wind back through the thickets of journals and gardens and botanical drawings and colonial papers of the seventeenth, eighteenth, nineteenth, twentieth centuries?

If gay men are the flowers of Jarman's beloved queer dodder vine, when can its other parts speak? Leaves and stipes, roots and rhizomes.

I am hungry. For more.

There is a line through this chapter on flowers and gay men, on hunger and scarcity, and on grief. There is the tang of the sacred and the Christological. And I want to keep it tied to the part of this book that will not forget the colonial legacies of British horticulture, agriculture, land acquisition and biocapital.

* * *

It is not hard to trace Jarman's nature-writing back to the Romantic traditions of poets like William Wordsworth – whose pantheistic sense of the sublime in the natural world came under fire from Aldous Huxley in his essay 'Wordsworth in the Tropics'. Huxley pours scorn on Wordsworth for his failure to understand the brutality of Nature, for making it too simple, too unexpansive and, fundamentally, too Eurocentric.

Outside Britain, from her garden in Vermont, from her childhood of British colonial rule in Antigua, Jamaica Kincaid hates Wordsworth and his daffodils. Or at least she did. She writes and rewrites this familiar, ambivalent hatred. The protagonist in her novel *Lucy* detests them, since she was forced to memorise them as a child and then, after her move to the United States, is commanded to 'appreciate' them by her employer, Mariah.[12] The 'gun-to-the-head' colonial violence of *that Wordsworth poem* conditioned into the bodymind of Kincaid, and the concomitant dislike of daffodils, recurs in her fiction and essays for decades – until, eventually, the flowers of evil become flowers that she grows in her Vermont garden.[13] Decades of writing and gardening and processing the trauma of British colonial education systems, and eventually Kincaid comes to the point where she has planted 5,500 daffodil bulbs in her own lawn. In a short essay from 2007 for *Architectural Digest* she writes:

> For 20 years now I have lived in Vermont, a state that falls in a climate suitable for this genus. For many of those 20 years I have gone back and forth with the daffodil: I love it, I do not love it. But I live in this place where there is true spring, a place where the four seasons repeat themselves one after the other in the usual order and the sight of the daffodil is a true joy. In any case, I view spring itself as such pleasure that I have come to believe that the earth and its workings are meant to result in this season, spring.[14]

Jarman follows the daffodil to its other end: its bulb, not its flowering swards. Where Kincaid heals herself, Jarman seeks the daffodil's anaesthetising, medicinal, palliative uses. He describes the root of the word *narcissus* – the Latinate term for the daffodil – from Pliny's *narkê*, Socrates' 'crown of the infernal gods', and the Roman introduction of the daffodil to British soils, since they carried it in their packs to numb the nervous system. The last line of his diary entry on Thursday 23 February 1989 reads, 'Narcissus, narcotics, self-absorption: benumbed retreat into self.'[15]

I love both these garden writers for their ambivalence. Their willingness to about-face from beauty to misery, violence to planting gives me that *both, and* feeling. Daffodils seed their creative practice. Out of plants come metaphors. Who knows how deeply Jarman plumbed the dodder vine he describes as film: 'Film has twisted itself like a serpent through my life, a rampant dodder pushing out life-sucking tentacles into every nook and cranny.'[16]

A few sentences later, he writes about the biography of Eric Gill, the sculptor and typeface designer associated with the Arts and Crafts movement. Gill was also a predator who sexually abused his sisters and daughters – this is even described in the biography that Jarman was reading. In his diaries Jarman writes of Gill as 'eccentric, even silly'.[17]

I have other names for a rapist. I see the complexity in understanding the relationships between life and art – I do – but I refuse to elide suffering, and I refuse to skirt over abuses of power that aren't so much dodder vines as iron rivets bolting together the edifices of patriarchy.

The path to canonisation always begins with being human, in all its erroneous, complex, difficult, messy, frustrating, wrong, violent, fallible humanness. If Jarman is becoming canon, ascending to the lofty heights of national treasure, the story of the fallible human is as important as the story of the saint. Both, and.

***

Gertrude Jekyll doesn't appear in *Modern Nature*. This is curious, because her life's work was clearly influential for Jarman, who, it is said, owned a copy of her book *Colour Schemes for the Garden*. She wrote about dodder vines too – though the name I would use for the most invasive plant of my garden is bindweed. I'm often struck by bindweed's beauty: its bottle-green heart-shaped leaves and white ear-trumpet flowers. My relationship with bindweed is one of negotiation. Bindweed and I take note of one another. I pull it up; it regrows. We know the drill. But Jekyll calls the dodder a 'vegetable vampire, suck[ing] the blood of other plants'[18] Jekyll's vampire, Jarman's serpent.

Jekyll was a garden designer, known for the introduction of the herbaceous border into gardening. She adopted colour theory, drawn from Michel-Eugène Chevreul's nineteenth-century writing, and, via her arts education from the likes of John Ruskin and William Morris, studied impressionist painting in depth, especially the work of J. M. W. Turner. She travelled widely in her youth with women's rights activists like Barbara Leigh-Smith Bodichon. And, as her sight became significantly impaired, the rumour is that she took up gardening as a painterly response to her creative impulses, which could no longer be satisfied at short range. She teamed up with the architect Edwin Lutyens to create a house and garden, first at Munstead Wood in Surrey. Together they were commissioned all over the UK to build homes and design gardens – including Great Dixter, which would become the home of gardener Christopher Lloyd. Though Lutyens and Jekyll parted company later, Jekyll went on to design gardens in Britain, France and Ireland. And at Lindisfarne Castle, on Holy Island, off the coast of Northumberland, to which queer members of the Bloomsbury set like Lytton Strachey were often invited by Edward Hudson, owner of *Country Life* magazine. In her planting, Jekyll designed 'drifts' that would flow from one to the other in paintbrush-loads of colour: a style you can still see at Kew Gardens along their Great Broad Walk Borders, thought to be one of the longest herbaceous borders in the world.

Jekyll appears only briefly in Jarman's last book, *Derek Jarman's Garden*. Its calmly animated photographs of Jarman, and the garden, and his last trip abroad to Monet's garden in Giverny, were taken by Howard Sooley. Sooley was a friend of Beth Chatto, who Jarman met in Dungeness in June 1990, and a keen plantsman responsible for much of the planting at Prospect Cottage. Jarman described Sooley as 'a giraffe that has stared a long time at a photo of Virginia Woolf' – all complimentary, if incongruous.[19] And Jarman notes of his garden: 'Jekyll's observations about the use of colour in gardens are nowhere more apposite than here. Also, certain plants do not fit in – daffodils in the shingle are the most surreal. [...] Dog roses grow here, bleach bone and skeletal.'[20]

It is in this book that I learn that Jarman's dodder is not bindweed, but *Cuscuta epithymum*, a rootless, parasitic plant with long scarlet tendrils, and a tendency to wrap itself around gorse bushes, fusing itself with the stems and seeking out new hosts by scent. No wonder Jekyll and Jarman were both interested: to me, the dodder is a neither/nor, both/and kind of a plant. A queer weed, parasitic and symbiotic, strident and cosexual.

Jarman and Jekyll both trained in fine art before diversifying into filmmaking and gardening, respectively. And towards the ends of their lives, amid their experiences of visual impairment – Jarman's from the effects of AIDS-related illness and AZT medication; Jekyll's from a degenerative eye disease – they wrote about colour. Jarman, of course, in his book *Chroma* (1994) and in his dazzling film *Blue* (1993). Jekyll in 14 books and thousands of articles, but most prominently in *Colour Schemes for the Flower Garden* (1908). There she writes about not just colour as a tool of garden design but colour as emotion, colour as mystic connection to the natural world. Of a woodland in winter, she writes: 'Today there is a thin mist; just enough to make a background of tender blue mystery three hundred yards away.'[21] Blue of distance. Blue of love.

Leafing through the hordes of writing about Jekyll, astonishingly little material directly describes her as queer. Perhaps like the contemporary wave of social conservatism in wider politics, British horticulture is not quite ready to meet the tender blue queerness in its midst. There are hints of it: in a 1981 pamphlet by Joan Edwards on the history of embroidery, Jekyll features as 'Embroiderer, Gardener and Craftsman'. Writing on Jekyll's early life, Edwards says that Jekyll 'was apt to say she was more of a boy than a girl in her activities and ideas, delighting to go up trees and play cricket, take wasps' nests after dark, and do dreadful things with gunpowder, and all the other boy sort of things. With amused affection her mother called her "my oddity Gertrude."'[22] Gertrude the oddity. The queer fish. Edwards' biography continues: in Jekyll's early career as an artist, she painted animals – which Edwards links to the work of renowned French lesbian painter Rosa Bonheur. Later, she associates Jekyll's embroidery and textile practices with May Morris, the daughter of William Morris, an expert in embroidery whose lifelong companion, Mary Lobb, was described contemptuously by Evelyn Waugh as a 'hermaphrodite'.[23] The dodder vine's tendrils grow across the garden histories of Jekyll. Queerness follows her.

Jekyll was nonconformist, unmarried, child-free, radical in her feminist politics, fat in her later years and uncompromising in her clothing choices while working in her garden, which she preferred to the company of high society that followed her work. Lutyens called her 'Aunt Bumps' and first met her dressed all in blue. The unsubstantiated, unreferenced rumour is that, influenced by Van Gogh's boot painting, William Nicholson painted Jekyll's boots (1920) after Jekyll refused to sit for him because of her discomfort about her body shape being given visibility in painting.

I see her. And her discomfort at being forced into the visible world.

Jekyll influenced the work of other queer horticulturalists before Jarman – the Bloomsbury Group for one, especially the gardens of Vanessa and Duncan Bell at Charleston in Sussex, and Roger Fry at Durbins near Guildford.[24] Her work also powerfully shaped the horticultural pedagogies of Beatrix Havergal and Avice Sanders, the queer couple who founded Waterperry Horticultural School in the 1930s. Havergal became the archetypal figure for Roald Dahl's

Miss Trunchbull in *Matilda* – Dahl sent a photograph of her to Quentin Blake to illustrate the book. Knowing Dahl's misogynistic propensity to make masculine women villainous, this isn't surprising. But given Dahl and Havergal's shared love of gardens and horticulture, and the proximity of Waterperry to Great Missenden, Dahl's home for the last 20 years of his life, it's also reasonable to speculate that their relationship wasn't unfriendly.

I devour website after website, digitised collections of archives, blogs, searching for Jekyll's queerness. The archives and library of the Museum of English Rural Life bring up traces, tendrils, spidery lines of connection. I search for any links at all to other suffragists like Fanny 'Rollo' Wilkinson, another quasi-queer woman who was the first Principal of Swanley Horticultural College; but I only come up against that peculiarly Victorian phrase, 'queer fish' – the term Jekyll's father used to describe her. The lineage of queer women gardeners and horticulturalists – women and non-binary people too, who went against the grain of the constrictions of femininity – is so long that I bridle at the invasive prurience of outing Jekyll's sexual partners. Asexuality is also a queer identity, a strain resistant to the monocultures of heterosexual life.

And Jekyll's involvement in suffrage and in early horticultural training for women already speaks volumes at a time of asphyxiating constrictions on women's movement, economic practices, education. Queerness – living at odds with the cultural environment in which one lives – is all over Jekyll's gardens, railing against the vast 'natural' landscapes of garden designers like Capability Brown, reintroducing flowers, medicinal plants, beds at close quarters to the home, with paths easy to tread for people with visual and physical impairments.

Shingle is not easy to tread. But the shingle of Jarman's Prospect Cottage is now a site of pilgrimage, for queers and art lovers and gardeners.

When I can walk again, when my pain levels have subsided, when travel is possible, there are other places to which I would like to make my own queer garden pilgrimages. To the queer gardens of Jekyll and Jarman, Havergal and Lloyd, Delany and O'Keeffe.

And I am hungry, so hungry for more.

fire::rage::summer

10

love in the mist (on wildflower meadows, queer kinship and grief)

A few years ago, we planted a meadow in our shallow front garden. Planted is the wrong word: planting is for seedlings that need hospitable soil-permanence to survive. We raked gravel, scattered wildflower seed, watered, and waited. After a few weeks, tiny plantlets sprouted, like it was no task to thrive in ground that had previously been a plot for cat shit and crisp packets. The serrated leaves of salad burnet and the occasional cornflower, tall cocksfoot grasses and feathery protrusions of yarrow grew squashed in beside one another, an unstructured, messy community in the small five-foot-deep patch between the front windows of our home and the street beyond. In May last year the oxeye daisies opened simultaneously. For a short while a few square metres of waving white-and-yellow heads resembled the flowered pasture you might think of in midsummer, breathing gently for miles. This year, it is already early June and the daisies are barely in bud. The magnolia sits behind this riot of green life, observing in its silent, hundred-million-year-old ways. It had its feast weeks ago. Beyond the shonky pallet fence, poppies and red valerian have self-seeded between gaps in the paving stones.

Year on year, I forget the sadness that comes with summer. It is supposed to be a time of plenty: gorgeous golden-hour light, blue skies, warmth, the return of time outdoors, long hours of talk winding into the night. But I find myself awake at four in the morning, ruminating.

It is an anniversary of sorts – a year, two years, three, more, since I left a full-time, open-ended contract as an academic – the only career I had ever known. There was a before and an after, but the precise moment of the pivot is occluded. I wasn't present to it.

So instead I draw on my body's intuition. My body knows in the fabric of sensation that I walked away. In Ursula Le Guin's short fable 'The Ones Who Walk Away from Omelas', bright, young, vigorous people go about busy industrious lives while a filthy, starving, miserable child lives in a prison cell underground, begging to be released. Its allegory haunts me. The intolerable things that must be tolerated, in order to remain. And the haunting feeling of turning your back on everything that is familiar.

* * *

Queer ecology in a garden is about the untamed and unpruned. As Palestinian visual artist Jumana Manna points out, differentiations between weed and plant are made all the time in a garden, 'where ideas of the familiar and foreign, native and invasive, the border and its transgression, are installed. Like state formations, gardens are defined by who is curated and who is cared for, pruned, contained, against the unwelcome intruders.'[1] Decisions rule about a plant's appropriateness or suitability, and what falls beyond the garden's always-failing borderlines. Gardens, like states, enact borders – who is tended, who is torn out.

Ecology is also subject to similar differentiations. Ecology is a human-made concept, no matter how much we might wish to decentre humans from it.

In a spiral of chorus and echo that feels familiar to me now, I am introduced via Susanna Grant and Rowan Spray's pamphlet *From Gardens Where We Feel Secure* to Indigenous writer Dennis Martinez' concept of kincentricity, 'a unique Indigenous cosmology and relationship to nature [...] one of equality.' As Martinez explains, 'the Indigenous kincentric model is based on a gifting ethic ... where gifts cannot be owned but have to be passed on to others in the community.'[2] It is a familial model, whereby the natural world, plants, fungi, more-than-human animals and humans exist in a continuous ethical contract with one another – an Original Compact based on love, mutual care, respect, abundance and restraint. If 'ecology' is the cold, clinical post-Enlightenment term, kincentricity is its warmer, older, land-based ancestor – less concept than covenant.

Kincentricity is Indigenous knowledge with heart and spirit. Its ecologies are forms of living knowledge: they are land-and-people-based, relational and endangered as Indigenous peoples around the world are forced off the land to which they are so intimately connected. Successions of empire and colonialism, agrarian and industrial revolution, and capitalist mass-farming technologies have repeatedly assailed locally embedded knowledge. So has the larceny of language.

Across Europe variations on the theme of racial purity steal from the language of land intimacy. 'De souche' – of ancestral roots (another arboreal reference) – is how white French lineage is described, for example. In Britain, a word like indigeneity leaves a sour taste in the mouth. Used interchangeably with whiteness by extreme right-wing political factions, it gained traction under the ultranationalist British National Party in the 2000s and continues to misappropriate the rights demanded by minority ethnicities and communities, serving instead the interests of white supremacy.[3] On an island subject to millennia of occupations, trade agreements and cycles of dependency on other land masses, not to mention the legacies of violence that are an endemic condition of European empire-building,[4] there is no skin pigmentation that plausibly indicates who is or is not Indigenous. It makes more sense to consider Britain's imperialism as an opposing, extinguishing colonial force to kincentrism and Indigenous land relations.

I long to know what place-loving knowledge was already lost, buried in the land I care for. And what kincentric circles remain in those still powerfully connected to the land they tend.

In a much more prosaic sense, it feels warming to consider the wildflowers in my front garden as my kin. The deadnettles and ribwort plantain that spring up through the pavement, the huge wild rose that showers me in petals as I walk past my neighbour's front garden; the insects that inhabit it and the birds who scuttle in to feast on invertebrates; the cats and foxes who stop to drink from the half-barrel pond we rolled into our five-foot front patch the moment we moved in. They are all part of the small world I tend and watch, and they bring me more happiness than I can possibly reciprocate.

The natural world holds inconceivable complexity. It also encompasses a richer, earthlier erotic–ethical connection that I call queer because it is certainly not straight. Queer kincentrism, perhaps.

* * *

On my way to my weekly therapy sessions, which by the early summer of 2021 had only recently resumed in person, I walked through the car park of a large Sainsbury's store. Outside a metre-high sign, bolstered in place by heavy stone feet, stated that the store proudly supports members of the LGBTQ community.

What does it even mean for a supermarket chain to 'proudly support'?

Pride month exists because of death. Not just the deaths of Black trans women Marsha P. Johnson and Sylvia Rivera who fought for queer rights during the riots against police brutality at the Stonewall Inn, Greenwich Village, New York City on 28 June 1969. Both Johnson and Rivera died before their time, as has so often been the case for trans people, denied adequate healthcare and often living in poverty because of employment discrimination. The deaths of countless queer people from homophobic violence, or state-sanctioned attack, or discrimination or failures in the legal system to provide sufficient protections for living and dying; this is why Pride month exists.

Pride does not exist because of joy. It exists because of death, and grief, and rage. This is what Grace Petrie sings about in her angry queer folk song 'Pride'; what Amethyst Kiah sings in 'Tender Organs': the exquisite and agonising viscera of alone-togetherness.

June is the month of grief and rage. I forget this every year until it comes around.

As I walk past the superstore and the blocks of flats by the road that connects to it, I see that the long meadows, which formed in May in the encircling communal gardens, have been mown and turned into yellowing scurf.

What is 'no mow May' for, if June is razed to stubble? To extend that ecological contract just one month further, only to rescind it?

And what is the point of Pride month and 'proudly supporting' and flag waving in June, if a month later it all goes back to the same colourless outfit, the same shorn meadow, the same enchanted city with the same damned, miserable child cowering in the basement?

Gardens are grief-orchards, and gardening an act of grieving and return. The black seeds of love-in-a-mist (*Nigella damascena*) sit in an envelope on my desk, where they have sat for two years, after being gathered from my neighbour's garden and generously gifted to me, and I have failed. The ranunculus bulbs given to me by another kind and thoughtful friend still sit in my kitchen drawer, and I have failed. I do not know why I plant some seeds and fail to plant others. They are reminders of gifts unreciprocated, failures unsealed, where I have not maintained that Original Compact with the land and my community.

Midsummer is a time for mourning, just as midwinter is a time for celebration.

* * *

Reading Timothy Morton's 2010 article on queer ecology, it has not aged well.

The written voice all the way through this piece is a bugle: clarion, solo. In it I hear refrains of mocking, aggressive, amygdalan play. Intellectual fisticuffs. I hear the refrain of the 'harmless' academic who is 'just debating'. Whose arms are not in the dirt but in a sealed room somewhere, talking about ecology as if it were just words.

Perhaps I am being unfair, and these are not echoes from Morton's writing, but the bugle voices I have heard all my life. Morton is one of the biggest names in Ecocriticism, a curiously shaped field that comes mainly from studies of English Literature, but ranges vastly across the humanities and environmental sciences to support its thinking. The piece cites copiously from Richard Dawkins, whose 'just debating' style has repeatedly been used to launder attacks on trans and Indigenous people, and anyone beyond his rationalist mirror.

One phrase in Morton's essay catches my breath. Anger roils. 'The garden variety environmentalisms, with their vitalist webs of life, have ironically strayed from materialism.'[5]

I am used to the language of academic prose because I used to practise it – the cerebral combat that turns reading into conflict, not conversation. Beneath the words I sense the scorn for gardening, for small cultivation, for the daily interrelations of beings.

If there is a 'garden variety' environmentalism, so what? A dandelion is a garden variety; so is clover, chickweed, yarrow, ragwort, corn marigold, common knapweed, ladies' bedstraw, fireweed, green alkanet, any number of wildflowers that grow in gardens, as weeds or (in)tended plants. The biodiversity of invertebrates even in small urban gardens is vast. Rhetoric poorly disguises prejudice masquerading as fact – as if a garden did not already contain multitudes of difference; as if basic cultivation renders habitats common, vulgar, inferior.

Why is it that gardens so rarely feature High Academia's vision of queer ecology?

The bugle voice of Morton has softened since 2010. The tides of their affiliations have shifted, perhaps not coincidentally since their non-binary gender was acknowledged in published form in *All Art Is Ecological.* In their short book, designed for publics, not narrow academic audiences, they say, 'How about just visiting your local garden centre to smell the plants?'[6] You don't need to stray that far. Why not close your eyes on an overland train platform and let your nose locate the scent of soil? It will be there, somewhere, close by.

I wonder what Morton's bugle makes of the counter-chorus of weeds and micro-ecosystems in the middle of this new decade. Filling the leadpipe, pouring from the bell.

The materially different conditions under which gardening flourishes or fails are never perfect – at the back of a house, on the mooring beside a boat, an arrangement of stones in the small one-metre-square frame of earth known as the tree pit at the foot of an urban tree, on a tiny plot of disused and potentially contaminated land – as many sites of urban agriculture are and were once. If garden varieties are looked down upon as failing, inadequate, wrong in some way, then so too are plant lives, stone lives, pond lives, grass lives, trash lives, the lives even of the overenthusiastically weeded municipal flowerbed.

Though Morton has changed tack, their past words carry with them the odour of that muscular white scorn. Disregarding the minor and the unremarkable. Removing the human in order to elevate it above the soils from which you, I, we came.

If I plant a violet in a desert, it will die. If I bury tulips in damp woodland, not the full sun these mountain-dwelling plants need, they will not reflower. I am in relation to the plants I tend. They are my community, and I am theirs. I may not always do right by them, but take me out of the equation and everything will certainly not be alright.

At one point, many points, I thought that wiping out my own existence would do nothing but good. My garden taught me differently.

* * *

I am beginning to understand why it is that garden journals and almanacs are so popular. The almanac understands what the human body forgets: no summer is the same summer, even before climate crisis. Almanacs offer an anchoring in continuity and change.

When I observe my garden, I am also asking questions. What does the queer community – the historical chorus I am assembling from the tails of archives and histories and contemporary retellings – think of summer, and seasons? How does the grief-laden seasonal change I experience relate to the seasons observed by Virginia Woolf or Octavia Hill, queer co-founder of the National Trust? And how does that queer community speak to kincentrism?

Woolf haunts my queer gardening thoughts, as she should, from *Orlando* to *Mrs Dalloway*; more so even than Vita Sackville-West, a far more accomplished and recognised gardener, whose histories of disinheritance are also entwined with her journeys across gender boundaries. In Woolf's *A Room of One's Own*, the gardens of Oxbridge become the textured substrate of her reflections on what makes it possible to write, and for women to be writers.

The gardens are a place where she sees the histories of Oxbridge unfolding, particularly the foundation of the women's colleges, like Newnham at Cambridge. In the garden at 'Fernham', as she calls it, she opens the door onto 'the beauty of the world which is so soon to perish, has two edges, one of laughter, one of anguish, cutting the heart asunder.'[7] I read this, nodding: laughter and anguish are familiar edges, especially in summer.

My garden is the place where I feel the most inept. I am always waiting for some authority figure – a parent, an elder, a more experienced gardener – to tell me that I am doing it all wrong. And yet the conversations I have had about gardening with people who have gardened their whole lives make it clear that doing it wrong, making mistakes, failing and failing again are the ways that gardens are made. No bugle: all weeds and anthills, blackfly infestations, mulched ground and failed plants.

Woolf's essay is full of failure too: failure to know, failure to research, failure to write in a linear way. She knows it – where there is an expectation of straightforward academic prose, instead she turns to her imagination, to see what it is she is envisioning and wrap it in words. She writes slant, though with less awkwardness than the queer poet Emily Dickinson, who requested that we tell our truths obliquely.[8]

And still there are the many women and non-binary people whose slides along the queer variance from feminine to masculine, from gay to straight, leave traces no more marked than moth dust trapped in the leaves of a book. Where my wild little front patch gave me room to breathe, their histories of cultivation remind me that I am never alone.

* * *

In the early part of the 2020s, battles raged against the leadership of the National Trust, led principally by journalists in right-wing broadsheets. Articles poured from the *Daily Telegraph* denouncing the Trust for its 'woke' agenda, for its 'politicisation' and 'dumbing down', for being 'divisive' by celebrating queer history or recognising colonial complicity.[9] The conversation has moved on since then, seeking other targets for the promotion of scientifically biological essentialism under the banner of 'common sense'. Denial is a powerful tool.

So here's an undeniable thing: Octavia Hill, co-founder of the National Trust, lived in queer companionship with a woman, Harriet Yorke, for the last 30 years of her life. She and Yorke are buried together in Holy Trinity Churchyard, Crockham Hill, Kent. Earlier in her life, Hill also had a passionate affair with Sophie Jex-Blake, the first cis-gendered woman surgeon in the UK, and one of the Edinburgh Seven said to be the first group of women enrolled as undergraduates at any university in the UK. I say cis-gendered because there were indeed other surgeons before her with more complex genders, like James Barry, who qualified as a surgeon in 1813 and in 1817 performed one of the first successful Caesarean sections in Western medicine, and whose assigned gender at birth was only made public upon his death in 1865.

The seeds of the National Trust were nurtured by queer women. This isn't an over-exaggeration. Octavia Hill did not marry, did not have children, did not participate in the heterosexual matrix that for several centuries has attempted to supplant millennia of gendered and sexual complexity in human life. Her relationships with women are accounted for. Who Octavia Hill loved and how she lived are on record.

Queerness and gender fluidity have always been part of the landscapes of Britain. They are suppressed by the same hands who systematically deny that post-Renaissance Britain was a colonising nation upon whose hands will always be the blood of the peoples it wittingly or unwittingly subjugated and destroyed.

Am I angry? Yes, I am.

***

My garden is a history. Its plant populations are my friends, allies, co-travellers and compasses. Some travelled with me for seven years before finding ground. Some preceded even that. My garden is an odyssey of temporary living, a collection of pots growing year on year, some of which have found a place to thrive. It is not a planned garden, so much as one that arrived through accumulation and error.

And I also notice – because the last year has been a year of observing the passing of time with ever more acute focus – that summer has come late to the garden. By mid-May the irises are still forming their elongated bud-pupae, when a year earlier they had been in full bloom for weeks. The English lavenders – always later than expected – are tense and green. The peony buds will never open: I watch them shrivel in tightly wadded darkness. This is my fault. I moved the plant when it was about to burgeon, and now I am punished by its silence. Of course, I am over-anthropomorphising: replanting disturbed the delicate mycelial balance of soil, root and plant, broke networks and starved the peony stems when they most needed nourishment to flower. If anything, I am the punishing one.

Seasons change, but they change changeably.

There is change in the bottom of the garden too. Where the shed once stood, and a series of railway sleepers formed a raised bed, and the lemon verbena, and the dogwood and the hibiscus, there is now flattened earth. The garden stops abruptly along the line of the raised roots of the cherry tree. Behind it is a building site, waiting. This is in long anticipation of the pre-fabricated cabin; the garden room that will become my writing space.

I am aware of the incredulous privilege of such a thing. To have access to enough land and capital to build a structure that creates an extra room, in a city where during successive pandemic lockdowns many people had no access to outdoor space that they could steward for themselves. During the COVID years of the early 2020s I spoke to artists who, fed up with the endless time indoors, turned part of the land surrounding their block of flats into a community herb garden. A writer friend told me about his relationship with his Indian rubber plant: its scars from drought or overwatering are signs of a shared emotional life of isolation and grief. Many channelled their frustrated creativity through their relationships with plants.

This land, this building to come, is precious and I am grateful. If I had not walked away from my version of Omelas, I would not have had the intuition to know that a room of my own was what I needed. But a need it is: a private space for queer, lopsided, writing-gardening solitude in a city of millions. A garden room of my own, to rephrase Virginia Woolf. My garden variety of ordinary-extraordinary life rhythms.

* * *

The first two days of June magically transformed. From the downpours and chills of May emerged flowerbeds more abundant than I had ever seen them. Cardoons planted the previous year became huge stegosaur spikes; the white clematis has spread the length of a fence on its sunny side, covered in creamy flower-heads with four large petals, spread wide for worker bees to gorge on. The *Dicentra formosa* – now renamed *Lamprocapnos spectabilis* – with its obscene pink hearts and white phallic stamens reached its peak, retracting as the sun beat more strongly. The artemisia, whose fresh, silver scent makes me want to rub my face in its soft lace, opened, fractals cascading out of its stems. The honeywort, which I grew from seed last year, somehow survived the winter. Its mauve-purple flower-heads filled with the tinny buzz pollination tactics of bumblebees, vibrating the head of the flower to release a shower of pollen and nectar. Interspecies sex in action.

Some of the more noticeable plants in the garden were there before we arrived. The spotted laurel that I do a terrible job of pruning each year, the weigela with its variegated white and pink flower bells and the large cherry tree, the sedum that grows tall by the pond, and the Italian arum that multiplies its veined green arrowheads, tucked under a dry, shady spot. We have populated the garden with beloved plants. The dark purple, almost-black irises shooting up their heads were bought from the now-defunct Darsham Nurseries in Suffolk, who closed their doors for the last time in early 2020. And the self-seeders feel like a reward: white foxgloves appear in the garden in different places; *Alchemilla mollis*, weeping globular tears. The pink wild geranium, herb robert, has found homes in any available crevice, in the small gravel sidings along the path, any place with a tenuous link to growing medium.

* * *

In the last few days of June 2021, grey and green, news of the death of the queer critic and scholar Lauren Berlant arrived.

I felt a guilty sense of relief that here, finally, was a tangible, clear-hearted reason to grieve. None of the vague, gaseous grief that permeates the sweating cellar of midsummer.

Grief settles in the passing of an incredible writer and scholar who named the mystic artefact of cruel optimism upon which much of capitalism is premised – when what you desire is an obstacle to your own flourishing. I want to re-read *Cruel Optimism*, to fathom its depths in my own seas of feeling. I have spent a long time swimming in the dark, trying to numb, suppress and *un-feel* the grief and fury that stack up, day on day – that stacked up, day on day, while I was working in an environment never intended to sustain anything but the most privileged forms of life: namely wealthy white men and those who circle in their orbit, whose primary affiliations are to the orders and structures of power itself.

I am not some crazed Shakespearean witch screaming from the preludes of his plays, misogyny carried on the air like dandelion seeds. I am as ordinary as the chorus in Sophocles' play *Antigone*, or as much as Anne Carson's translations will allow of ordinariness. As Berlant said, 'The ordinary is, after all, a porous zone that absorbs lots of incoherence and contradiction, and people make their ways through it at once tipped over awkwardly, half-conscious, and confident about common sense.'[10] Once you have broken the surface of madness, common sense is no longer a place of confidence. There is madness in the ordinary.

In Berlant's work, gardens appear as suspicious places of bourgeois intervention. In the suspicious garden of Berlant and Kathleen Stewart's flash fiction/essay, 'Projects', 'a team of beautiful young women dressed like field ecologists built the new walkway and lined the front of the house with the cast-iron plant / rosemary, irises, and sage to hide the stucco.'[11]

In the story, the women who build and plant are undermined, literally, by 'John', the partner of the narrator, and by the termites who fly up through the floorboards from the underground lair John has built beneath the house. The structural deficits of capitalism and patriarchy uproot the planted world.

What would it have been for someone like Berlant to feel connected to plant and animal worlds that neither hide stucco artifice nor threaten the existence of a home?

It's no coincidence that, at the time I began a career in academia, I also began to build a garden. Gardens were my antidote.

* * *

Reading Susanna Grant and Rowan Spray's pamphlet on wild plants, I learn about plant blindness. Developed by US botanists Elizabeth Schussler and James Wandersee, one of the symptoms of this condition of disconnection from the natural world is 'Thinking that plants are merely the backdrop for animal life', and 'overlooking the importance of plants to one's daily affairs'. Perhaps that's where 'blindness' is the wrong metaphor, because unseeing is not an experience of impairment, but a willed denial, a failure to look at what is already connected to nature in the small, the bourgeois, the urban and the profane.

Plant blindness is a social phenomenon, more like the strange condition that certain non-disabled people seem to experience when they move uncomfortably close to a wheelchair, tripping over the chair user and potentially harming everyone. Or the way a non-disabled person might try to navigate someone moving slowly with crutches or a frame on the pavement by suddenly rushing past them, or attempting to squeeze between their co-walking friends.

I've often exchanged quizzical looks with loved ones in wheelchairs and on crutches when this happens. I see the unseeing eye of the passer-by, and I know it's not blindness. Not an experience of visual impairment. It's a social and cultural pattern buried in a person: to make invisible what it is inconvenient to see.

I want to see what is inconvenient to see. To get in among the weeds and cultivars, the cow parsley and the wild carrots. To see the Q where it is inconvenient to see it.

* * *

The relationship between humans and ecology is anything but nothing. Garden variety is scorn that runs deep.

I would rather follow poet and writer Tamiko Beyer's manifestations of queer eco poetics:

> The double colon of queer::eco::poetics breathes new life into co-opted, saturated forms, wrestling both queerness and greenwashing away from corporate /mainstream speech acts. It holds queerness in all its discomforts and embraces the entirety of ecology (ecology of language, of human creation, of thought, emotion, *and* of the 'natural' world).
>
> A queer::eco::poetics holds on simultaneously to the outsider status of queerness while working to disrupt the distinctions between outside and in, natural and unnatural, normal and freakish. A poetics of the porous.[12]

Queer::eco::poetics embraces the garden variety as much as it does the wild endangered present and its precursors. Not either/or, but both, and. Here are a set of values older than anything a well-recognised academic authority might conceive of. Stewardship. Kincentrism. Abundance.

I want to get away from the Victorians and the modernists, wonderfully queer though they were. It's a rich seam, but it feels too easy, too obvious now that I see it. The Q in the Victorian-modernist garden is visible enough to meet with dominant culture's attempts to eliminate it. I am looking closer for queer kincentrism. In my wildflower meadow. In the burgeoning tomatoes on my allotment. In a connection to land that feels like home, while tending my tender queer grief.

* * *

This summer's solstice was something I never saw. Much as I would have liked to rise before dawn, the gathering energies of the season overwhelmed me as usual. I crave the long, dark night, the quiet dreaming hours of winter to temper the rapid shift into restlessness and grief. I was born facing the wrong way: wishing for night-long vigils in winter and endless sleep in summer. I am not ready for the tilting of the axis: it always comes too soon. When summer has barely begun, it is already meeting its decline.

I share my grief in queer kincentric circles. Grief in a death never more present than in the abundance of life. Grief in the seed packet unopened on my desk. Love in the mists between.

11

tomato, skin, kin (on wolf peaches, persecution and wild edibles)

Blisters run along the soles of my feet, as if long, flat worms had buried themselves there. Each year these blisters appear, as tender skin fails to harden quick enough to meet with London's sudden shift from wet spring to sweaty summer. I prefer my feet bare: the sensitivities of my skin mean wounds form easily in the friction of textiles. Bruises, swellings, scar tissue, red weals, rashes, skin infections, broken veins, eczema, dermatitis: these are not friends. But I recognise them well.

There is a French expression, *à fleur de peau*. It is difficult to translate, but it means something like the first flush of the skin. The tenderest moment, the most exquisite (vulnerable, painful) sensation. Hypersensitivity or, if you look at it the other way round, attunement. This is the thin cloak of self that wraps around my body. I am always *à fleur de peau*. Clumsy and accident-prone. Tender and responsive. My skin bruises easily: press it just a little and there will be a blue-green thumbprint the next day.

I have always understood the thinness of my skin to be genetic – part of the collection of predispositions that come with red hair, hypermobility, translucent skin. Amid all the structural advantages of whiteness, my ultra-pale body burns on contact with the sun. My summers are regularly blighted by oedema: as the temperature rises, joints swell and skin tenses with fluid. These are the minor complaints that make up a life. The medication I take only exacerbates them, transforming me into a swollen, highly photosensitive skin-creature.

Raging, burning, tomato-red.

* * *

In search of names for my tomato skin, I find myself drowning in them.

Solanum lycopersicon is one of the tomato's Latin binomial classifications, though that too is constantly reframed. Adjusted to a window of language that does not fit.

Lycopersicon is a mistranslation from Galen, the medieval medicine man. I remember him from my GCSE history syllabus, though of course it's not true that he is medieval: he was a classical Roman physician. His writing, among others (Pedanius Dioscorides for one), became the fetishised script of medieval European medical care (that is, if you didn't visit your local witch or *sage-femme*, whose extensive herbalist knowledge would in the Renaissance period become a sign of devil-worship). Galen, who for centuries was synonymous with Western medicine, at one point refers obscurely to an Egyptian plant used to ward off wolves. This wolf-defending plant's juices have an unpleasant odour; it is toxic but also contains powerful medicinal properties. It's possible that this wolf-poison may have been a member of the *Solanaceae* family: perhaps mandrake (*Mandragora officinarum* L.). Or one of the nightshades: deadly (*Atropa belladonna*) or woody (*Solanum dulcamara*).

Incidentally, Atropa was one of the three classical Greek Fates: she severs the thread of human life spun by Clotho and measured by Lachesis.

Renaissance botanists were somewhat hazy about geography. North Africa, Turkey, Egypt became synonymous with all far-off places. Everywhere that was not Europe was yonder. In Europe's orientalising imaginary, a plant from Egypt might as well be a plant from South America: the Old World was the New World. Both were, according to early modern botanising colonisers, distant and subject to the hunt for bio-productive species. And so botanists of the sixteenth and seventeenth centuries weave this thread of magical thinking into the golden cloth of mythology, to seal up a tear in the knowledge of the classical world that destabilised the Renaissance one.

In the midst of the tomato's curious arrival in Europe from South America, Galileo's *Dialogue Concerning the Two Chief World Systems* (1632) was battling and losing against worldviews that placed the earth at the centre of the universe. If our universe is geocentric, and Europe the centre of that earth, then everywhere else is simply other. 'Turkish' plants are the same as South American plants. The tomato from South and Central America thus becomes known, retroactively, to an earlier empire who named an entirely different plant species.

And so the tomato's naming becomes wrapped up with a mapping of otherness onto Eurocentrism. The cloth of life from which the tomato is spun is severed on contact with Europe.

The Renaissance desire to cling to pre-existing classical medical frameworks and pre-Copernican geocentrism is not at all surprising: we cleave to earlier agendas (and rumours, and stories) all the time. As David Gentilcore points out in *Pomodoro! A History of the Tomato in Italy*, 'The New World had the potential to lead investigators to call into question the entire cultural system on which their naturalistic knowledge was based.'[1] New knowledge – or rather, knowledge that is new to those who meet it – shakes up old systems. That unfamiliarity breeds fear. Fear, and repression, and a desire to return to older, increasingly tenuous knowledge systems – and then, a grim fixation upon those systems, no matter how systematically they are dismantled. Several centuries later the small but emphatic cult of flat-Earthers is still going strong. And now quiet revolutions in the sex and gender wars mean that some seek comfort in a familiar past, while others move forward. Some grasp at the bastion of belief in binary gender, while others, like Judith Butler, patiently demonstrate all the ways in which evolutionary, endocrinological, anthropological, botanical, sociological evidence points in the opposite direction.[2]

* * *

I wanted this to be a story of sensuous growth and renewal, with bowls of sun-sweetened tomatoes drenched in olive oil and salt and home-grown basil shared over long summer lunches. And yet where I find myself this season is in a pit of rage, fighting off stomach pains where I hold fury down.

I had intended to write about the wonder of sowing tomatoes in late March or early April. Watching tiny leaves push through the surface of the lightly padded soil. Noting how they grow into stronger, hairier seedlings (something in me loves tomato hairs – a fragrant furry covering to protect and sustain). The acts of sustenance that lift seedling to pot to cold frame, hardening them off over the course of weeks, to transfer to the allotment, aligned on strings hung from a wooden frame up which they become strong trusses of fruits, red and yellow and waiting to be plucked. Planting basil between the rows as a companion that sweetens the fruit, wards off pests and tastes delicious.

I wanted to write about food sharing and permaculture. Instead I find myself locked in a battle between sleeplessness and irritable bowel syndrome, anxiety crawling across my skin like tiny red ants.

I guess I am in serious trouble. Which is why I turn to edible plants.

* * *

This is the advice, or perhaps the prophecy, of Zheng Bo, artist and advocate of fern kink: whenever we get into serious trouble we turn to edible plants.

His *Survival Manuals*, where he copies the knowledge of books on edible weeds, are archival work, digging for the traces of survival strategies in the most catastrophic of times. During the nationwide famine in China in 1961 that followed The Great Leap Forward (1958–60) the Communist Party published *Shanghai's Wild Edible Plants*, to help its people survive the starvation it had caused. Survival is key: finding ways to exist on the thinnest, most inhospitable and barren of grounds, when all else has failed. Survival is indifferent to political orientation too: *Taiwan's Edible Plants*, published in 1945, was written by Japanese colonialists at the end of World War II, five months before Japan's surrender.[3] On Zheng's website, he translates words from the text's preface: 'At this critical moment of the sacred war, the survival of the empire depends on winning the war on food.'[4]

Wild edibles – foraging – are found at the site of something much bigger. The forces of totalitarianism and colonialism meet in those narrow inches of soil. Foraging is a tool for survival and resistance; it is also subject to the racialising forces of geopolitical conflict.

No wonder I couldn't write about the quiet joys of seedlings. Food plants are part of something larger: sites of conflict and cultivation that cast back through the centuries, and begin always with a wild counterpart.

* * *

The wild tomato, *Solanum pimpinellifolium*, has fruits barely a centimetre in diameter, and scraggy plants that cling to the land with ferocious tenacity in a narrow stretch of South America from Chile to Peru. I notice how wildly accounts of this currant-tomato vary. One cultural history of the tomato describes it as an 'aggressive colonizer that grows like a weed from northern Chile to Peru-Ecuador'.[5] But a 2015 article from the Smithsonian Institution's quarterly magazine indicates quite the opposite: that the wild tomato is rapidly losing the habitat it once colonised to intensive agricultural methods.[6] The tone of this article harbours a colonising flavour itself; while complaining about Peruvian agriculture's devastating effects on wild tomato habitats, it recognises in passing that the USA is the only member of the UN *not* to have signed the Convention on Biological Diversity in 1992, which established protocols by which genetic resources like seeds and plants required informed consent from donor countries, and profit share from the commercialised results of any research. And while it's certainly the case that environmental protections have themselves been exploited to support colonial expansion elsewhere in the world, the Smithsonian article carries the vernacular of the colonial 'protector': trying to save plants from the Peruvian farmers who know not what they do.

A convention designed to limit colonising exploitation is claimed to inhibit environmental protections. Because environmental protections are the privilege of the colonising power, and never the colonised. Sounds familiar.

* * *

On my train journeys to therapy, my mind folded inwards.

Midsummer is a time of celebration. In summer 2021 anti-vaccination protests paraded through London whistling and waving and rejoicing in collective rage, wishing death upon death for the sake of suspicion and computer chips.[7]

What came up over and over in therapy was bile, and grief.

Like the many plagues before it, the COVID pandemic unleashed not only a virus but also a feast of ghosts, spirits and scapegoats, a medieval rise in killing suspicions, fears of death projected onto others; death spirals aligned with fear, retrenchment, suspicion, ill-will. I felt its movements below the surface of things.

And as I watched the anti-vaxxer protesters stream past the Embankment Bridge beside the Thames in July warm with the ripeness of summer, I saw a virulent strand of self-righteousness, a conviction of personal autonomy, individual fear or discomfort taking precedence over the needs of the wider community. It is a political strategy. I saw it in 'gender critical' spokespeople too, keen to align actual widowhood with the hypothesis of the wife who 'loses' her husband because they begin their gender transition.[8] As if all griefs could not be held together. As if the highest grief must be allocated to (white, always white) female, cisgender, 'gender-critical' tears. As if grief were not a both, and situation.

The grief roiled. Indigestion, pain, bloating were the inevitable consequences. My angry gut woke me at night, made sitting for any period of time untenable. Eating was a constant skirmish, as hungry or full or sated all things felt the same. Pain, discomfort, unease.

* * *

As I've come to expect in my voyages through the history of botany, the tomato underwent a series of name claims – territorial pissings, if you will – between sixteenth-, seventeenth- and eighteenth-century European botanists. While in the 1550s Pietro Antonio Michiel collected it under all its names, including *Lycopersicon galeni* (Galen's wolf peach), and in 1571 Francisco Hernandez confused the tomato for the tomatillo (now known as *Physalis ixocarpa*), Joseph Pitton de Tournefort added a new binomial in his 1694 volume *Élémens de la botanique*: *Lycopersicon esculentum* (edible wolf peach). He was succeeded by our friend Carolus Linnaeus in his 1753 *Species Plantarum* who placed the tomato genus within the *Solanum* family to create *Solanum lycopersicum*. Phillip Miller's revised fourth edition of his *Gardener's Dictionary*, published the following year in 1754, bypasses Linnaeus to return the tomato to Tournefort's *Lycopersicon*, introducing *esculentum* to situate the tomato in a whole new genus.[9]

But the name more commonly used – *tomato* – comes from the Náhuatl (Indigenous Mexican) word *xitomātl*, describing the fruit's substantial growth, water content, navel-like depression and plump size.

Gaining weight and taking on water in the summer heat: I identify.

The *miltomātl* was reserved for the tomatillo, the fruit whose husk dries out and bursts to reveal the smooth green (or yellow, or purple) beneath. This husky-smooth, suggestive fruit was far too clitoral for Spanish physician Hernandez who heaped moral opprobrium on the plant for its 'venereal and lascivious' appearance.[10]

Feminine sexualisation as a tactic of colonial control? Sounds familiar.

***

In my small corner of South East London, high summer arrived, leaf canopies packed so thickly they block out the light in the middle of the day. My front garden was a haywire assemblage of daisies, salad burnet, white frothy heads of yarrow, purple knapweed and red valerian, shifted sideways where cats and foxes made daybeds. Self-seeded lemon balm plumed everywhere. Meanwhile in the back, the cardoon became a nine-foot spiked angel with silver wings and four tiny heads.

During that wet, warm, grey summer so typical of England's perfidious temperament – everything grew. Everything, including the vast explosion of slugs and snails that destroyed all but one courgette plant in the allotment, stripped tender lettuce seedlings, bean shoots and peas. Uncontainable and legion in number, I picked them off and threw them into my neighbour's untended garden. How dramatically my relationship to them had shifted since my gentle solidarity with the previous autumn's lemon verbena snail. In Erika Lopez's queer hybrid graphic novel *Flaming Iguanas*, her protagonist, Tomato, reckons with this too. She speaks of her guilt about pouring salt on slugs, hearing their screams in the night.[11] I don't pour salt on slugs, or snails. I don't put down slug pellets. I don't do anything to them at all. Though my partner goes out at night to collect them, and I don't ask questions.

That summer was not the best weather for tomatoes, who demand high sun to grow tall. In the allotment they remained squat, stunted, waiting to grow up the twines hung for them from the wooden frame. The slugs and the snails circled, waiting too.

* * *

Like all official-sounding botanicals, the tomato's Latinate binomial has muddy origins. Notwithstanding the orderly claims for knowledge made by naming, this particular one began with a spelling error. If the ancient Greeks and Romans never made it to Peru, then whatever Galen's plant was, it probably wasn't a tomato. And the name of Galen's non-tomato, the part toxic, part curative plant-pharmakon from North Africa was *Lycopersion*.[12]

The *persion* part is, apparently, untranslatable. But it makes me think of *compersion*, the emotion conferred by polyamorous communities to the pleasure gained from one's lover's pleasure with another lover. A radical pleasure, pleasure of and for the unknown (or well-known) third or fourth or fifth. Sympathetic fellow feeling, with an overtone of eroticism; another term for vicarious joy, the mirror emotion of jealousy or envy. There is joyful, erotic, subversive sensuality in Galen's tomato, despite its co-option into sixteenth- and seventeenth-century classificatory systems.

Lycopersicon was the word that stuck: its yarns spun out of the desires of European Renaissance scientists to bind themselves to classical wisdom, shoring up the black holes in knowledge that they encountered abruptly when travellers, expeditioners and missionaries returned from their travels to the 'New World'. And then, in the same breath, the wider structures that are always twinned with science come out to play: superstition, fear, patriarchy. *Lyco*, drawn from the ancient Greek *lycos*, refers to wolves, werewolves and beasts. It is one of several reasons for several hundred years of tomato-based suspicion, and why the tomato was in Renaissance Europe considered to be a carrier of evil, poison and witchcraft. Its proximity to the hallucinogenic nightshade family made it as suspect as mandrake, henbane or hemlock.

Persicon is mentioned in Pliny the Elder's *The Natural History* (77–79 AD): a broad-leaved, large-rooted plant suitable for sciatica and 'inguinal complaints', 'diseases of the groin' and other faintly sexual illnesses.[13] *Persicon* alludes to the persica malus, the term first used by Europeans to describe the peach on its journey from China via Persia to Europe.[14] In German, the term was transliterated into *Wolfpfirsich* – the wolf peach. By the time Linnaeus got hold of the mythology of the tomato, its folklore and European oral histories had become a part of its naming. The wolf peach.

From Galen's peachy queer *persion* comes the botanical equivalent of a witches' spell. The tomato is where the *persicon* of Tournefort and Linnaeus and Miller becomes peach; the lascivious, dangerous, lupine fruit. And anyone who has ever eaten a sun-ripened beefsteak variety will know how close it comes to that peachy taste. A ripe, queer peach of a tomato.

(And I think to myself: the vision of alt-indie rapper Peaches screaming *boys wanna be her* in the mid-2000s as she crowd-surfs in a darkened Pontins entertainment hall, rented by the brilliant and now defunct UK indie festival All Tomorrow's Parties).

Peaches and queers and angry sex politics. Now *that* I am hungry for.

***

Tomato skins are vulnerable to bursting, exposing their flesh to airborne moulds, which set in, rotting the fruits as they sit on the vine. If the plant is left thirsty, then overwatered, the fruits develop what is appealingly called blossom bottom rot. The fact of it is unattractive. A nasty brown rash forms at the base of the fruit, which gradually decays and moulders, then drops to the ground, unripened, for slugs to feast on.

This damp year at least, my allotment tomatoes did not suffer from blossom bottom rot. Plunge a finger into the soil and it came out damp; brown sediment scooped in the crescent of my fingernail. The regular, unrelenting rains served the tomatoes and the weeds a heavy dose. The ground gave pliably underfoot as bindweed burst out beneath paving stones and bark chippings.

***

The tomato *Solanum pimpinellifolium*, like its kin, the three sisters of squash, corn and beans, was first cultivated by ancient Mesoamerican cultures (see that line between culture and cultivation? It is far older than you think). The tomato is an indigenous food plant,[15] first transported to

Europe in the mid-sixteenth century, and there viewed with suspicion for several hundred years, before it became ubiquitously adopted and embedded, particularly in the food cultures of Italy and Spain. What we know to be a tomato has only become so because of its entwined millennia with humans, who have cultivated, bred, saved seed, overwintered, replanted, again, again, again, over a longer time than writing – longer than naming – though not quite as long as mark- or art-making.

Tomatoes are almost-human anthropochores, who have danced with humanity for millennia. The human flesh-cloaks preceding you, me, us have made the tomato larger, juicier, more fruitful and more consistent. This has often made tomato plants more susceptible to fungal and viral damage, suffering far more in drought and pestilence than their wild relatives.

In saving skin and kin, the cultivated tomato is less well prepared to face the apocalypse. Plant biologists and tomato breeders have returned to the wild tomato to seek out the genetic traits of disease resistance, to help retain the milder, larger, more vulnerable and tender skin of the edible tomato cultivars. Kin-tomatoes.

* * *

In wild edibles the artist Jumana Manna found room for survival and kin. *Wild Relatives*, her film from 2018, explored the complex politics of seed banks in Syria, Lebanon and Norway, after an international agricultural centre in Aleppo was forced to relocate to the Bekaa Valley of Lebanon during the Syrian civil war in 2012, and was forced to laboriously replant its stocks from backup stocks at the Svalbard Global Seed Vault. I read about Manna's relationships to weeds in spring 2020, while I was managing the edible and inedible weeds of my own allotment. In lockdown with her parents in East Jerusalem she wrote about decades of foraging in the wild plains around their home, for *za'atar* (thyme) and *'akkoub*, tumble thistle, also known as *Gundelia Tournefortii* (here another botanical friend, Tournefort of wolf-peach naming, makes a cameo appearance). Manna's story intertwined histories of Palestinian foraging and cooking, successive attempts by the Israeli government to reduce, constrain and destroy Palestinian-Arab populations, and the relationship between government-led attempts at ecological preservation and ideologies designed to either eradicate or monetise millennia-old Indigenous relationships to the land. Released in 2022, her subsequent film *Foragers* combined archival footage with documentary and staged reenactments of court hearings where Palestinian foragers have been prosecuted for pursuing the generational traditions of foraging for *za'atar* and *'akkoub*.

Manna writes that, despite the growth of Traditional Ecological Knowledge programmes in Canada, Australia, Aotearoa (New Zealand), Indigenous foraging in Israel falls on the prongs of government policies designed to prohibit, outlaw, regulate and mount suspicion of foraging as a dangerous, contaminating act.[16] By turning foraging into witchcraft, which must therefore be treated with the utmost suspicion, environmental protections become a mechanism of colonial inversion. Herbalist practices of land-knowledge and stewardship are intentionally transformed into dangerous unknowable forces of darkness. It is a colonising, misogynistic (because food gatherers are very often women, because knowledge practices about food and cooking and home medicine and land are often held by women), dominating process.

Environmental protections are of course not a bad thing, nor should governments avoid introducing policies designed to manage and support ecological biodiversity. Manna identifies the ironies of pine forest planting following the establishment of the state of Israel, where the monocultural planting of pines funded by the Jewish National Fund (JNF) created high towering forests on desert, heath and scrub that was once rich in forageable foodstuffs. While the JNF attempted to recreate Eastern European landscapes for populations of Ashkenazi Jews, the pines shed acidic needles that shifted the pH balance of the soil and killed off other plants, vastly reducing the land's biodiversity. And when they burned, the pines communicated forest fires with alacrity where previous ecosystems had restricted their spread. The trees were planted to help the European Jewish settlers feel more at home in a desert landscape. But they were created in denial of Indigenous ecological relationships between plants and food and earth and fire, despite the presence of Indigenous populations – like Palestinian Arabs, like Bedouins – who could have taught them, had they had the opportunity to be heard.

Nothing is as simple as it seems. Not even planting trees.

* * *

Lycanthropy, the study of werewolves, is where the tomato, member of the mystical nightshade family, found a home. It was believed, like the other nightshades – mandrake, for example, which is both poisonous and hallucinogenic if taken in the right quantities – to possess the properties of dark magic. At the time of the colonial 'discovery' of the tomato, the witch hunts and witch trials, that European project of mass cultural misogyny, was in full flow. The tomato's botanical relationship to mandrake also smeared it with the same taint of witchery, wolf transformations and other satanic rituals.

Nightshades – the devil's food – were described as part of the unguents that witches were said to smear on their bodies and broomsticks so as to take off and fly. In 1627, Francis Bacon wrote in his *Sylva Sylvarum* about this witches' ointment, made up, apparently, of the 'fat of children digged out of their graves', together with 'the juices of smallage, wolf-bane, and cinque-foil, mingled with the meal of fine wheat' together with 'soporiferous medicines' like 'henbane, hemlock, mandrake'.[17]

Primordial nightshade lube on a giant flying dildo. This is not too much of a stretch, since sexual perversion was a perennial accusation against women during the centuries of the 'witch craze' in Europe. As historian of witchcraft Anne Llewellyn Barstow identifies, misogyny and sexual violence were the consistent components of the persecution of women. These moments of pandemonium reached a peak in the seventeenth century, where patriarchal misogyny gave way to torture and extreme violence, leading to implausible and sometimes impossible claims about what witches could (or could not) do.[18]

This hypersexualised, misogynistic vision of witches and tomato-based unguents is, as scholar Michael Ostling has pointed out, a fiction entirely constructed through words: 'The ointments' principle ingredients are neither babyfat nor belladonna, but words: cried out in coerced confessions, written in defense of the devil's power or of the sufficiency of a naturalist human science. The ointment exists only in and through arguments about it: despite its seeming physicality, it is a product of discourse.'[19] Words and stories determine the structures of culture and knowledge.

The more I read about witchcraft, shamanism and European and South American rituals, the less confident I feel about extricating fact from fiction, life from mythology. Were there witches? I don't know. Did they use nightshade lube? Probably not. Was there fear that the evidence of the emerging world encountered by colonisers would contaminate existing Eurocentric knowledge, based as it was on classical Greek and Roman texts? Yes. Was there a mass cultural psychosis about women and witchcraft? Almost certainly.

So why does the *idea* of the witches' brew exist? Why were women sexualised and demonised as its possessors?

To uphold the power held in the fields of botany, theology, history. Of course.

And why is women's non-reproductive sexuality so frightening to structures of power?

Ah yes, I remember now.

Estimates vary wildly on the number of people murdered during the 250-year-long European femicide, which emerged as Europe transitioned into Renaissance globalist empire: from 45,000 to almost half a million.[20] It was a particular kind of cultural psychosis, twinned with the rise of European colonialism. And since the witch trials drew to a close in the mid-eighteenth century, it has not ended but simply transformed into differing shades of hatred towards women.

That's a whole lot of misogyny to swallow in the name of a small, squishy wolf peach.

* * *

Visual artist Taraneh Mosadegh's series of untitled paintings, *Tomato Resistance*, speaks decolonial tomato mythologies.[21] Her panels are often small – only 8 inches by 9.5 inches – with the smallest the size that analogue 35mm photographs used to be – 5 inches by 7. Each one reveals a single tomato plant in near-silhouette. Sometimes the fruits sit heavy on a branch, weighting the plant down as its fingers reach skyward. The roots curl in the shallows at the base, observing the contours of the earth they rest upon. I want to use the word *eldritch* about these paintings, to acknowledge their power, as if they were illustrations from a storybook of tomato fables. In them I see the crabbed hands of the Baba Yaga, or Medusa's snaking hair. These are paintings that know the tomato's magic. They reveal the nightshade traces of the more-than-human, the opposite of the colonial sadism that transformed the tomato vines on Aztec terraces into the tender skins of the beefsteak and the gardener's delight.

* * *

While many languages in Europe and Asia have borrowed and built their own *tomātl*-based words, another one appears: *pomodoro*, the golden apple that spreads from Italy to Lithuania, Ukraine to Azerbaijan and Uzbekistan. It is another grasp backward in time, to Greek myth. The three goddess-nymphs, the Hesperides, were protectors of a tree with golden apples. Their dragon protector was slain, and the golden apples stolen by Herakles during his 12 labours. (Incidentally, it was on one of Herakles' other jaunts that he killed the red monster, Geryon, and his little red dog.)

Tomatoes were first described in the mid-sixteenth century, not long after Europeans invaded Peru, as 'mala

Peruviana' or 'Pomi del Peru'.[22] Both draw on the Latinate *malus* or *pomum*, for apple. Golden apples, love apples; the tomato is confused with plants both distant and close-to: the mandrake, the pomegranate.

As *pomi d'oro*, tomatoes were not always red, nor are they the only plant-based foodstuff straddling the boundary between botanical fruit and culinary vegetable. Pumpkins, peas, olives, rhubarb, peppers, corn, cucumbers, aubergines, cucumbers all gleefully transgress the fruit/vegetable binary; all originating outside Europe. And though the apple (*pomo, pomme*) is no relative of the tomato, the mandrake certainly is part of the nightshade (*Solanaceae*) family and was considered to have aphrodisiac properties.

There is more to be said about this relationship to sexuality, especially of the feminine kind. The mandrake is part of the Old Testament narratives of Leah, Rachel, Jacob and their children; it is part of the feminine reproductive lineage of the three monotheistic religions.[23] The much more ungodly tomato was also habitually confused with the aubergine (eggplant), as well as other nightshades. Fruit and vegetable cross many paths via the sixteenth- and seventeenth-century European coloniser struggles to own, define and control food plants and the worlds they came from.

* * *

Tomato, beetroot, carrot – all these carmines are familiar taunts from my early life. I was a fat child with flame-red hair. Early on I was taught shame about my size and my height ('such a big girl for her age!'). Shame about my translucent, semi-porous skin and genetically aberrant hair followed shortly afterward.

The most exciting part of reading the Arabian Nights was, I remember, how often the highest compliment given to a woman's beauty was her *skin like the moon*. My skin is luminous under sunlight. Any exposed area of skin shines so brightly for a moment that it looks like it is lit from the inside. That is before, if left unprotected, it turns pink, then angry, blistering red. I have often found this embarrassing when in Mediterranean climates, surrounded by bronzed bodies on beaches where I shelter under umbrellas and hats, scarves and sun cream, protecting myself from the sun that the leonine in me craves.

Skin like the moon as a compliment for its paleness was something it took me a while to discover. It is part of uncovering whiteness as a privilege, even as my skin makes me suffer.

Because where I am not white I am red.

Red is the colour of my skin, hair, flesh, eyes, blood.

Red like a tomato, a beetroot, a dragon.

Red like Anne Carson's queer, miserable Geryon in *Autobiography of Red*, the monster whose beautiful tender outsiderness his queer lover Herakles breaks into fragments.

* * *

That summer, I did not visit the allotment for weeks. Pulled down into the underworld of work, I channelled my energies away from myself to find some way to make positive, gentle change in a world hostile to positivity or gentleness.

Unlike the previous summer, which was full of consistent heat and ripeness, the summer of 2021 was more like an interstitial space between spring and autumn. Though there were wildfires and marine heatwaves in British Columbia, Britain received rains upon rains, with slugs and snails filling every open-standing orifice. And then a heat so intense it felt as if my brain had melted. Not a time of abundance.

How can I write about something as delicate and as queer as a tomato skin? Or about my own skin, which, in times close enough to remember in too much detail, felt flayed, stripped, like someone had blanched and peeled me, with no filter between the magnitude of the world and my innermost, palpating self?

Geryon, the red monster of ancient Greek fragments, monster who is out of time, outside time, grappling with time and place and the words of others he never understands, knows how. At the outset of Carson's playful, creative translation of these fragments, Geryon's child-self builds a sculptural autobiography out of a cigarette glued to a tomato, hair made from a ten-dollar bill ripped and bonded to its soft skin. As a young man in Argentina, he sits in a café with Nazi philosophers whose jokes and words he does not understand, trying badly to conceal his true queer monstrous nature, and failing, because his stuffed overcoat so clearly indicates the deformity of his black lace wings beneath. He waits for food and his mouth comes alive when he tastes the red pimento hidden within an olive. A plate of tomato sandwiches arrives, and he eats, deliciously. He calls himself a philosopher of sandwiches – and yet what he is eating is himself; the tomato he transformed into autobiography, when he was too young and slow with words to form himself in language.

How can I write about the time when I existed somewhere in the space between Geryon's tomato glued to a cigarette and his slippery tomato sandwiches?

The times when words failed – because they always fail, in the end.

I can't.
Tomatoes are my queer kin and skin.
Oh, Geryon.

* * *

Lycopene, the bright red carotenoid hydrocarbon pigment that colours tomatoes, carrots, watermelons and other fruits and vegetables, is an antioxidant. It can slow down the progression of some cancers, reduces levels of LDL cholesterol while increasing HDL, can protect against sunburn and UV damage, delays the onset of cataracts, reduces pain, protects brain health and maintains bone strength. All this in a tomato. Many tomatoes – it takes a lot of raw *lycopersicons* to make up a regular and significant dose of lycopene, red as the blood of wolves.

In 1960, doctors observed a middle-aged mother of three admitted to hospital with shoulder pain and orange discoloration in her palms and the soles of her feet. She had been drinking two litres of tomato juice a day for two years. Her condition became known as lycopenemia.[24]

I instinctively want to know more about this woman, and why she religiously drank tomato juice. But when I read that she was, apparently, 'fat', something clicks into place.

That old chestnut (tomato).

Obsessive patterns of thinking and doing brought on by the social stigma that clings to fat, femme bodies. Who told her drinking two litres of tomato juice a day was a way to reduce the size of her fat body?

More importantly, who taught her, and in how many ways, that her fat body was unacceptable?

* * *

By the time the last tomato crop in the allotment was ready, blight had swept across the site, foreclosing the end of the tomato season. Blight is an annual event: moved in from the east coast of England and blown westwards by summer rains, every plant is affected eventually, save the varieties bred specifically for their resistance. On our plot, the more easterly red tomatoes succumbed quickest, despite my attempts at stripping the leaves to protect the ripening fruits. The older variety, 'yellow submarine', lasted longer and cropped more vigorously. Their thin skins, fast ripening and tendency to burst seemed to offer them some protection.

There is no organic cure for blight: it is a fungal disease whose spores travel via water (rain and low winds are its perfect environment). The affected plants must be burned or buried, and since bonfires were not permitted because they affect air quality, I dreaded visiting the one crop that had successfully outwitted snails, slugs, waterlogging and all the other difficulties of an overly wet, mild summer. Late summer is the time of fire – forest fires, as well as campfires. Fire as a tool of ritual cleansing. Fire in the belly.

* * *

An acquaintance once insisted that others perceive him to be belligerent, because he is afraid of judgement. I believe he was trying to explain his own vulnerability, whilst abrogating responsibility for the cruelty – particularly towards women – he wielded to protect it. There is a link, of course, between vulnerability and cruelty: it is another way of describing what Marshall Rosenberg identifies in his theory of nonviolent communication. *Violence in any form is a tragic expression of our unmet needs.*

I remember violence. And not all vulnerabilities require cruel expression. This much my tender skin knows well.

There is a similar tonal quality of vulnerability, cruelty and violence in the story of the tomato, wild and cultivated. A fear of unknowing, of failure to supply a rational, scientific answer to the arrival of a plant that placidly refused to fit the convenient structures of a millennium of knowledge derived from ancient Greek and Roman texts. A fear that to *unknow* was to *lose knowledge* was to be *judged as ignorant* was to *die*. Unknowing would induce an irrecoverable shame, a shame worse than death, which no status-holding physician or botanist could countenance.

What this fear of unknowing transformed into, ran concomitantly with, was the violent reduction of the rest of the world into a non-European 'other'; mounted on the back of misogyny that destroyed the lives of hundreds of thousands of women and the communities they upheld. Fear of judgement; the unmet need to be seen as knowledgeable, as powerful, as invulnerable, is at the root of a great deal of colonial violence. This is patriarchy at work. Knowing this does not stop the violence itself.

When I look at the Renaissance facts of the tomato, and the colonial masculine Renaissance bodies who ordered and structured the universe as a way of knowing and therefore controlling the world; the twinned suspicion of the tomato as a poisonous nightshade, as a witches' brew; the rise of the misogynistic mass murder of women; what I am thinking is that science perpetually misses a trick when it tries to communicate itself in exclusively rational terms.

While the Eurocentric rational mind was being built between the fifteenth and eighteenth centuries, witch fever burned through Europe like an untamed, unstewarded forest fire. And of course, it wasn't only witches who were persecuted: this was also the time of the wars of religion (is there any other kind of time?). And while antisemitism was hardly invented during the Renaissance, it certainly experienced a groundswell, if you can call it that, along with the Orientalism twinned with colonial exploitation. What comes with scientific projects is a determination to deploy that science to shore up or allay the fears, superstitions, insecurities, anxieties, discomforts of those in power. The fallout of control and a sensed, felt, anguished loss of it is always violence.

The sunny wolf peach, with its plump navel and acidic juices, is the perfect place to hide away all those filthy fears.

* * *

Next year I will not plant too late. Next year I will sow enough seeds for spares in case of slug catastrophe. Next year I will slough off the old skin of the year before, make a bed of cut flowers, build a frame up which to trail pumpkins. Next year. The security of gardening is thinking of the year to come, because of what already has been.

By the light, bright, breezy mornings of early October, blight had shrivelled all the remaining leaves of my tomato plants, and turned sturdy stems brown. We lifted them in a brief half hour between rain clouds, picking what tomatoes we could, leaving the bruised remains as yellow and red pinpricks among clods of earth.

* * *

Roiling guts, tender skin and tomatoes. Dear, queer Geryon, the tomato-eating monster with black lace wings. The tomato-based unguent spread on a witch's broomstick. The clitoral *miltomātl* on its travels around the world.

These things pass through queerness by means of the suspicion they incite. Suspicion of otherness (which in a way is much too easy to frame, given the suspicions that, for example, queerness, bisexuality, genderfluidity and trans-ness all arouse in colonial binaries).

Often a thing becomes suspicious or dangerous not because it is in itself a danger, but because of the failures it reveals in the powers that interrogate it. The tomato's acidic juices and nightshade leaves disclose irrational and misogynistic fears twinned with the emergence of 'rational' science; with it, ultimately, the incendiary fear of otherness that ripped through Europe, burning witches and Jews and Gypsy, Roma and Traveller communities and colonised others that did not, has never truly ended.

The tomato changed the face of the world, just by existing in tandem with the humans who cultivated it. It is a queer, tender, anti-patriarchal wolf peach. As kin-tomato, it embodies culture and cultivation entwined.

As queer skin-tomato, it is one long tender blister, across the soles of my feet.

12

burn (on fire, flow and succession)

The courtyard of the flint cottage is filled with pink hydrangea and spindly yellow sprays of fennel. Its flanks face the sea at an angle, braced as it has been for seven hundred years against the North Atlantic squalls.

This is the furthest I have travelled in over a year: the two hundred or so miles from east to west along England's lowest points. We are so close to the ocean that the cloud line often draws back half a mile before the coast begins, revealing a thin sliver of blue sky and high stratus cloud, on which we sit, like an island of an island, looking out over the white sea. Even when it is cloaked by grey cloud, light glows electric. There are wild orchids in roadside verges, and as we scramble down to the beach, the escarpment churns up honey scent from wide bands of purple heather. Though I am nowhere near so high, nor nearly so remote, their intense colour reminds me of Nan Shepherd's summertime passage through the Cairngorms in *The Living Mountain*, a book which begins with rock and ends with being.

In one of her last lines, Shepherd writes: *The thing to be known grows with the knowing.*

This is the way I know about the Q-trail, the Q-tendrils, the Q-roots that wind through everything, but especially the garden.

What is to be known – the violet cloaks of honey-scent, the rush of the sea at the cliff base, the queerness of gardens – grows with the knowing.

* * *

The succession community is the ecological term for what grows once the forest has burned. Sifting the ashes, finding the germ of new growth, is part of the practice of knowing the Q in garden, gardener, gardening.

Where are my queer gardening allies? Where can I look for them?

Barbara Hepworth, who planted her Trewyn studio garden in St Ives with the South African-born composer Priaulx Rainier in 1949, died in 1972 in a fire caused by her last cigarette smoked in bed, in a mistimed interval as sleeping pills took hold. She and Rainier were 'intimate friends' – and Rainier herself died unexpectedly of a heart attack in 1986, while holidaying in the French Alps with her partner, June Opie.[1]

When Daphne du Maurier, author of the queerest and most intense of fiction about masculine obsession, died in 1989, her ashes were scattered at Kilmarth, the dower house of the Menabilly estate in Cornwall. Menabilly was her lifelong muse, her retreat, her writerly home, and the inspiration for Manderley at the opening of her most famous novel, *Rebecca*.

Josephine Baker, whose performances lit up the sky, and whose gardens at the Château des Milandes in the Dordogne in France she tended with such care, died of a cerebral haemorrhage in 1975, four days after the hugely popular opening of the comeback revue she needed to support her family after losing home, partner and fortune.

These queer gardening artists did not so much go up in flames as fly, coruscating, out of life. I am not romanticising death. But since the 2020s began in viral times and continues in brutality, death is always close. It cleaves to those living outside of the straight, white, cis-gendered norm. So death must remain.

Death is not grief. Grief is what is left behind.

I want to stare into the flames to uphold the dead. To understand what grows after their fuel is spent.

* * *

In a simple white playsuit, Josephine Baker waters her collard greens.

Hard to imagine she – lover of Frida Kahlo and infamous French novelist Colette, the first Black woman to feature in a major film in 1927, the anti-fascist fighter whose revues enabled messages to be passed between members of the Resistance, the only woman to speak at Martin Luther King's Washington March in 1963, she of her rainbow tribe, 12 adopted children from nations across the globe that long predated the clans of Angelina Jolie and Madonna – hard to imagine her *gardening*.

Hard to imagine the young bare-breasted girl with kohl rimmed eyes and provocative banana skirt calmly watering vegetables. But there she is, hair swept back behind her ears, right arm bent high above her shoulders, the fingers

Figure 3 Josephine Baker watering plants. Courtesy of Getty Images.

of her right hand curled around the can's handle as water sprays through the rose. In the uncanny optical illusion that photographs sometimes create, something strange has happened to her left hand – it's half-lost, a shadow pressed against the base of the watering can, fingers gently cupping where spout meets drum. Left forefinger supports. Her eyes are downcast, observing the flow.

Examining her gestures this closely reminds me that, of course, Baker is a dancer. Each movement is carefully controlled and choreographed. See the way she stands, legs planted evenly against the ground. Her upper torso tilts towards her work. Only her slim biceps, and the sinews in her neck, reveal that this activity might be demanding or laboured under the weight of water. The work of a dancer makes physical labour invisible (though of course there are dancers who sought to make that labour visible again – Pina Bausch for one). Josephine's dancer body makes what her body can do, what her body *did* do, look as simple, as unthought and intuitive as turning on a tap, as filling a watering can. Bausch exposed the effort of the effortless. Baker, gardening, renders effort invisible.

It's a beautiful watering can. The big metal drum is large enough to hold – what, a gallon of water, maybe two. That's a good ten kilograms hanging from the handle, plus the weight of the can itself. Even if it were made of the lightest aluminium, it is still a heavy burden.

And yet, Josephine Baker carries the weight of water lightly, with delicacy, strength and grace.

* * *

St Ives is filled with people vacationing along the seafront. Despite the squalls of rain washing in from the sea, there are children in wetsuits dabbling in the waves, scores of people and their dogs dipping in and out of fish and chip shops, stalls selling crabbing kits, arcades and storefronts with inflatables and fridge magnets.

Barbara Hepworth's studio and garden are tucked down a quiet back street. The museum has low vitrines filled with newspaper cuttings of Hepworth's success, and tiny black-and-white photographs of her, her family, her children. Upstairs in the light-filled room that was her gallery sit small casts of the larger works, protected by the high sloping roof and white walls. And then, the garden: lush with Japanese wood anemones; dense planting from which rise her huge bronzes, meeting the earth between land and sea. Her workshop studio and her conservatory are preserved as she left them: blocks of marble stand like a giant game of chequers, waiting to be brought in.

In this small green landscape, I imagine Priaulx Rainier arriving with stacks of seed-grown pots to plant along the stone terraces, while she and Hepworth speak of sound hewn from rock. And there, at the edge of the garden, is the summer house, where Hepworth slept in a narrow single bed with a creamy white counterpane. The summer house has French doors and one small window. Did she – did they – awake one morning, arms and legs entangled, seagulls circling overhead?

White, the colour of dreamless sleep. White wood anemones. Dressed in bone white among white marble, the summer house is an immaculate and tiny palace of death. I do not know what to do with this knowledge. The whole museum feels as if it is waiting for Hepworth's eternal return. We are simply visitors passing through.

Late summer is the time of fire – forest fires, campfires. Fire in the belly. I wonder what I would feel if, instead of the immaculate white counterpane, I saw scorch marks.

* * *

What other weights did Baker carry in her lifetime? I don't know if I am projecting my own sensations, walking to and from the allotment water butts as late afternoon and early evening slowly blends during the late August reprieve of summer. I make space to remember the years that have gone by: the tender plants that in 2020 grew furiously in the summer heat, in 2021 were annihilated by gastropods and fungal disease, in 2022 submitted to drought.

In her white playsuit, Josephine looks calm. She isn't, for once, arresting the camera with her eyes – either to command her regal feminine sexuality in ways that brought her extraordinary degrees of fame, and no small amount of wealth, or to become playfully and erotically double-gendered, to cross her eyes, to play the fool, to dress up as the little sailor, to confuse spectators with her capacity for femme sensuality and boy-like trickster charm.

I'm drawn again to Anne Cvetkovich writing about queer femme and butch sexuality in *An Archive of Feelings*.[2] That what butch sexuality reveals, endorses, takes the deepest pleasure in, is allowing femme sexuality to flourish. To flourish in a way that heterosexual male sexuality fears. The femme whose receptive sexual appetite is so unquenchable that straight desire cannot satisfy it. Rather than considering it a source of dread or disempowerment, though, butch sexuality *encourages* femmes to own this powerful, vast ocean of desire. Not to be estranged from it, but to take it into their bodies and express it as loudly, as vibrantly, as fully as it is possible to do so.

I remember reading Cvetkovich and thinking, *ahhh*. The sheer relief of finding my past self in language, in Cvetkovich's book, is love laid bare. I was once that kind of femme. And yet, maybe there were always elements of the butch. The granite inside. The unfailing loyalty. The need to be held in sympathetic resonance. Both, and.

I wonder how often Josephine Baker's vast sexuality was simply allowed to be. Channelled as it was into popular dance revues, metropolitan French primitivist fetishes in the 1920s and 1930s, and then wartime nursing, anti-fascist espionage and Black civil rights activism. I look at the way she holds the watering can in that photograph, eyes lowered to the plants she is watering and I think: there is sexuality here, too. An oceanic Black femme sexuality built in a contract between earth and flesh, which is not for me, and never was. And yet, I see her, and the tendrils of her desire, and they move me.

Is Josephine Baker's life as a Black queer woman as hidden as her life as a gardener? How did I know she was queer before I knew about her queer relationships? What kinds of rumour vine twists and plies through my consciousness, saying to me, *I know*?

What is that queer feeling where you know, you *know* from a part of you that has no language, that *recognises* before it sees? And sometimes you don't know you know until the truth emerges, and then you think, *ahh. Yes.*

In queer circles this is a widespread joke: the gaydar. The knowing. But what is it, exactly? What is that knowledge that is deeper than words? The thing you knew before you knew? The way I know there is queerness in gardening and there are gardens in queerness. How does this knowing grow?

The thing to be known grows with the knowing.

* * *

On my fortieth birthday I am walking through the New Forest in Hampshire. The day is bright with the sounds of the tree canopy, the dual carriageway that lies beyond it, the construction work not far beyond its borders and, maybe, the distant hum of the power station that, it seems, haunts all flatlands in England – Dunwich in Suffolk. Dungeness.

The New Forest is new to me: I didn't know about its magic. The eerie flatness of the sea plain, the heather and gorse heaths at its borders, the ponds and small rivulets that I am sure are where bog spirits hide. And then, entering the forest, the long, wide lines of sight, where over centuries every branch has been trimmed to pony height by generations of equine teeth. The forest is dense enough to mass trunks of birch, beech and oak for miles; but that five-foot canopy line also reveals what would be obscured in places without the interdependent relationship between forest and horse. As families trundle by on mountain bikes, leaving behind the crunch of grit and the occasional whine of a tired-legged child, walking the forest on foot reveals its textured character. A quiet fattened by the whirr of crickets.

Silence and stillness often bring activity with them. When I meditate, it's only then that I find the curious itch on my nose, or a familiar ache in my hip. These internal cues show me to myself; the always-moving me that scatters like a butterfly pair rising from the brambles.

In the mid-afternoon mugginess, we stop, while my feet ache and my mind dissipates between log piles, bracken and beech. In the calm between the scudding trails of cycling families, a tiny muntjac deer appears a hundred metres or so in front of us, off the forest path. There are benefits to choosing footfall over pedal power. The forest comes to you.

* * *

Brief moments of contentment and singularity amongst plants and soil. Why is the pleasurable cultivation of gardens so often excised from the record? I have many more questions about Josephine Baker's gardening, about this spectacular woman whom the world truly did not deserve.

I am no doubt projecting again – since who knows what the purpose of the publicity shot was. In the Getty images database, amongst the many, many images of Baker in performance, on set, ready to project her dancing body, there are only a few of her gardening. And yet, it's hard to imagine what wouldn't feel like contentment, watering a row of greens in the summer, between espaliered peach trees growing against the wall beyond. Crouched among the heads of Shasta daisies. Lying on a garden bench, legs waving in the air.

Baker didn't just garden in one place: she brought gardening with her. By 1931 she had already lived a life more expansive than most people manage in a lifetime. She cultivated land. She dominated stage and screen. She became an icon as renowned as Greta Garbo and Marlene Dietrich. We don't hear about Garbo and Dietrich gardening. Do we? Or did their ambivalent femme natures include a desire to cultivate too?

The project of queer gardening goes back a long way. Unearthing garden love grows with the knowing.

* * *

The New Forest contains its own scorch marks: heaths where the black silhouettes of tree stumps are slowly overgrown with new saplings. Controlled fire has always been a practice of tending land: it is a form of Indigenous knowledge that is beginning to be recognised in ecological conservation. I see no fire on our visit, but I see what came after.

During and after the pandemic, my horizons witnessed a shift of such magnitude I have no idea whether they will return to what they were before. What constitutes 'far' changed in my vocabulary. In Cornwall and Hampshire, I travelled vast territories. The details of geography and folklore and gardens within the UK's borders felt wide and rich; things I have opened my eyes to because looking elsewhere became charged with the freight of a new geopolitics, and a renewed sense of the ecological damage of air travel. The routes I travelled were between ideas and things, soil and sky, the turbulent now of the twenty-first century and the eras before it whose mistakes we may be condemned to repeat.

In the cool clear chills of December 2019, I visited my friend J in Berwick-upon-Tweed. I was living through the height of the inferno of anxiety and depression and she, with quiet tenderness, helped to reconnect me to what lay beyond the wildfires, even while they were still burning. For a few days, she welcomed me into the rhythms of her household: her children's bathtimes and bedtimes and school runs; a frozen, exhilarating swim in the North Sea; meeting for a drink with an artist friend, talking about writing and art-making in the spaces that life makes between. If I had known this would be one of the last of my travels before the pandemic, would I have appreciated more our short walk across frost-flecked ground between castle walls, to the golden, windswept beach, empty except for us, launching into the sea for a few moments before retreating, skin alive with pins and needles, fingers fumbling with towel and buttons?

Illness shrank my world to the shape of my home, sometimes my bed only. I fought it in the kind of inevitable, flailing way that made no difference at all. It's an easy metaphor to compare depression and anxiety respectively to drowning and burning. Drowning is fighting water, which only claims in the end. And burning only stops when the fuel is spent. Fighting both yielded nothing but more instability. It was surrender – to my bed, my home, and occasionally my garden and allotment – that brought something akin to a state of broken, still-smouldering grace. While my brain was on fire; while I was drowning in the smoke, the world beyond drew smaller and smaller around me. I waited for the flames to lose their fuel. And when my inner landscape had, once again, become blackened frames and scorched earth, I began again.

* * *

Though a garden is a garden, and land is land, the ways it gets talked about shifts through time. Just like sexuality, the language isn't ever the same. In Baker's biography, this is what Maude Russell, another showgirl who worked with Baker at the Standard Theatre, Philadelphia, said:

> Often ... we girls would share a [boarding-house] room because of the cost. ... Well, many of us had been kind of abused by producers, directors, leading men – if they liked girls. ... And the girls needed tenderness, so we had girl friendships, the famous lady lovers, but lesbians weren't well accepted in show business, they were called bull dykers. I guess we were bisexual, is what you would call us today.[3]

Baker's last marriage to Jo Bouillon was, like Vita Sackville-West's marriage to Harold Nicolson, a lavender one. They both had extramarital relationships with women and men respectively, while raising their 12 children in a chateau in the Dordogne.

Image upon image of Baker as a showgirl fills my screen as I search the Getty Archive. Some with her children. A scant few of her in military dress, receiving the Croix d'honneur, or at demonstrations with Martin Luther King Jr. And two photographs of her alone, in her gardens. One smiling to the camera, crouched in a bed of daisies. The other, gaze cast downward, watering her collard greens.

* * *

In lockdown – even before lockdown, in the grip of debilitating illness, I walked and walked the same circular routes each day. It was a matter of survival to learn what does not remain the same, what changes through the seasons, what plants retreat and unfurl over the passage of the seasons, during rare frosts in late winter, warm spells in early spring, torrential rains in early summer. I needed to learn about change to fend off the stasis of living death that called to me all the way through my illness, to work through my fractured identity, and through a pandemic that UK government seemed intent on proliferating into multiple viral variants by opening up early, locking down late and showing a thorough disinterest in the preservation of life.

It was a gradual, painful enlargement to a half-hour radius on foot, running from our allotment plot to the crest of the South London ridge that folds over into central London. From the adjoining parks to the small strip of river where a heron picks insects in its shallows, that was where I walked, audiobooks firmly pressed into my ears to block out the sounds of other people.

I turned to the land to cultivate a contract with the living world. One that did not force me to rely on the thin film of civilisation that seemed so intent on killing. Especially in those early days of lockdown, where the slowness of the UK government's reactions cost so many lives.

And so I walked. I walked, calling upon fellow travellers to walk with me, through the riverbed or along the treetops or in the cloud line that draws back land from sea. I walked in my small urban landscape, alongside those spirits of places with even a touch of nature, a footprint of magic.

* * *

What have I discovered in this process of seeding and cropping, nurturing and propagating my queer garden of queer gardeners? Besides the obvious: that a queer archive barely exists at all and therefore it is essential to make one. To fashion it from the earth, rake it from the ashes, just as So Mayer invites in *A Nazi Word for a Nazi Thing*: 'The history we carry is our history, each of us an anarchive, perhaps of untaken photographs and destroyed films, of work we will never have the opportunity to see or make, but also of the yearning to make that impossible work possible.'[4]

The succession community is the name for the plants that grow after the fire. And for me, another word for anarchive is garden: I can propagate cuttings from other offshoots (Baker the star, Hepworth the artist, du Maurier the writer), reconnect them with images (Josephine in her gardens in 1931, in 1937; Barbara in hers in 1956), draw the lines between them that whisper: Garden. Land. Cultivation. Pleasure. Sexuality. Flame.

Even if I can't see the seed catalogues or the planning schedules of that sexuality, even if what I see in a garden is the sediment of what others have made and designed and nurtured before, I can see the Q in the gardens of the past. And especially in Baker I see the turning back of many kinds of reckonings, constructing her body in this way or that, as an exotic showgirl, spy, mother of 12 children, activist, a precariously young girl fleeing abuse and poverty.

Baker was all of these things, and she also was a gardener. Look at the photograph. Look! There she is, in her garden, making her own bond with earth and life. Does it matter whether she did this once or a thousand times? Not really. Besides, gardens themselves are evidence of time. Gardens do not emerge without tending. Once is not nearly enough. They are the summary of slow work. Patience. Willingness to fail. Willingness to succeed too.

Their existence is testimony to the repetition of labour, skill, desire.

***

Brexit, before illness, before and after COVID, shrank my horizons all over again. Forged in the last 25 years of European politics, the identity that had given me the right to live and work freely beyond Britain's borders, that same identity so precariously balanced on the tides of government sentiment moving back and forth over the last five years, was finally, decisively broken apart on the British shoreline in 2020. Since I'm untied by blood or kin to another country in any citizenship-providing sense of those terms, I am instead boxed in along the sealine of this small, racism-saturated island. The same one I hated when I was ten, and the one I continue to loathe now.

But it's a loathing of the country's self-concept, not of the land. An aversion to national politics, and not the shorelines and forests that have brought me peace when I have needed it most. Until recently, I had built much of my life on running away: keeping a sea channel's distance between me and the world I grew up with. Sometimes I wish I had taken the plunge sooner, kept that ocean between me and home more consistently, more extensively, more powerfully, and built another identity altogether. Except that the North Sea at Berwick and the tidal pools of Cornwall remind me that the land is not to blame for the shadow veil of politics that claims to govern it.

***

Josephine Baker lost her gardens to debt; she and her children were swept up in the arms of Grace Kelly – or rather, Princess

Grace of Monaco, along with Prince Rainier. Grace Kelly, who has a hybrid tea rose named after her.[5] This was after Josephine's queer husband, Jo, had departed to Argentina in 1960; after her home, the Château des Milandes, was repossessed by creditors in 1968. Only seven years before she died in 1975 from a brain haemorrhage, having only just returned to the stage in order to meet her debts.

And Barbara Hepworth died of a five-minute interval turned the wrong way: her sleeping pills kicking in too quickly; her cigarette taking too long to burn out. Her garden remains. As does Baker's.

Gardens are not eternal things; they are passing too. They occupy a strange temporality: seasonal, annual, but also changing, evolving. They do not quite operate in human time, and nor do they operate in the time of trees. According to scholar Jill Casid, gardens possess a curious space-time, between imagination and reality, archival record and present moment.[6] Gardens are sites of colonial dominance and spaces of queer resistance. They sit somewhere in between; symbolic of richness (both material wealth and spiritual abundance) and yet without labour they proliferate and disappear under overgrowth. They carry with them the traces of colonial botany, mass extraction, the Middle Passage, the unending trauma of diaspora, and yet also the space of repose and resistance.

Repose and resistance: this is what I see in the photograph of Josephine Baker in her garden. What I most want to see is Josephine Baker's gardens as she grew them in the 1930s, to be then, *now*. A way of connecting, as my own queer tendrils reach for her. This, of course, is what I will never see. I will only see the traces in the land, even if I make it as far as the high walls of the Villa Beau Chêne, or the public gardens of the Château des Milandes, or the museum that is dedicated to her there.

Baker became a naturalised French citizen in 1937, seeking to escape the pressures of living as a Black woman in mid-twentieth-century America; donning a new identity that enabled her to live a fuller life. In August 2021, she was the first Black woman to enter the Panthéon in Paris – the greatest honour France can bestow upon a dead soul. But her body remains buried in Monaco. What has been interred at the Panthéon is earth. Soil taken from the places where she lived – Missouri and France and Monaco – was placed in a cenotaph; a ceremonially empty tomb.

Terre natale, (trans)literally birth earth, is a concept both amorphous and central to French Enlightenment thinking and colonial identity, symbolic of difference and the violent repression of it, and yet so metaphorically potent that it becomes ritualised at the highest forms of government cultural practice. Baker's birth earth is both French and American, and neither. This both and neither stance is what I have aspired to.

Presuming stability where there was in fact none, for a decade or two I lived halfway between Britain and Europe. When that house of cards toppled, I was at first enraged. A righteous fury at a government who willingly opted for the worst possible solution for its people to fill the pockets of its mates, at government-backed campaigns that broke electoral laws[7] and invited interference in democratic process from abroad through programmes of disinformation fuelled by social media.[8] Indignation at the curtailment of such fragile rights as freedom of movement, which I was only ever afforded because of the unearned privilege of living in a particular time and place. Frustration from a body whose mobility I took for granted despite the physical restrictions of pain. Shame at the dependency my rights always had upon the restrictions of freedom for others.

And yet, the land roots me here. I question this too, whether it had to be *this* land, the small square mile in South East London that I have inhabited more or less constantly over the last decade. Or perhaps I was drawn towards the land I lived in as the inevitable result of those world-contracting internal and external events. In three tightening concentric circles – illness, Brexit, COVID – my world became so small that I had to find a way to live it by becoming small too.

By investing in what is local, a community of sorts, I also found a slackening of self, an opening of my own interior borders to a small, gentle, queer world of urban nature, ecology, garden-making. That I transitioned from cosmopolitan citizen of nowhere to diminutive, land-dwelling earth-creature, at a time when my conditions left me with no other option but to travel the uneven track and newly lain woodchip walkways between the segments of the allotment plot: this is not exactly coincidence, not exactly choice. It was the way of being available to me, and it was the one I embodied too.

Not *terre natale* – birth earth – but *terre vivante.* Living earth.

* * *

I can imagine pulling a luscious leaf from the greens Baker has just watered, tearing a piece and placing it in my mouth. The warm glow in the back of my neck that comes from eating something plucked moments from where it was grown. Baker watering and smiling in her garden just on the outskirts of Paris, or her chateau in the Dordogne, surrounded by babies and children as she wished to be in the 1950s, or alone and at home as she was in the 1930s. (Was she ever alone? There was a photographer to take these images too ...)

I can imagine her as I do these things in my own small allotment.

Of course the story is more complicated than this. The appearance of the maternal idyll that Baker cultivated in the 1950s was also part of a considered publicity drive. The 'Village du monde' that she aimed to create at les Milandes, was specifically developed as a tourist attraction; her children were thus lined up as part of this larger-scale performance of a different facet of Josephine Baker, the global mother figure significantly distanced from the showgirl image she projected in the 1920s and 1930s. But this is why these two photographs of Baker in her garden in the 1930s are so fascinating to me. They are the opposite of glamour: in place of theatrical set constructions and the drapes of haute couture, a young woman stands or sits, surrounded by vegetation. The photographs are clearly taken for some kind of audience, but a fundamentally different one to those engaged in Baker's star persona. This is a different Baker, in a different milieu.

* * *

Hard not to conceive of those years of pandemic and illness as lost, abandoned to waiting and worrying, quietness and boredom, and death.

And cultivation too: stories of gardens in pots, in small front plots, on boats, by the sea, on balconies, a social force of return to cultivation as a way to work through sudden shifts in time, in waiting, in mourning.

Where was I in this? In the process of recovery, binding myself to my allotment and my garden to remember my place in the universe. When the world slowed to my pace, I was not alarmed; merely surprised that such a deceleration could ever happen.

It is not always easy living as a slow person, prone to periods of debilitating chronic illness, in a fast world. I am reminded of writers like Anne McDonald, who first wrote about Crip Time as the slowed, meandering, cyclical time produced in her disabled body: 'I live life in slow motion [...] I am forced to live in your world, a fast, hard one.'[9] Pandemic time brought pace alongside my own version of Crip Time, and I felt ...

Relief. In the midst of the trauma of a global pandemic, I felt relief. I was ashamed too, for being in a position where there was reprieve in the slowing down, with some modicum of security that did not plunge me into precarity. Guilt for not working, and shame at being on prolonged sick leave, that was certainly a part of it.

I reconfigured my relationship to the world in the form of a dicotyledon. I planted seeds. Found joy in germination. I – we (since gardening is never purely solitary) tenderly transferred those tiny plants into bigger pots, protecting them in my newly acquired cold frame. We enriched the soil in the garden and the allotment; scattered wildflower seeds to build a meadow of borage in the raised bed; grew chamomile and cerinthe, wild hyssop and basil. And tomatoes, squashes, courgettes, beans from seeds we found and saved when we took over the allotment, two years ago.

I lived in this world a few square miles in diameter for several years. It was not terrible. I was fortunate. And this is so curious to me, because living through suicidal ideation, day after day, did not feel lucky.

And yet, when the pandemic threw up short boundaries, I could live within this tiny biosphere through the means of small living, which depression, among other things, had taught me how to combine. Fortune and survival from loss.

I do not know if I will ever fully understand this contradiction. That I went into a pandemic wanting to die and came out of it with a tenuous but nonetheless powerful sense of my place in the world, in this small stretch of land, this small village in London, this small garden and allotment. My vision of life shifted and I do not know if my old sense of what I should be – part of a well-educated cosmopolitan elite for whom international travel is as natural as breathing – will return. Where did craving for newness go? I leant into my fear and found gardens in which to cultivate my lacklustre, imperfect, amateur sense of ungendered self. Not luscious sweeps of vista, but small, earth-bound attention.

Messy, generative, and small. So small.

* * *

On a week-long retreat in summer 2019 (how long ago that summer seems) I spent a day alone and in silence, journeying through the land. Respecting the wisdom that solitude carries with it, I walked a few miles of the river Dart in south Devon, around the boundaries of the Sharpham Estate, home to the Sharpham Trust, an organisation dedicated to the practice of mindfulness and nature connection.

During that day of mindful solitude, I brought with me a copy of Alice Oswald's epic poem *Dart*, with no intention at first other than to sit for a while and read. But instead, and because there was no-one there to see, I read to the river, whispering passages over the valley and down towards the tidal waters. I read the Dart back to itself. I did not expect a response, let alone a silent conversation with the sloping woodland and curves of pasture.

I sat by the river shore, a mile or so beyond the edges of Totnes. A dunlin observed me from a branch, as I sat looking over the shallows. When you are silent, animals come: earlier that week, while splitting wood for the boiler, a bluetit watched me and the noisy machine from only a few feet away.

That day, I saw the spirit of my queer friend K. For years she wrote exquisitely, tenderly, about queer bodies, about inclusive queerness, about how queer embodiment dances in and around the moving image. She had incredible bodily intuition from decades of life as a professional athlete, and a mind filled with reflection, determination and gentleness.

By the shores of the Dart, the summer after her death, she was there. As I walked along the line of the river and up the crest of the hill, she followed. There was a long, slow conversation, but I don't think it had words. At intervals, I found her in a tree, or in the sun beating down on my head as I trudged through game-scented meadows. She was in the sounds of the trout by the reed beds, who came up to the river's brown surface as I sat beside its swell. She was in the letter shapes of the estuarine valley as I watched small sailing boats tack towards the sea. She was there when, dodging horseflies, I caught sight of a stone shaped uncannily like a number, embedded in the bridle path scored into the fields. One. The first step.

I saw her, and her queer spirit danced.

epilogue: verbena, knotweed, biopolitics (on queer art ecologies)

Years have passed since I last pruned and dried swatches of lemon verbena on my kitchen countertop. My garden has changed its shape and orientation. The vibrant scarlet stems of dogwood now press close to the rear wall of the flat. There I have planted bluebells for the spring. The hibiscus, whose lilac flowers once dominated its sunny centrepoint, is dead. It suffered from a late frost that damaged its tender shoots, and when I moved it to another, shadier bed, it floundered. Shoots withered; bark fell from its branches. Even when it was centre-stage, its leaves were regularly spotted with fungal growth.

What is lost also returns in different forms. Thoughts and gardens move in spirals.

When I began writing the essay whose tendrils of thought sought out the Q, it was never my intention to write a whole book about queer gardens and gardening. I wrote to tend the queer tenderness of the garden through my fingers. When those queer vines touched the histories of colonial botany, queer gardeners, radical farmers, animated compost, poly-gendered plants, allotment communities, I wrote to scratch the itch I couldn't soothe until I wrote it out of my body. Queer is not who you sleep with, but how you are already part of the world. How you take up (or don't) a place within it. bell hooks understood queer as a way of learning to live. Drawing from her wisdom, the Q in garden makes space for queerness to bloom.

And though plants don't care about gender wars and the erasure of queer history, what I learn from them speaks to me about both. Plants thrive on strangeness, because they have embarked on queer companionship for millions of years, like the tiny beetles who still pollinate the *Magnolia stellata* in my small front garden. I am learning to be strange in the company of other, older strangers.

The commitments I make to plants in how they grow and die give me a home for the twisting, awe-filled strangeness that is the life-force of sexuality. Through them, I learn how strangeness is only estranging because centuries of Euro-Western cultural life that come before me have deemed it to be so.

Fear of strangeness takes many forms. When national newspapers in the UK attack charitable organisations that dare to examine their own suppressed histories – their colonial entanglements, their queer inheritances – what they defend is not tradition but a myth of purity. A belief that to be English, or orderly, or civilised, is to remain untouched by the blood and compost of the past. The same fear animates the reflex to police belonging, to draw tight the borders of what counts as home. Even with a different government in power to the one when I began writing this book, the choreography of containment continues. The rhetoric softens, but the habits of exclusion endure. What lies beneath is not the solidity of earth, but the ephemerality of ideas.

Beyond these islands, other borders remind me what enclosure and the forces of exclusion are capable of. The ongoing genocide in Palestine, where life itself has been reduced to rubble, exposes, again, the recurring question: who is permitted to belong to land, and who is made alien? Who gets to root, and who is uprooted? Who writes the record, and who is written out?

The same logic condemns the weed, the rodent, the queer body, the migrant. Beings deemed to occupy the spaces others have claimed. Each unsettles a hierarchy that imagines itself as natural. Biopower begins with this fear: the need to decide what is life, and what is not life, what lives and what is to be killed, and counts as life worth tending. If you cannot handle your fear, you make it others' responsibility to confine themselves to cultivations of your making. If you cannot tolerate your fear and you have the power to enforce the confinement of others, then you begin a journey of violence that will never conclude. This is biopower: the ordering of life through violence.

The much-maligned French theorist and historian Michel Foucault wrote about this concept, expressed as a claim that 'One had the right to kill those who represented a kind of biological danger to others.'[1] Foucault has been regularly misunderstood by right-wing politicians in the USA and the UK, who position him, without reading him, as a cipher for moral relativism or meaninglessness, blank intellectualism. But what he was most interested in was the conditions of human life. What makes life liveable. What makes life recognisable as life to others.

And although Foucault was talking about human biopower, I cannot help but return to weeds – to the so-called biological dangers claimed on behalf of Japanese knotweed. It is not poisonous or a threat to human life, and peer-reviewed evidence remains inconclusive about its wider ecological risks.[2] What is clearer is that knotweed can halt the mechanisms of capital by rendering a building unmortgageable.

The risk lies not in the plant – not even in its breaking up of foundations – but in capitalism's compulsion to regulate the odds in favour of value accumulation. Rather than understand how knotweed spreads through soil disturbance and redistribution of rhizomes, acknowledge the disruptions caused by nineteenth-century plant-hunting and colonial botany, consider how indigenous ecosystems naturally balance fast-growing species and what we might learn from them; instead, the lending and insurance markets designate knotweed as a biohazard, something to be feared and eradicated.

That logic – a plant represented as a danger to life because it threatens capital – runs throughout Euro-Western agriculture and economics. You might see it in the 1532 Preservation of Grain Act, which ordered England's people to eradicate all animals deemed 'vermin' when famine struck. The problem was never the pine martens or badgers, but centuries of deforestation, loss of land stewardship and the poor living conditions that produced crop failure and disease. As Roger Lovegrove notes in *Silent Fields: The Long Decline of a Nation's Wildlife*, the organised persecution of animals has indelibly marked Britain's landscape and its cultural attitude to pests.[3]

It is a category error to destroy plant and animal life in defence of capital or comfort. Killing creates cascades of consequence with effects we barely comprehend. And yet that error is old. So old.

I'm not saying that knotweed's rapid growth – up to a metre a month – isn't worrying for nearby households. Knotweed is not ecologically harmless: there is growing evidence that knotweed increases soil erosion on riverbanks, for example.[4] But its biohazard status justifies mass destruction through glyphosate-based herbicides that are themselves biocides – killers of *all* life. The plant's tender shoots are edible; its roots long used in Chinese and Japanese medicine as anti-inflammatory and antioxidant. Glyphosate, by contrast, is one of the world's most widely used herbicides – 'the most sprayed and distributed chemical substance in human history',[5] described by the WHO as probably carcinogenic.[6] One of the world's most ubiquitous chemicals, it is now present in everything from medical gauze to menstrual hygiene products.[7] It is genotoxic, harmful to microbial soil biodiversity and saturates food, water and human tissue with consequences still unknown.[8]

Worse: overuse will eventually make it useless. As Stefano Mancuso notes in *The Revolutionary Genius of Plants*, some populations of *Amaranthus palmeri* are now completely resistant. Using the same weapon will not only poison the world; it will no longer work. The means of control (glyphosate) become more hazardous than the supposed hazard (knotweed). By declaring a plant a biological danger, the right – indeed the requirement – to kill it becomes paramount, regardless of the wider repercussions. In the plant world as in the human one, this execution of biopolitics reproduces consequences we can neither measure nor fully understand, now and in the future.

The same question holds for people as for plants: who is allowed to grow?

It is never about destroying just one plant. Each destruction affects the world, marinating in watercourses and soil biota, and in the placental cells of the yet-to-be-born. Biopolitics is about who deserves to live and who deserves to die: the problem is that this cycle of thinking, developed by successive models of post-Enlightenment power, will not think us out of climate crisis, or vulnerable ecosystems, or housing precarity, or regressive binary models of sexuality and gender.

The poet and Black feminist activist Audre Lorde was right in so many ways when she said that the master's tools will never dismantle the master's house.[9] As Dennis Martinez says, 'The framing of solutions to sustainability problems involves the very economic forces and belief systems that have caused the problems in the first place.'[10] Sustainability is only the answer, if the question is about maintaining the status quo. As Leanne Betasamosake Simpson says, 'the cultural and the political are joined and inseparable, and they are both generated through place-based practices – practices that require land.'[11] An intimate, decolonised, kincentric relationship to land is a model of ecological cohabitation that places upon all of us a demand. Stop thinking about the land as instrumental. Stop ignoring the land. And yet: how to unthink European colonialism's instrumentalisation of land, ecosystems and sexuality, when it saturates every aspect of British culture? How to learn to listen to the wisdom that comes from elsewhere?

Home is an important place – the most important one we will ever have. Threats and disruptions to that home, including the incursions of tree roots into failing urban infrastructures like London's Victorian sewerage systems, or the rapidity of Japanese knotweed growth and its capacity to undermine foundations and riverbanks alike, are alarming. Loss of house is a terrifying thing: loss of home and land still more so. The freedom to stay in one place or to move is a fundamental human right – and yet this right also carries with it the responsibility to care: for the immediate environment, in community with the small world you tend. Being unable to tend and care is a brutal severance from the world that upholds you, a disconnection from land that is the doubled arrow of suffering for people who are dispossessed or unhoused, whose migration has been forced by colonisation, war, violence and economic instability, or who are incarcerated.

If biopolitics defines who must die, abolitionist gardens imagine who might live together – and how. The US-based artist jackie sumell has been making gardens in her practice for over a decade. The Solitary Gardens project (https://solitarygardens.org) arose through her lengthy conversations with US prison inmates in solitary confinement, the first of whom was Herbert Wallace, a wrongly convicted former Black Panther activist who spent more than 40 years in solitary confinement, and who died from liver cancer three days after his release in 2013. As sumell and Wallace corresponded by letter, they built visions of Wallace's dream home, which became the collaborative art project *The House That Herman Built* (formerly *Herman's House*). Wallace dreamed most of gardens, beyond the borders of his cell, around his imagined house. Three squares of gardens filled with flowers.

This set the seed for the Solitary Gardens, a way of honouring Wallace's memory but also of making visible one of the most hidden populations in the US – the estimated 80,000–100,000 people incarcerated in solitary confinement, of whom the overwhelming majority are Black and/or people of colour. From 2019 onward, through letter correspondence with Tim James Young on Death Row at San Quentin State Prison in southern California, sumell built a prototype of Young's imaginary garden, guided by his drawings and writings. Young was kept in a human-sized cage for upwards of 22 hours a day, which during the pandemic increased to 'quarantine' 24 hours a day, with abysmally poor access to PPE or adequate healthcare. But his vision of freedom is one that curls like vines through the cracks in the walls of his six-by-nine-foot prison cell. The cell-garden envisioned by Young, with an unfettered ocean view, protected by the tall waving stalks of sugar cane, with plantings of chard and kale, lima beans, potatoes and pumpkin, became the first solitary garden, co-designed and implemented by sumell and a team of interns at the Institute of Arts and Sciences at the University of California Santa Cruz.

As Young writes in his letters published alongside the project, 'I have always made the connection that there is a direct line from slavery to incarceration. I have always made the connection that prison and mass incarceration are just forms of modern-day slavery.'[12] In lines of connection winding through major cities in the US, from New Orleans to Philadelphia, Houston to New York, the solitary gardens have grown, becoming a series of collaborative, participatory art projects between volunteers and host organisations, and those incarcerated in solitary confinement. Each time a connection is made, a conceptual one is forged too, spreading the understanding of slavery's implicit and explicit role in the construction of long-term imprisonment.

Each garden has as its blueprint the standardised architecture of the six-by-nine-foot cell used for solitary incarceration in US prisons. The sculptural forms of the bed, sink and toilet are installed using fibreglass frames and a form of cob cement that sumell describes as *revolutionary mortar*: materials derived from the waste products of the cotton, sugarcane, tobacco and indigo industries (the key crops historically produced from chattel slavery), tamped down collectively by volunteer communities. This slow, collective process also creates the slowed time and space of collaborative, slowed conversation; for the side-by-side exchanges about racial injustice, health and repair that those working in community-based arts recognise as the spaces of healing. Without the didactic confrontation of lecturing, learning flourishes. Once the immovable architectures of the solitary garden are built through this slow, manual labour, what little floor space that remains is turned over to planting – vegetables, herbs, shrubs and flowers, directed and guided by letters from the incarcerated, and grown and tended by volunteers.

The gardens build land-tending connections between those most removed from soil and earth and tending, confined and alone, and communities who collectively take on the responsibility for realising the solitary gardeners' wishes. Each garden is a collaborative, temporary structure, supported by a network of people who with each growing season develop land-based, organic models of transformative justice. The gardens are not just a site to discuss abolitionism without didacticism; they nurture abolitionist practices of cultivation that serve and depend on all the communities they touch. In opposition to the racist structures of incarceration and the torture of solitary confinement the gardens make community, cultivation, care. Each garden remakes home as something shared, not owned.

How can I show you the Q in the Solitary Gardens project?

It's more of a Nan Shepherd kind of a knowing. A *thing to be known that grows with the knowing*. The struggle to show how cultivation was never owned solely by structures of white colonial heterosexuality, despite its attempts since at least the emergence of European empire to master and dominate. How cultivation bears the scars of chattel slavery as much as European pillaging of the world's resources. How the desire to tend and cultivate transcends the courtyards of English manor houses or the wealth of British aristocracy. How strangeness is not unnatural, how man-made structures create the walls that make others estranged and how, with perseverance, life finds a way through. Nature is far from simple and almost never binary. All the while the Q speaks to a need to breathe, to grow, to look out over an ocean view, as Timothy Young describes in his very first letter to sumell at the start of the Solitary Gardens project. Land-tending, love of land, is part of the Q's sprawling vines. And the Q of Garden is marked by the histories and exclusions of sexuality and race. *Both, and.*

The Q is a call to build relationships between you and the land you live on, the earth you might aspire to live with; to do it even if all you have is a single pot of soil. Because once you begin to build relationships with a plant, they will show you how limited, how laughable it is for you and them to ever have been constructed as non-entwined beings.

I wrote this book in response to a boundary call. But what emerged was a call to a community – to many small communities of people with queer feeling, who live in relationship to land. People who want to rebuild that bond. I imagined this book being passed between hands, kept in allotment sheds, shared in seed libraries and book libraries, read at gatherings on the days that mark the changing of the year, online or offline, in parks or community gardens, on balconies or in living spaces with just one small, beloved houseplant.

Much more than an identity or a sexual orientation, queerness is a kinship system. I see this book alongside the many queer collectives already doing the precious healing work of ecologising and botanising, composting and grieving. The Hildegard von Bingen Society for Gardening Companions, developed by performance artists Sophie Seita and Naomi Woo as a collective of queer gardeners connected to the mystic arts of twelfth-century mystic and visionary Hildegard von Bingen. Decolonising Botany, established by artist-duo Breakwater (Taey Iohe and Youngsook Choi), a collective of artists and researchers focusing on the relationship between colonising systems of knowledge production and nature, science, ecology and migration. Queer Ecologies, the collective of Ama Josephine Budge, Hari Byles and Linden Catherine McMahon, working in Tower Hamlets Cemetery Park from 2022 to 2023. Queer Botany, the project run by Sixto-Juan Zavala with Lili K Bright that affirms the relationships between queerness and nature. Queer Nature, an organisation based in Washington State in the USA, which runs place-based environmental training and skillshares, primarily for the LGBTQIA* community. US artists and scholars Annie Sprinkle and Beth Stephens' long-term project and life-paths as ecosexuals. Environmental humanist Catriona Sandilands, credited with originally coining the term queer ecology back in 1994. The Institute of Queer Ecology in Miami, Florida, USA.

Home, like queerness, multiplies; it refuses singular soil. These are just a few of the organisations and people whose inspiration, kinship or contact have sustained me over the last few years. There are many more: queer ecologies have a pulse and energy that resonate globally. There are no doubt many more who I have not yet met. I am still observing the queerness of nature; learning from the many communities whose approach to the natural world encompasses a rainbow spectrum of queer, decolonising land love.

This book is a call to them too; a whisper that says, *hello. We are here.*

How many people answered that call to connect with land when successive lockdowns forced them to live small, hyperlocal lives? A few years ago on an early September evening, as summer drifted gently into autumn, I walked along Piccadilly in London and I saw window-fronts installed with small trees and strips of wheat, each individually set in place to create a simulacrum of 'nature' as London's design and fashion houses deem it to be. Nature was briefly in fashion again, but only because fashion had responded to the call that came first from people, and the plants in their care, in their too-small, barely affordable homes.

The Q in Garden is a *both, and* situation. It is a collaborative labour of tracing and imagining, working with soil and body, and memory, and the fine-tuned intuitions of craft and care and cultivation. It is a gentle, radical project of transformative justice. The world as it has been constructed through centuries of whiteness that are also centuries of straightness and binary gender, colonial capital and botanical-biological orderings of knowledge; this world is a dense loam to shift. And peeling back just one corner of that mantle is heavy work. So much heavier than the clay soils of London where I dig or, as I learn more about no-dig methods and soil preservation, *don't* dig my allotment and garden.

It is also small, skilled, playful work, allowing the tendrils of the tender Q to grow, stretch, find sunlight and pleasure between the cracks of a system that it was never meant to survive. Permitting my own tender shoots to entwine with other human, animal, plant beings, to whisper the Q that was always there in the garden, the yard, the walled *pairidaēza*, is pleasurable and joyful, in the midst of chaos and pain on a global and interpersonal level.

The Q in sumell's Solitary Gardens project, in Sharon Lockhart's *Double Tide*, in Zheng Bo's fern-loving sexualities, in Derek Jarman's cinematic gardens, in Octavia Butler's Earthseed trilogy. In the mind-your-own-business flooding the flagstone corners at Sissinghurst, in the knees of the swamp cypress at Leonardslee, in the couch grass roots of my compost pile, in the flowers of the small *Magnolia stellata* in my front garden, in the tomatoes in my allotment, in the wild orchids on the verges of North Cornwall.

The Q where words fall apart and become queer::eco::poetics, after Tamiko Beyer.

The Q in garden is the breath you dare to take
each time you walk barefoot on the earth.

Each time you expose
(breathe in)
your exquisite tenderness
(breathe out)
and your vulnerability
(breathe in)
and your strangeness
(out)
to the strange earth-world
(in)
you cannot fully know.
(out)
And yet, it holds you.

notes

prologue: broken earth

1 bell hooks, 'Are You Still a Slave? Liberating the Black Female Body', Eugene Lang College, Tuesday 6 May 2014, https://www.youtube.com/watch?v=rJkohNROvzs (accessed 13 February 2026).

2 Joan Roughgarden, *Evolution's Rainbow: Diversity, Gender, and Sexuality in Nature and People* (Berkeley, CA: University of California Press, 2013 [2004]), pp. 225–231, and Ross Brooks, 'Darwin's Closet: The Queer Sides of *The Descent of Man* (1871)', *Zoological Journal of the Linnean Society*, 191 (2021), 323–346.

3 Derek Jarman, *Modern Nature* (London: Vintage Books, 1991), p. 3.

4 Data drawn from the Joint National Conservation Committee's analysis: https://sac.jncc.gov.uk/site/UK0013059 (accessed 5 November 2025).

5 For more on the idea of grievable life, see Judith Butler, *Frames of War: When Is Life Grievable?* (London: Verso, 2016).

introduction

1 Olivia Laing, *The Garden Against Time* (London: Picador, 2024); Toni Morrison, *Paradise* (London: Vintage Classics, 2024 [1997]); Jamaica Kincaid, *My Garden (Book)* (New York: Farrar, Straus and Giroux, 2001).

2 Marcus Tullius Cicero, From 'To Varro, in Ad Familiares IX, 4'. Original Latin: *Si hortum in bibliotheca habes, nihil deerit.*

3 Feminist Hebrew Bible scholar Barbara Deutschmann is particularly interested in the cultural significance of interpretations of

the Eden myth and the wider effects of gender oppression that have resulted. See *Creating Gender in the Garden: The Inconstant Partnership of Eve and Adam* (London: T&T Clark, 2022).

4 Sharae Deckard, *Paradise Discourse, Imperialism, and Globalisation: Exploiting Eden* (London: Routledge, 2009).

5 The relationship between imperialism, gender control and landscaping is spelled out in Jill H. Casid's book *Sowing Empire: Landscape and Colonization* (Minneapolis: University of Minnesota Press, 2005).

6 For more on the transmission of knowledge about abortifacients from South America and the West Indies to Europe, see Londa Schiebinger, *Plants and Empire: Colonial Bioprospecting in the Atlantic World* (Cambridge, MA and London: 2004).

7 Roughgarden, *Evolution's Rainbow*.

8 For more on this, see Banu Subramaniam's *Botany of Empire* (Seattle: University of Washington Press, 2024).

9 Stefano Mancuso, *The Revolutionary Genius of Plants* (New York: Atria Books, 2018).

10 Wolf D. Storl, *A Curious History of Vegetables: Aphrodisiacal and Healing Properties, Folk Tales, Garden Tips, and Recipes* (Berkeley, CA: North Atlantic Books, 2016), p. 2.

11 Anna L. Tsing, *The Mushroom at the End of the World: On the Possibility of Life in Capitalist Ruins* (Princeton, NJ: Princeton University Press, 2015), p. 18.

12 Casid, *Sowing Empire*, p. 129.

13 Michael Moon, Eve Kosofsky Sedgwick, Benjamin Gianni and Scott Weir, 'Queers in (Single-Family) Space', *Assemblage*, 24 (1994), 30–37, p. 30, https://doi.org/10.2307/3171189

14 See 'queer (adj.)' and 'queer (v.)' in online etymology dictionary, https://www.etymonline.com/word/queer (accessed 13 February 2026). William Sayer's short article 'The Etymology of Queer' also makes the case for the word's long-standing existence, particularly in association with strange, twisted, misaligned, sloping or oblique positions. William Sayers, 'The Etymology of Queer', *ANQ: A Quarterly Journal of Short Articles, Notes and Reviews*, 18:2 (2005), 17–19, https://doi.org/10.3200/ANQQ.18.2.17-19

15 Combahee River Collective, 'The Combahee River Collective Statement', copyright © 1978 by Zillah Eisenstein, https://americanstudies.yale.edu/sites/default/files/files/Keyword%20Coalition_Readings.pdf (accessed 7 November 2025).

16 K. E. Altieri, R. R. Audh, J. M. Burger, T. G. Bornman, S. Fawcett, C. M. B. Gwinnett, A. O. Osborne and L. C. Woodall, 'The Transport and Fate of Microplastic Fibres in the Antarctic: The

Role of Multiple Global Processes', *Frontiers in Marine Science*, 9 (2022): 1056081, https://doi.org/10.3389/fmars.2022.1056081

17 James Dinneen, 'Ocean Acidification Is Reaching Deeper Waters', *New Scientist*, 24 November 2024, https://www.newscientist.com/article/2458149-ocean-acidification-is-reaching-deeper-waters/ (accessed 9 November 2025).

1 Q is for garden (on heritage, passing and bothness)

1 Kincaid, *My Garden (Book)*.

2 'Lemon Verbena: A Lemon-Scented Herb From South America', *SPICEography*, https://www.spiceography.com/lemon-verbena/ (accessed 13 February 2026); and S. Gattuso, C. M. van Baren, A. Gil, A. Bandoni, G. Ferraro and M. Gattuso, 'Morpho-histological and Quantitative Parameters in the Characterization of Lemon Verbena (Aloysia citriodora palau) from Argentina', *Boletín Latinoamericano y del Caribe de Plantas Medicinales y Aromáticas*, 7:4 (2008), 190–198, p. 191, https://www.redalyc.org/pdf/856/85670402.pdf (accessed 13 February 2026).

3 'The woke National Trust risks trivialising our rich history; It is an act of modern narcissism to treat the past as if it were the present', *Telegraph Online*, 26 October 2020, https://link.gale.com/apps/doc/A639483196/STND?u=rdg&sid=STND&xid=f567e22d (accessed 6 November 2020).

4 Thank you So Mayer for this brilliant image.

5 Some digitised images from the Radev Collection are available via Bridgeman Images: https://www.bridgemanimages.co.uk/en/collections/RADEV-COLLECTION (accessed 13 February 2026).

6 The author Dorothy Parker is attributed with the witticism 'they lived in squares, painted in circles, and loved in triangles.'

7 Elliott Kennerson, 'Everything You Never Wanted to Know About Snail Sex', *KQED*, 14 March 2017, https://www.kqed.org/science/1446777/everything-you-never-wanted-to-know-about-snail-sex (accessed 13 February 2026).

8 Vita Sackville-West, 'The Garden', 1915, The Garden Museum Collections, https://www.gardenmuseum.org.uk/collection/the-garden/ (accessed 3 February 2026).

9 'From the Archive: Vita Sackville-West on Her Garden at Sissinghurst (1950)', *House and Garden*, 30 May 2025, https://www.houseandgarden.co.uk/article/vita-sackville-west-on-sissinghurst-garden (accessed 3 February 2026).

10 'From the Archive: Vita Sackville-West on Her Garden'.

2 kewrious (on queer bodies and transgressive gardening fashion)

1 Derek Jarman (dir.), *The Garden* (1990); Virginia Woolf, *Kew Gardens* (Richmond: Hogarth Press, 1919); Elizabeth Tova Bailey, *The Sound of a Wild Snail, Eating* (Chapel Hill, NC: Algonquin Books, 2010); Patricia Highsmith, 'The Snail Watcher', in *The Snail Watcher and Other Stories* (London: Doubleday, 1970), pp. 1–9.
2 Zheng Bo, *The Garden of Earthly Delights*, ed. Stephanie Rosenthal (Berlin: Silvana Editoriale, 2019), p. 58.
3 Catherine Horwood, *Women and Their Gardens: A History from the Elizabethan Era to Today* (Chicago: Ball, 2010), ebook, 'Swanley Misses', paragraph 4.
4 Fiona Davidson, *An Almost Impossible Thing: The Radical Lives of Britain's Pioneering Women Gardeners* (Beaminster, Dorset: Little Toller, 2023), p. 71.
5 Horwood, *Women and Their Gardens*, 'Swanley Misses', paragraph 15.
6 Laurence Philomene, *Puberty* (Atlanta, GA: Yoffy Press, 2022).
7 John C. Fout. 'Sexual Politics in Wilhelmine Germany: The Male Gender Crisis, Moral Purity, and Homophobia', *Journal of the History of Sexuality*, 2:3, Special Issue, Part 2: 'The State, Society, and the Regulation of Sexuality in Modern Europe' (January 1992), 388–421, p. 398.
8 For more on the Allen-Browns, Ada and Decima, see Davidson, *An Impossible Thing*, pp. 137–153.
9 Horwood, *Women and Their Gardens*, 'Not Ladies in Any Sense of the Word', paragraph 17.
10 Bonny Ling, 'Let's Really Talk About Slavery and Cotton', *The News Lens*, 26 April 2021, https://international.thenewslens.com/article/150156 (accessed 13 February 2026).
11 Alexis Pauline Gumbs, *Undrowned: Black Feminist Lessons from Marine Mammals* (AK Press: 2020), p. 13.

3 arboretum, or the feeling of trees (on genderqueer forests and herb women)

1 Pınar Ateş Sinopoulos-Lloyd, 'Queer Futurism: Denizens of Liminality', 31 December 2017, https://www.queernature.org/queer-futurism-denizens-of-liminality (accessed 13 February 2026). (First published in Youth Passageways' *Confluence Journal*, 2:2.)

2 Glynis Ridley, *The Discovery of Jeanne Baret: A Story of Science, the High Seas, and the First Woman to Circumnavigate the Globe* (New York: Crown, 2010), pp. 13–41.
3 Londa Schiebinger, 'Jeanne Baret: The First Woman to Circumnavigate the Globe', *Endeavour*, 27:1 (March 2003), 22–25, p. 22.
4 Shreya Dasgupta, 'At 2,624 years, a bald cypress is oldest known living tree in eastern North America', *Mongabay*, 16 May 2019, https://news.mongabay.com/2019/05/at-2624-years-a-bald-cypress-is-oldest-known-living-tree-in-eastern-north-america/ (accessed 13 February 2026).
5 Patrick Barkham, 'How Britain's oldest tree became "sexually ambiguous"', *Guardian*, 2 November 2015, https://www.theguardian.com/environment/shortcuts/2015/nov/02/britain-oldest-tree-fortingall-yew-change-sex (accessed 13 February 2026).
6 Schiebinger, 'Jeanne Baret', p. 23.
7 Schiebinger, 'Jeanne Baret', p. 22.
8 Ridley, *The Discovery of Jeanne Baret*, pp. 84–89.
9 Ridley, *The Discovery of Jeanne Baret*, pp. 159–161.
10 Michael Sturma, 'Dressing, Undressing, and Early European Contact in Australia and Tahiti', *Pacific Studies*, 21:3 (September 1998), 87–104, p. 91; and Candace Lin, 'J.B', in exhibition catalogue *Candace Lin: A Hard White Body*, curated by Lotte Arndt and Lucas Morin, *Bétonsalon Centre D'Art et de Recherche*: *BS*, 22 (2017), 12.
11 Ridley, *The Discovery of Jeanne Baret*, p. 189.
12 For more detailed analysis, see for example Vanesa Medina Godoy, '(In)Visible Histories: Postcolonial Histories of Gender and Sexuality through the Lens of South African Visual Activism', *Global Histories*, 7:2 (January 2022), 39–52, http://dx.doi.org/10.17169/GHSJ.2021.475
13 Roughgarden, *Evolution's Rainbow*, p. 45.
14 Rachel Holmes, *The Secret Life of Dr James Barry: Victorian England's Most Eminent Surgeon* (London: Bloomsbury, 2020 [2002]), p. 20.
15 Ursula K. Le Guin, 'Direction of the Road' in *The Wind's Twelve Quarters & The Compass Rose* (London: Gollancz, 2015), p. 253.
16 Brian Hare and Vanessa Woods, *Survival of the Friendliest: Understanding Our Origins and Rediscovering Our Common Humanity* (New York: Random House, 2020).
17 Paul Gilbert, *The Compassionate Mind* (London: Constable, 2010).
18 Peter Wohlleben, *The Hidden Life of Trees: What They Feel, How They Communicate. Discoveries from a Secret World*, trans. by

Jane Billinghurst (Vancouver and Berkeley: Greystone Books, 2016); Suzanne Simard, *Finding the Mother Tree: Discovering the Wisdom of the Forest* (New York: Knopf, 2021).

19 Rebecca Solnit, *Orwell's Roses* (London: Granta, 2021), p. 126; Sascha Pare, 'Pando: The world's largest tree and heaviest living organism', *Live Science*, 4 November 2024, https://www.livescience.com/planet-earth/plants/pando-the-worlds-largest-tree-and-heaviest-living-organism (accessed 13 February 2026); Michael C. Grant, 'The Trembling Giant', *Discover*, 14:10 (1993), 82–90, https://www.discovermagazine.com/planet-earth/the-trembling-giant (accessed 13 February 2026).

20 Eric J. Tepe, Glynis Ridley and Lynn Bohs, 'A New Species of *Solanum* Named for Jeanne Baret, an Overlooked Contributor to the History of Botany', *PhytoKeys* 8 (2012), 37–47, p. 45, https://doi.org/10.3897/phytokeys.8.2101; Schiebinger, 'Jeanne Baret', p. 25.

4 hands in the mud (on labour, gesture and earth connection)

1 Audre Lorde, 'The Master's Tools Will Never Dismantle the Master's House' (1984) in *Sister Outsider: Essays and Speeches* (Berkeley, CA: Crossing Press, 2007), pp. 110–114.

2 Robin Wall Kimmerer, *Braiding Sweetgrass: Indigenous Wisdom, Scientific Knowledge, and the Teachings of Plants* (London: Penguin, 2020), p. 9.

3 Kimmerer, *Braiding Sweetgrass*, p. 209.

4 Richard Dawkins, 'Myths do not belong in science classes: Letter to the Royal Society of New Zealand', 4 December 2021, https://richarddawkins.net/2021/12/myths-do-not-belong-in-science-classes-letter-to-the-royal-society-of-new-zealand/ (accessed 13 February 2026).

5 See, for example, Elinor Cleghorn's book on the histories of gendered and racialised inequality in healthcare and medicine, *Unwell Women: Misdiagnosis and Myth in a Man Made World* (New York: Dutton, 2021), or Stephen Jay Gould's work on the racialisation of intelligence, *The Mismeasure of Man* (New York: WW Norton, 1981).

6 Dawkins was stripped of his 1996 award of 'Humanist of the Year' after his comments disparaging trans and Indigenous communities were made public in 2021. See 'American Humanist Association Board Statement Withdrawing Honor from Richard Dawkins', 19 April 2021, https://americanhumanist.org/news/

american-humanist-association-board-statement-withdrawing-honor-from-richard-dawkins/ (accessed 13 February 2026).
7 Kimmerer, *Braiding Sweetgrass*, p. 213.
8 Kimmerer, *Braiding Sweetgrass*, pp. 214–15.
9 Solnit, *Orwell's Roses*, p. 155.
10 'Soft-shell clams', Maine Sea Grant, University of Maine, https://seagrant.umaine.edu/maine-seafood-guide/soft-shell-clams/ (accessed 13 February 2026).
11 'Clam industry growing as climate change warms Gulf of Maine', *AP News*, 19 December 2021, https://apnews.com/article/climate-environment-and-nature-maine-bangor-3d07401dcb068e27a467fd63d6fb4f66 (accessed 13 February 2026).
12 Stockholm Environment Institute, Climate Analytics and International Institute for Sustainable Development, *The Production Gap Report 2025*, http://productiongap.org/2025report (accessed 8 February 2026).

5 compost (on medium, matter, mutter, mother)

1 Roxanne Harde, '"I got everything in me": *Fraggle Rock*'s Trash Heap, Spirit, Earth, and Connection', *The Lion and the Unicorn*, 35:2 (April 2011), 158–175.
2 Eli Clare, *Exile and Pride: Disability, Queerness, and Liberation* (Durham, NC: Duke University Press, 2015 [1999]), p. 145.
3 Jennifer Frazer, 'Dying trees can send food to neighbors of different species', *Scientific American*, 9 May 2015, https://blogs.scientificamerican.com/artful-amoeba/dying-trees-can-send-food-to-neighbors-of-different-species/ (accessed 13 February 2026).
4 Sarah Franklin, 'Staying with the Manifesto: An Interview with Donna Haraway', *Theory, Culture & Society*, 34:4 (2017), 49–63, p. 52, https://doi.org/10.1177/0263276417693290 (accessed 9 February 2026).
5 Annie Sprinkle and Beth Stephens with Jennie Klein, *Assuming the Ecosexual Position: The Earth as Lover* (Minneapolis: University of Minnesota Press, 2021), pp. 6–10.
6 Sprinkle and Stephens, *Assuming the Ecosexual Position*, p. 91.
7 Sprinkle and Stephens, *Assuming the Ecosexual Position*, p. 2.
8 Herman Melville, 'Bartleby the Scrivener: A Story of Wall Street', from *The Piazza Tales*, https://moglen.law.columbia.edu/LCS/bartleby.pdf (accessed 9 February 2026).
9 Sprinkle and Stephens, *Assuming the Ecosexual Position*, p. 25.

10 Sprinkle and Stephens, *Assuming the Ecosexual Position*, p. 142.
11 Kim TallBear, 'What's in ecosexuality for an indigenous scholar of "nature"?', *Indigenous Science Technology Society*, https://indigenoussts.com/whats-in-ecosexuality-for-an-indigenous-scholar-of-nature (accessed 7 January 2022).

6 roots and radicals (on recovery dreams, radical politics and rebuilding)

1 A. Colman, 'radical', *A Dictionary of Psychology* (Oxford University Press, 2008), https://www.oxfordreference.com/view/10.1093/acref/9780199534067.001.0001/acref-9780199534067-e-6944 (accessed 6 January 2022).
2 M. Allaby, 'radical', *A Dictionary of Plant Sciences* (Oxford University Press, 2019), https://www.oxfordreference.com/view/10.1093/acref/9780198833338.001.0001/acref-9780198833338-e-5718 (accessed 6 January 2022).
3 *Online Etymology Dictionary*, https://www.etymonline.com/word/*wrād- (accessed 13 February 2026).
4 Kimmerer, *Braiding Sweetgrass*, p. 56.
5 Rose Collis, *Portraits to the Wall: Historic Lesbian Lives Unveiled* (London: Bloomsbury, 1999), pp. 140–143.
6 Michael Bloch, *Closet Queens: Some 20th Century British Politicians* (London: Little Brown, 2015).
7 Eve B. Balfour, *The Living Soil* (London: Faber and Faber, 1943), p. 10.
8 Balfour, *The Living Soil*, p. 10.
9 Balfour, *The Living Soil*, p. 181.
10 Peter Kropotkin, *Fields, Factories, and Workshops Tomorrow or Industry Combined with Agriculture and Brain Work with Manual Work* (London, Edinburgh, Dublin and New York: Thomas Nelson & Sons, 1912), available via The Anarchist Library, https://theanarchistlibrary.org/library/petr-kropotkin-fields-factories-and-workshops-or-industry-combined-with-agriculture-and-brain-w (accessed 9 February 2026).
11 Peter Kropotkin, *Mutual Aid: A Factor of Evolution* (New York: McClure, Phillips & Co., 1902), available via The Anarchist Library, https://theanarchistlibrary.org/library/petr-kropotkin-mutual-aid-a-factor-of-evolution (accessed 9 February 2026).
12 Balfour, *The Living Soil*, p. 185.
13 Angela Y. Davis. 'Radical Perspectives on the Empowerment of Afro-American Women: Lessons for the 1980s', *Harvard Educational Review*, 58:3 (August 1988), 348–353, p. 353.

14 'Statement by the United Nations Special Rapporteur on the rights to freedom of peaceful assembly and of association at the conclusion of his visit to the United Kingdom', 21 April 2016, https://www.ohchr.org/EN/NewsEvents/Pages/DisplayNews.aspx?NewsID=19854&LangID=E (accessed 13 February 2026).

15 Gurminder K. Bhambra, 'First, citizens were turned into immigrants. Now we're being stripped of political rights', *Novara Media*, 15 December 2021, https://novaramedia.com/2021/12/15/first-citizens-were-turned-into-immigrants-now-were-being-stripped-of-political-rights/ (accessed 13 February 2026).

16 Nisha Kapoor, 'Citizenship deprivation at the nexus of race, gender and geopolitics', *Verso Books*, 22 February 2019, https://www.versobooks.com/blogs/4250-citizenship-deprivation-at-the-nexus-of-race-gender-and-geopolitics (accessed 13 February 2026).

7 seed/lings in space (on seeds, science fiction, speculation)

1 Kimmerer, *Braiding Sweetgrass*, p. 49.

2 adrienne maree brown, *Emergent Strategy: Shaping Change, Changing Worlds* (Edinburgh: AK Press, 2017), p. 23.

3 Octavia E. Butler, *Parable of the Sower* (New York: Open Road Integrated Media, 2012).

4 brown, *Emergent Strategy*, p. 26.

5 Zakiya McKenzie, *Testimonies on the History of Jamaica Vol. 1* (London: Rough Trade Books/Garden Museum, 2021), n.p.

8 magnolia, fern (on prehistory, polygenderedness, erotics and shame)

1 Juan M. Losada, '*Magnolia virginiana*: Ephemeral Courting for Millions of Years', *Arnoldia*, 71:3 (2014), 19–27.

2 Dave Goulson, *A Sting in the Tale: My Adventures with Bumblebees* (London: Jonathan Cape, 2013).

3 Ashleigh Milner, 'An introduction to understanding honeybees, their origins, evolution and diversity, *Bee Improvement and Bee Breeders Association (BIBBA)*, https://bibba.com/honeybee-origins/ (accessed 17 July 2022).

4 Roughgarden, *Evolution's Rainbow*, p. 45.

5 Roughgarden, *Evolution's Rainbow*, p. 49.

6 Evelleen Richards, *Darwin and the Making of Sexual Difference* (Chicago: University of Chicago Press, 2017), p. xviii.

7 Brooks, 'Darwin's Closet', pp. 327–329.

8 Bruce Bagemihl, *Biological Exuberance: Animal Homosexuality and Natural Diversity* (New York: St Martin's Press, 1999).

9 So Mayer, *A Nazi Word for a Nazi Thing* (London: Peninsula, 2021), p. 31.

10 Hannah Shewan Stevens, 'Were do not resuscitate orders illegally placed on disabled people?', *Each Other*, 22 June 2021, https://eachother.org.uk/were-do-not-resuscitate-orders-illegally-placed-on-disabled-people/ (accessed 13 February 2026). See also Care Quality Commission, 'Review of Do Not Attempt Cardiopulmonary Resuscitation decisions during the COVID-19 pandemic' Interim Report, November 2020, p. 2, https://www.cqc.org.uk/sites/default/files/20201204%20DNACPR%20Interim%20Report%20-%20FINAL.pdf (accessed 13 February 2026); and Care Quality Commission, 'Review of Do Not Attempt Cardiopulmonary Resuscitation decisions during the coronavirus (COVID-19) pandemic: our methodology', 29 January 2024, https://www.cqc.org.uk/publications/themes-care/review-dnacpr-decisions-during-coronavirus-pandemic-methodology (accessed 13 February 2026).

11 Green Deane, 'Sweetbay Magnolia', *Eat the Weeds, and Other Things Too*, http://www.eattheweeds.com/magnolia-viginiana-how-sweet-it-is-2/ (accessed 13 February 2026).

12 Young-Jung Lee, Yoot Mo Lee, Chong-Kil Lee, Jae Kyung Jung, Sang Bae Han and Jin Tae Hong, 'Therapeutic Applications of Compounds in the Magnolia Family', *Pharmacology & Therapeutics*, 130:2 (2011), 157–176, https://doi.org/10.1016/j.pharmthera.2011.01.010

13 Johann Wolfgang von Goethe, *Goethes Sämmtliche Werke. Vollständige Ausgabe in zehn Bänden. Mit Einleitungen von Karl Goedeke, Neunter Band* (9th volume) (Stuttgart: Verlag der J. G. Cotta'schen Buchhandlung, 1875). p. 197. Digital edition available via https://archive.org/stream/goethessmmtlich99goetgoog/goethessmmtlich99goetgoog_djvu.txt (accessed 11 February 2026). Author's translation.

14 For more on Merian's relationship to Labadism, see Kim Todd, *Chrysalis: Maria Sibylla Merian and the Secrets of Metamorphosis* (London and New York: I. B. Tauris, 2007).

15 Kerry Lotzof, 'Maria Sibylla Merian: metamorphosis unmasked by art and science', *Natural History Museum*, https://www.nhm.ac.uk/discover/maria-sibylla-merian-metamorphosis-art-and-science.html (accessed 13 February 2026).

16 Londa Schiebinger, 'Exotic Abortifacients and Lost Knowledge', *The Lancet*, 371:9614 (2008), 718–719, https://doi.org/10.1016/S0140-6736(08)60330-X

17 Beth Chatto and Christopher Lloyd, *Dear Friend and Gardener: Letters on Life and Gardening* (London: Frances Lincoln, 1998), p. 167.
18 Vita Sackville West, *In Your Garden* (London: Frances Lincoln, 2004 [1951]), pp. 93–94.
19 Angela Y. Davis, *Blues Legacies and Black Feminism: Gertrude 'Ma' Rainey, Bessie Smith, and Billie Holiday* (New York: Vintage, 1998), p. 183.
20 Davis, *Blues Legacies and Black Feminism*, p. 183.
21 Davis, *Blues Legacies and Black Feminism*, p. 192.
22 Ruth Hayden, *Mrs Delany, Her Life and Her Flowers* (New York: New Amsterdam Books, 1980), p. 50, cited in Lisa L. Moore, 'Queer Gardens: Mary Delany's Flowers and Friendships', *Eighteenth-Century Studies*, 39:1 (Fall, 2005), 49–70, p. 52.
23 Moore, 'Mary Delany's Flowers', pp. 58–59.
24 Moore, 'Mary Delany's Flowers', p. 65.
25 Moore, 'Mary Delany's Flowers', pp. 63–64.
26 Zimra Chickering, 'Georgia O'Keeffe: the ultraliberal queer "security risk"', *The Emory Wheel*, 30 June 2021, https://emorywheel.com/georgia-okeeffe-the-ultraliberal-queer-security-risk-lets-be-perfectly-queer/ (accessed 13 February 2026).
27 M. Zastrow, 'Ferns Communicate to Decide Their Sexes', *Nature* (2014), https://doi.org/10.1038/nature.2014.16214; N. M. Atallah and J. A. Banks, 'Reproduction and the Pheromonal Regulation of Sex Type in Fern Gametophytes', *Frontiers in Plant Science*, 6 (2015), https://doi.org/10.3389/fpls.2015.00100
28 K. Gupta, S. Srivastava, G. Saxena et al. 'Evaluation of Phytoremediation Potential of Pteris vittata L. on Arsenic Contaminated Soil Using Allium cepa Bioassay', *Bulletin of Environmental Contamination and Toxicology* (2021), https://doi.org/10.1007/s00128-021-03291-8
29 Y. Foucault, T. Lévêque, T. Xiong, E. Schreck, A. Austruy, M. Shahid and C. Dumat, 'Green Manure Plants for Remediation of Soils Polluted by Metals and Metalloids: Ecotoxicity and Human Bioavailability Assessment', *Chemosphere*, 93 (2013), 1430–1435, https://doi.org/10.1016/j.chemosphere.2013.07.040
30 Karl Leif Bates, 'Nineteen species of fern named for Lady Gaga', *Duke Today*, 19 October 2012, https://today.duke.edu/2012/10/gagafern (accessed 13 February 2026).
31 David Whyte, *Crossing the Unknown Sea: Work and the Shaping of Identity* (London: Michael Joseph, 2001), p. 149. I am indebted to Jackee Holder for sharing this quotation with me at one of her early morning writing groups.

9 hungry gap (on gardening, mortality and seasonal dearth)

1 Kincaid, *My Garden (Book)*, p. 216.
2 Kimmerer, *Braiding Sweetgrass*, pp. 303–309.
3 Ann Cvetkovich, *An Archive of Feelings: Trauma, Sexuality, and Lesbian Public Cultures* (Durham, NC: Duke University Press), pp. 57–60.
4 adrienne maree brown, *Pleasure Activism: The Politics of Feeling Good* (Chico, CA and Edinburgh: AK Press, 2019).
5 Radclyffe Hall, *The Well of Loneliness* (London: Penguin Classics, 2015).
6 Anoosh Chakelian, 'Free school meal scandal: Why the government is failing to feed people during the pandemic', *New Statesman*, 12 January 2021, https://www.newstatesman.com/politics/health/2021/01/free-school-meal-scandal-why-government-failing-feed-people-during-pandemic (accessed 13 February 2026); Lucy Campbell and Sally Weare, 'Rashford: something "going wrong" with free school meal deliveries', *Guardian*, 12 January 2021, https://www.theguardian.com/education/2021/jan/12/not-good-enough-marcus-rashford-condemns-free-school-meal-packages (accessed 13 February 2026).
7 Anoosh Chakelian, 'Revealed: the £208m food box rip-off: our exclusive analysis shows the government paid private contractors almost double the retail value for food parcels containing items that were barely edible', *New Statesman*, 16 October 2020, https://www.newstatesman.com/world/uk/2020/10/208m-food-box-rip-off-private-outsource-government-contract-covid-coronavirus (accessed 13 February 2026); Jack Monroe, 'No-one who has experienced food poverty would stand by and let it spread like this', *Guardian*, 11 September 2020, https://www.theguardian.com/commentisfree/2020/sep/11/no-one-food-poverty-let-it-spread-brexit-pandemic-coronavirus (accessed 13 February 2026).
8 So Mayer, *A Nazi Word for a Nazi Thing*.
9 See Jill Liddington, *Nature's Domain: Anne Lister and the Landscape of Desire* (Hebden Bridge, West Yorkshire: Pennine Pens, 2003).
10 For more on the possibilities of a trans reading of Lister's diaries, see Charley Matthews, '"I feel the mind enlarging itself": Anne Lister's Gendered Reading Practices', *Journal of Lesbian Studies*, 26:4 (2022), 367–381, https://doi.org/10.1080/10894160.2022.2125142
11 Olivia Laing, 'Introduction' in Derek Jarman, *Modern Nature* (London: Vintage, 2018 [1991]), p. viii.

12 Jamaica Kincaid, *Lucy* (London: Picador, 2022 [1990]).
13 For more on Kincaid, Wordsworth and colonial resistance, see Jana Evans Braziel, 'Daffodils, Rhizomes, Migrations: Narrative Coming of Age in the Diasporic Writings of Edwidge Danticat and Jamaica Kincaid', *Meridians*, 3:2 (2003), 110–131.
14 Jamaica Kincaid, 'Garden inspired by William Wordsworth's dances with daffodils', *Architectural Digest*, 31 March 2007, https://www.architecturaldigest.com/story/gardens-article (accessed 13 February 2026).
15 Jarman, *Modern Nature*, p. 17.
16 Jarman, *Modern Nature*, p. 24.
17 Jarman, *Modern Nature*, p. 25.
18 Gertrude Jekyll, *Children and Gardens* (Woodbridge: Antique Collectors' Club, 1982 [1908]), p. 134.
19 Derek Jarman and Howard Sooley, *Derek Jarman's Garden* (London: Thames and Hudson, 2012 [1995]), p. 34.
20 Jarman and Sooley, *Derek Jarman's Garden*, p. 20.
21 G. Jekyll, *Colour Schemes for the Flower Garden*, 6th edn (London: Country Life, 1925), cited in Richard Bisgrove, 'The Colour of Creation: Gertrude Jekyll and the Art of Flowers', *Journal of Experimental Botany*, 64:18 (2013), 5783–5789, https://doi.org/10.1093/jxb/erm070
22 Joan Edwards, *The Fourth of Joan Edwards' Small Books on the History of Embroidery: Gertrude Jekyll, Embroiderer, Gardener and Craftsman* (Dorking: Bayford Books, 1981), p. 2.
23 See Janis Londraville, *On Poetry, Painting, and Politics: The Letters of May Morris and John Quinn* (London: Associated University Presses, 1997), p. 27. Waugh's derogatory comment is widely shared as a crucial detail about Lobb, which ignores its misogynistic intent and internalised homophobia.
24 Cheryl Capaldo Traylor, 'Bloomsbury and the Natural World' (MA thesis, Duke University, 2014), https://dukespace.lib.duke.edu/dspace/bitstream/handle/10161/9233/Capaldo%20Traylor,%20Cheryl%20Final%20Project-4%20(2).pdf (accessed 28 February 2022).

10 love in the mist (on wildflower meadows, queer kinship and grief)

1 Jumana Manna, 'Wild Relatives, 2018, The Water-Arm Series, 2019', in Stephanie Rosenthal (ed.), *Garden of Earthly Delights* (Berlin: Silvana Editoriale/Gropius Bau, 2019), p. 108.
2 Dennis Martinez, 'Redefining Sustainability through Kincentric Ecology: Reclaiming Indigenous Lands, Knowledge, and Ethics'

in Melissa K. Nelson and Dan Shilling (eds), *Traditional Ecological Knowledge: Learning from Indigenous Practices for Environmental Sustainability* (Cambridge: Cambridge University Press, 2018), pp. 139–174, p. 157.

3 Sasha Williams and Ian Law, 'Legitimising Racism: An Exploration of the Challenges Posed by the Use of Indigeneity Discourses by the Far Right', *Sociological Research Online*, 17:2 (2012), 1–12.

4 Caroline Elkins' book *Legacy of Violence: A History of the British Empire* (London: Bodley Head, 2022) discusses exactly this.

5 Timothy Morton, 'Guest Column: Queer Ecology', *PMLA*, 125:2 (March 2010), 273–282, p. 277.

6 Timothy Morton, *All Art Is Ecological* (London and New York: Penguin, 2018).

7 Virginia Woolf, *A Room of One's Own* (London: Penguin, 2004), p. 19.

8 Dickinson famously wrote 'Tell all the truth but tell it slant —' in poem 1263. From Helen Vendler (ed.), *Dickinson: Selected Poems and Commentaries* (Cambridge, MA: The Belknap Press of Harvard University Press, 2010), p. 431.

9 Christopher Hope, 'National Trust chief resigns amid "woke" revolt', *Daily Telegraph*, 26 May 2021, p. 1, link.gale.com/apps/doc/A663028354/STND?u=rdg&sid=bookmark-STND&xid=a578261b (accessed 13 June 2023); Christopher Hope, Robert Mendick and Craig Simpson, 'Fears National Trust could get more "woke" as head departs', *Daily Telegraph*, 27 May 2021, p. 12, link.gale.com/apps/doc/A663194607/STND?u=rdg&sid=bookmark-STND&xid=7961dedb (accessed 13 June 2023); Hayley Dixon, 'National Trust criticised over Pride plans; volunteers encouraged to wear rainbow face paint and glitter, amid growing concerns over woke agenda', *Daily Telegraph*, 15 June 2021, p. 11, link.gale.com/apps/doc/A665235442/STND?u=rdg&sid=bookmark-STND&xid=8b53c561 (accessed 13 June 2023); Hayley Dixon, 'National Trust to vote on whether Pride is a "divisive waste" of money', *Daily Telegraph*, 6 September 2022, p. 10, link.gale.com/apps/doc/A716231437/STND?u=rdg&sid=bookmark-STND&xid=c40d5153 (accessed 13 June 2023); Hayley Dixon, 'Vote on Pride ban for National Trust in England', *Daily Telegraph*, 6 September 2022, p. 10, link.gale.com/apps/doc/A716231603/STND?u=rdg&sid=bookmark-STND&xid=8047e5af (accessed 13 June 2023); Simon Heffer, '"The National Trust is skewing history so it is anti-British". Zewditu Gebreyohanes The 23-year-old leading the campaign against the politicisation of the conservation

charity talks to Simon Heffer about wokery and dumbing down', *Daily Telegraph*, 15 October 2022, p. 25, link.gale.com/apps/doc/A722478301/STND?u=rdg&sid=bookmark-STND&xid=5fodf8eo (accessed 13 June 2023).

10 Lauren Berlant, *Cruel Optimism* (Durham, NC: Duke University Press, 2011), p. 53.

11 Lauren Berlant and Kathleen Stewart, *The Hundreds* (Durham, NC: Duke University Press, 2019), p. 95.

12 Tamiko Beyer, 'Notes towards a queer::eco::poetics', https://doveglionlit.wordpress.com/2010/11/29/tamiko-beyer-notes-towards-a-queerecopoetics/ (accessed 13 February 2026).

11 tomato, skin, kin (on wolf peaches, persecution and wild edibles)

1 David Gentilcore, *Pomodoro! A History of the Tomato in Italy* (New York: Columbia University Press, 2010).

2 Judith Butler, 'Why is the idea of "gender" provoking backlash the world over?', *Guardian*, 23 October 2021, https://www.theguardian.com/us-news/commentisfree/2021/oct/23/judith-butler-gender-ideology-backlash (accessed 13 February 2026).

3 Zheng Bo, *The Garden of Earthly Delights*, p. 58.

4 Zheng Bo, 'Surviving Manuals', 2015–ongoing, http://zhengbo.org/2015_SM1.html (accessed 13 February 2026).

5 Clarissa Hyman, *Tomato: A Global History* (London: Reaktion: 2019), p. 17.

6 Barry Estabrook, 'Why is this wild, pea-sized tomato so important?' *Smithsonian Magazine*, 22 July 2015, https://www.smithsonianmag.com/travel/why-wild-tiny-pimp-tomato-so-important-180955911/?no-ist (accessed 13 February 2026).

7 Conspiracy theories abounded during the period of the COVID pandemic, drawing on combinations of right-wing online forums and populist disinformation. See for example, 'Coronavirus: Bill Gates "microchip" conspiracy theory and other vaccine claims fact-checked', *BBC News*, 30 May 2020, https://www.bbc.co.uk/news/52847648 (accessed 13 February 2026).

8 '"Trans widows" face being trapped in loveless marriages if their spouses no longer need their permission to change gender', *Daily Telegraph*, 20 June 2021, https://www.telegraph.co.uk/news/2021/06/20/trans-widows-fear-trapped-loveless-marriages-gender-law-changes/ (accessed 13 February 2026).

9 My sources for this account include: Gentilcore, *Pomodoro!*; Hyman, *Tomato: A Global History*; Mathilda Causse, Jim

Giovannoni, Mondher Bouzayen and Mhamed Zouine (eds), *The Tomato Genome* (Berlin: Springer, 2016); Charles M. Rick, 'The Tomato', *Scientific American*, 239:2 (August 1978), 76–89; J. A. Jenkins, 'The Origin of the Cultivated Tomato', *Economic Botany*, 2:4 (October–December 1948), 379–392; Monica Ozores-Hampton and Gene McAvoy, 'Tomato Varieties for Florida – Florida "Red Rounds," Plum, Cherries, Grapes, and Heirlooms', document HS1189, Horticultural Sciences Department, UF/IFAS Extension, original publication date March 2011, revised August 2014 (http://edis.ifas.ufl.edu); K. Annabelle Smith, 'Why the tomato was feared in Europe for more than 200 years', *Smithsonian Magazine*, 18 June 2013, https://www.smithsonianmag.com/arts-culture/why-the-tomato-was-feared-in-europe-for-more-than-200-years-863735/ (accessed 13 February 2026).

10 Gentilcore, *Pomodoro!*

11 Erika Lopez, *Flaming Iguanas; An Illustrated All-Girl Road Novel Thing* (New York: Simon & Schuster, 1997).

12 Andrew F. Smith, *The Tomato in America: Early History, Culture, and Cookery* (Urbana and Chicago: University of Illinois Press, 2001), p. 13.

13 Pliny the Elder, *The Natural History*, edited by John Bostock (London: Taylor and Francis, 1855), 27:113. Available as a digitised searchable database via Perseus: http://data.perseus.org/citations/urn:cts:latinLit:phi0978.phi001.perseus-eng1:27.113 (accessed 13 February 2026).

14 Dale E. Hammerschmidt and Michael J Franklin, 'The Edible Wolf Peach', *Translational Research: The Journal of Laboratory and Clinical Medicine*, 146:4 1 October 2005), 251–252, https://doi.org/10.1016/j.lab.2005.08.010

15 The style guide for my publisher is selective about capitalisation for the word indigenous, preferring capitalisation for humans but not for plants. This speaks, perhaps, either to the value placed on plant life or to the relative attribution of plants and humans to hierarchies of distinction.

16 Jumana Manna, 'Where Nature Ends and Settlements Begin', *e-flux journal*, issue 113, (November 2020), https://www.e-flux.com/journal/113/360006/where-nature-ends-and-settlements-begin/ (accessed 13 February 2026).

17 James Spedding, Robert Leslie Ellis and Douglas Denon Heath (eds), *The Works of Francis Bacon*, 14 vols (London: Longmans & Co., 1861–1879), Vol. 10, 664 [10.975] cited in Michael Ostling, 'Babyfat and Belladonna: Witches' Ointment and the Contestation of Reality', *Magic, Ritual, and Witchcraft*,

11:1 (Summer 2016), 30–72, p. 31, https://doi.org/10.1353/mrw.2016.0008

18 Anne Llewellyn Barstow, *Witchcraze: A New History of the European Witch Hunts* (London: Pandora/Harper Collins, 1994).

19 Ostling, 'Babyfat and Belladonna', p. 34.

20 Nachman Ben-Yehuda, 'The European Witch Craze of the 14th to 17th Centuries: A Sociologist's Perspective', *American Journal of Sociology*, 86:1 (July 1980), 1–31.

21 Taraneh Mosadegh, 'Tomato Resistance', https://www.taranehmosadegh.com/tomato-resistance (accessed 13 February 2026).

22 Jenkins, 'The Origin of the Cultivated Tomato'.

23 John M. Riddle, *Goddesses, Elixirs, and Witches* (Basingstoke: Palgrave Macmillan, 2010), pp. 55–58.

24 Peter Reich, Harry Schwachman and John M. Craig, 'Lycopenemia – A Variant of Carotenemia', *The New England Journal of Medicine*, 262:6 (11 February 1960), 263–269.

12 burn (on fire, flow and succession)

1 Oliver Soden, 'Priaulx Rainier: fearless and pioneering composer', *Engelsberg Ideas*, 17 August 2021, https://engelsbergideas.com/portraits/priaulx-rainier-fearless-and-pioneering-composer/ (accessed 13 February 2026).

2 Cvetkovich, *An Archive of Feelings*, pp. 57–60.

3 Lester Q. Stong, 'Josephine Baker's Hungry Heart', *G&LR*, https://glreview.org/article/article-959/ (accessed 13 February 2026).

4 So Mayer, *A Nazi Word for a Nazi Thing*.

5 Rosa x hybrida 'Princesse de Monaco'; bred originally by Marie-Louise Meilland in 1981 and named after Grace Kelly at her request: https://www.monaconatureencyclopedia.com/rosa-princesse-de-monaco/?lang=en (accessed 13 February 2026).

6 Casid, *Sowing Empire*, pp. xii–xiii.

7 See 'Brexit: Vote Leave broke electoral law, says Electoral Commission', *BBC News*, 17 July 2018, https://www.bbc.co.uk/news/uk-politics-44856992 (accessed 12 February 2026).

8 See Marco Bastos, *Brexit, Tweeted: Polarization and Social Media Manipulation* (Bristol: Bristol University Press, 2024), https://doi.org/10.2307/jj.9692580 (accessed 12 February 2026).

9 Anne McDonald cited in Petra Kuppers, 'Crip Time', *Tikkun*, 29:4 (2014), 29–30, https://doi.org/10.1215/08879982-2810062 (accessed 12 February 2026).

epilogue: verbena, knotweed, biopolitics (on queer art ecologies)

1 Michel Foucault, *The History of Sexuality, Volume 1: An Introduction*, translated by Robert Hurley (New York: Pantheon Books, 1978), p. 138.

2 C. Lavoie, 'The Impact of Invasive Knotweed Species (*Reynoutria* spp.) on the Environment: Review and Research Perspectives', *Biological Invasions*, 19 (2017), 2319–2337, https://doi.org/10.1007/s10530-017-1444-y

3 Roger Lovegrove, *Silent Fields: The Long Decline of a Nation's Wildlife* (Oxford: Oxford University Press, 2007).

4 Rébecca Matte, Maxime Boivin and Claude Lavoie, 'Japanese Knotweed Increases Soil Erosion on Riverbanks', *River Research and Applications* (11 December 2021), https://doi.org/10.1002/rra.3918

5 Vincenzo Torretta, Ioannis A. Katsoyiannis, Paolo Viotti and Elena Cristina Rada, 'Critical Review of the Effects of Glyphosate Exposure to the Environment and Humans through the Food Supply Chain', *Sustainability*, 10:4 (2018), 950, https://doi.org/10.3390/su10040950

6 IARC Monographs Volume 112: *Evaluation of Five Organophosphate Insecticides and Herbicides*, March 2015, https://www.iarc.who.int/wp-content/uploads/2018/07/MonographVolume112-1.pdf (accessed 13 February 2026).

7 Torretta et al., 'Critical Review of the Effects of Glyphosate Exposure'.

8 Ram Swaroop Meena, Sandeep Kumar, Rahul Datta, Rattan Lal, Vinod Vijayakumar, Martin Brtnicky, Mahaveer Prasad Sharma, Gulab Singh Yadav, Manoj Kumar Jhariya, Chetan Kumar Jangir, Shamina Imran Pathan, Tereza Dokulilova, Vaclav Pecina and Theodore Danso Marfo, 'Impact of Agrochemicals on Soil Microbiota and Management: A Review', *Land*, 9:2 (2020), 34, https://doi.org/10.3390/land9020034

9 Lorde, 'The Master's Tools Will Never Dismantle the Master's House'.

10 Martinez, 'Redefining Sustainability through Kincentric Ecology', p. 141.

11 Leanne Betasamosake Simpson, *As We Have Always Done: Indigenous Freedom through Radical Resistance* (Minneapolis: University of Minnesota Press, 2017) pp. 49–50.

12 Timothy James Young, letter to jackie sumell, 8 August 2019, https://www.timothyjamesyoung.com/solitarygarden (accessed 13 February 2026).

illustrations

acknowledgements

I often turn to the acknowledgements in a book first. I want to know where the author sits in constellation with those they love. The gossip is an additional bonus.

I'm not the best gossip, but I'm good at gratitude. So here are my thanks, my slow cat-blinks.

Anna Backman Rogers, for the moment you saw the spark of this book and told me to keep writing. Frances Morgan, for just-right advice that launched the first essay. Monica Suswin, for diving into writing with body, and soup at the kitchen table. Gaylene Gould, for the reflective, reparative, abundant time of emergence. Jessie Greengrass, for kindness and sea swims in the frost. Mathelinda Nabugodi for calling me in on the scent of magnolias. So Mayer, for every moment of holding, melting, co-thinking, firm and tender feedback, and learning how to be a leaf. Colin Michel for reparative reading and the both, and. Louise Hickman for tender crip collaboration. The early morning writing group led by Jackee Holder and Fiona Parashar, who made light in the dark.

Guy Baxter, Ollie Douglas and the whole team at the Museum of English Rural Life at the University of Reading, whose fellowship and financial support enabled me to get to know Eve Balfour a little better. Sarah Rigby at Elliot and Thompson, for publishing the partner piece to this book in *This Allotment* – and for that beautiful sunlit day with Marchelle Farrell at Charleston, when sparrows joined our revolutionary call. Sophie Seita, Naomi Woo and the Hildegard von Bingen Society for Gardening Companions for their generous collectivity and fun with risographs, film poems and fern frolicking. The Feminist Duration Reading Group for ongoing questing, questioning and queer reflection.

Fitzcarraldo Editions, the Nan Shepherd Prize and the Nature Chronicles Prize for giving the first seedling of this book a place to root. Saraband for publishing an earlier version of its first chapter. The Oak Spring Garden Foundation in Virginia, USA, for generous support during my residency, my equally generous interdisciplinary co-residents, and time to sit with the ghosts in the land. Casa Snowapple in Mexico City, and the international cohort who gathered to talk nature: Lars Horn, Nikki Dekker, Diana Del Angel, Mariken Heitman, Lina Parra Ochoa, Verena Blok.

My magnificent, tenacious agent Caro Clarke. My open-handed, thoughtful editor Tom Dark.

The digital gardens of the now-defunct Twitter that for a while held an abundance of queer accomplices and allies. The co-cultivators of the analogue allotment whose work lingers long after they left; the friends and neighbours who gifted plants and seeds.

Freddie Butler de Lacy and Jonathan Woods, who stand by with rituals, readings and wine. Amber Dowell, for wisdom and foolishness. Steve Joy, for laughter and tediously repetitive conversations about how to be me. Darren, for unconditional acceptance. Kalli and Alf, and every being in the garden, allotment, this small corner of the world.

And of course, the land itself, without which there would be nothing.

index

Literary and other works can be found under writer/artist names. Page numbers in *italic* refer to illustrations.